MBA for Healthcare

MBA for Healthcare

JOSEPH S. SANFILIPPO, MD, MBA
PROFESSOR OF OBSTETRICS, GYNECOLOGY &
REPRODUCTIVE SCIENCES
UNIVERSITY OF PITTSBURGH SCHOOL OF MEDICINE
PITTSBURGH, PENNSYLVANIA

ERIC J. BIEBER, MD, MSHCM
PRESIDENT AND CHIEF EXECUTIVE OFFICER
ROCHESTER REGIONAL HEALTH
CLINICAL PROFESSOR OF HEALTH SCIENCES
ROCHESTER INSTITUTE OF TECHNOLOGY
ROCHESTER, NEW YORK

DAVID JAVITCH, PHD
PRESIDENT
JAVITCH ASSOCIATES
ADJUNCT ASSISTANT PROFESSOR
HARVARD T.H. CHAN SCHOOL OF PUBLIC HEALTH
BOSTON, MASSACHUSETTS

**RICHARD B. SIEGRIST, JR., MS,
MBA, CPA**
DIRECTOR OF INNOVATION AND ENTREPRENEURSHIP
CO-DIRECTOR, HEALTH CARE MANAGEMENT PROGRAM
HARVARD T.H. CHAN SCHOOL OF PUBLIC HEALTH
BOSTON, MASSACHUSETTS

OXFORD
UNIVERSITY PRESS

OXFORD
UNIVERSITY PRESS

Oxford University Press is a department of the University of
Oxford. It furthers the University's objective of excellence in research,
scholarship, and education by publishing worldwide.

Oxford   New York
Auckland   Cape Town   Dar es Salaam   Hong Kong   Karachi
Kuala Lumpur   Madrid   Melbourne   Mexico City   Nairobi
New Delhi   Shanghai   Taipei   Toronto

With offices in
Argentina   Austria   Brazil   Chile   Czech Republic   France   Greece
Guatemala   Hungary   Italy   Japan   Poland   Portugal   Singapore
South Korea   Switzerland   Thailand   Turkey   Ukraine   Vietnam

Oxford is a registered trademark of Oxford University Press
in the UK and certain other countries.

Published in the United States of America by
Oxford University Press
198 Madison Avenue, New York, NY 10016

Library of Congress Cataloging-in-Publication Data
Sanfilippo, J. S. (Joseph S.), author.
MBA for healthcare / Joseph S. Sanfilippo, Eric Bieber, David Javitch, Richard B. Siegrist, Jr.
  p. ; cm.
Includes bibliographical references.
ISBN 978-0-19-933205-2 (alk. paper)
I. Bieber, Eric J., author.   II. Javitch, David, author.   III. Siegrist, Richard B., Jr., author.   IV. Title.
[DNLM: 1. Practice Management, Medical.   2. Interpersonal Relations.   3. Marketing of Health
Services.   4.   Quality Improvement.   W 80]
R728
362.1068—dc23
2015017987

This material is not intended to be, and should not be considered, a substitute for medical or other
professional advice. Treatment for the conditions described in this material is highly dependent on the
individual circumstances. And, while this material is designed to offer accurate information with respect
to the subject matter covered and to be current as of the time it was written, research and knowledge about
medical and health issues is constantly evolving and dose schedules for medications are being revised
continually, with new side effects recognized and accounted for regularly. Readers must therefore always
check the product information and clinical procedures with the most up-to-date published product
information and data sheets provided by the manufacturers and the most recent codes of conduct and
safety regulation. The publisher and the authors make no representations or warranties to readers, express
or implied, as to the accuracy or completeness of this material. Without limiting the foregoing, the
publisher and the authors make no representations or warranties as to the accuracy or efficacy of the drug
dosages mentioned in the material. The authors and the publisher do not accept, and expressly disclaim,
any responsibility for any liability, loss or risk that may be claimed or incurred as a consequence of the use
and/or application of any of the contents of this material.

9 8 7 6 5 4 3 2 1
Printed in the United States of America
on acid-free paper

CONTENTS

Congratulations! Whether you are new to considering business education or have an MBA, this book will complement your education and expedite your career path. I feel honored and privileged to comment on it.

You are living in perhaps the most rapid period of change in healthcare, with great uncertainty and many unknowns. We have moved from house calls by country doctors/physicians to solo family doctors/physicians to managed care and now accountable care organizations. All of this has produced great stress on patients and professionals. Let us embrace the challenge. Be leaders in the solution. United as health professionals, in our care and concern of patients, we can lead this industry and our nation to victory over the health crisis that we are living.

Many agree that the way to improve healthcare is to educate physicians and health professionals in business and leadership. Research suggests that having a physician chief executive officer (CEO) is connected to overall better quality patient care. In fact, in a list of the 300 best hospital and health system CEOs, 20% were physicians, when only 3.6% of hospitals overall are run by physicians. Although this is encouraging, many of these physician CEOs do not have formal business education. Just imagine how much more successful they could be with it. It is difficult to imagine any other industry in which this is the case.

I have been working on educating medical students and physicians in business for more than 20 years. I am repeatedly asked by students, physicians, and other health professionals whether a resource exists for targeted self-learning. None has existed until this book, aside from some online courses, a few healthcare MBA programs, and many nonhealthcare MBA programs.

As a health professional with business training, the career possibilities are endless. Organizations run by physicians with business training have included the American Medical Association, American Board of Pediatrics, Robert Wood Johnson Foundation, Kaiser Permanente, Geisinger Health System, university hospitals, and more. The last two surgeon generals had MBAs. Dartmouth-Hitchcock hospital has always hired CEOs who are physicians. And four of the five most recent CEOs of New Hampshire hospitals are physicians.

After obtaining my MBA, I had not foreseen that I would initiate an MD/MBA program and be President of the Association of MD/MBA Programs, making it possible for hundreds of medical students to obtain business training. Now, roughly half of all medical schools in the United States offer the dual degree. In the 2000-year evolution of medicine built on protecting patients from harm, we are equipping an army of health professionals to lead us. And the authors of this book are doing the same.

Following my MBA, I also became Chief Medical Officer of a system of non-profit community health centers. Where usually a physician would not serve on a finance committee, I was invited because of my business training. I believe it is imperative that a clinician who understands budgets be paramount to decisions made about spending.

Obtaining business training changed my career and my life. Not only do I have enhanced career satisfaction, I have confidence in making financial decisions for my family. The model of healthcare delivery for individual physicians has radically changed throughout my lifetime. In the early 20th century, all physicians were in solo practice. Now, 45% of physicians are employed by hospitals and health systems. Imagine feeling confident negotiating your own contract in such a case.

Furthermore, with more people enrolling in healthcare, the number of elderly receiving Medicare increasing at an alarming rate, and a national shortage of providers, the question is: who will care for all of these patients with and how will we pay for it? Again, healthcare professionals as leaders must be part of the conversation and lead the quest for the solution.

If all this unrest does not convince health professionals to become leaders of the solution, we will become part of the overwhelming problem. We must consider it a challenge, a call to arms to unite. We are best qualified to protect the sanctity of the physician-patient relationship. We will prioritize patients and make better-informed decisions. We could be in jeopardy of losing the vital decision making authority for our patients' well-being. It takes those who recognize the need for patient care to look hard enough for better solutions.

It is up to us as healthcare professionals to acquire business knowledge and take leadership of our industry into our own hands. Articles have emerged about the importance of this proposition in the *New York Times*, the *Financial Times, The Atlantic*, and other publications. Many feel that it is our moral responsibility as professionals to uphold the Hippocratic Oath and ensure that the interests of patients are put first. The health and welfare of patients must be paramount in the economic decision-making authority. This means we must master aspects of leadership beyond our traditional scope of training.

The genesis of this book is in the incredible challenge we are faced with of providing high-quality care that is cost-effective to individuals and the population, known as the "triple aim" goal of the Centers for Medicare and Medicaid Services.

These authors, including a physician with an MBA, have the insight and expertise to give us what is needed.

Early in the chapter on information technology in the healthcare industry (Chapter 3), the authors acknowledge that technology will drive the future of healthcare but that it is imperative that the patient be engaged in order for behavior change leading to better health to occur. The authors state that this engagement begins with customer satisfaction, and they provide useful tools and strategies to achieve this. In the discussion of change management, the authors state that we must understand the patient's perspective and expectations and deliver solutions. Then they provide a formula for doing this successfully.

The chapter on leadership (Chapter 4) includes a list from Harvard of the "worst leader traits" versus those that propel leaders to have "high impact." The section on values forces leaders to think about who they are, what values they have, and what "future life position" they want. Communication describes professionals who are mindful, respectful, empathetic, and good listeners, which builds trust with the patient. And the chapter on competitive marketing (Chapter 13) gives great advice on engaging the different "generations" of patients. And the chapter on entrepreneurship (Chapter 16) reviews how to evaluate good ideas that meet market needs. Many health professionals are not aware of their creativity until they are challenged to express it. I know a cardiac robotic surgeon in business school who cannot wait to develop and market his ideas.

The purpose of this book is to provide the necessary skills to inspire you to take hold of your own destiny and that of your patients. This education will change your perspective—like a new pair of glasses. You will see healthcare through the lenses of clinical medicine and business. Although medicine strives for healing, business strives for efficiencies, and our profession is desperately in need of both in order to continue our traditional humanitarian values in this new century. Enjoy!

Maria Chandler, MD, MBA
President, Association of MD/MBA Programs (www.mdmbaprograms.org)
Director, MD/MBA Program, and Associate Clinical Professor of Pediatrics
Associate Clinical Professor, Paul Merage School of Business
Chief Medical Officer, The Children's Clinic
University of California, Irvine

As time progresses, it becomes of paramount importance for clinicians and allied health professionals to understand the basics of healthcare management. Increasing visibility of managed care and value-based purchasing, the uncertain future of independent medical practices, and the intricate facets of marketing and competitive advantage have taken on enhanced and increasingly important meaning. OB no longer stands for obstetrics but "organizational behavior," which per se is extremely germane to all healthcare providers. The arena of "information technology" is a continually moving target, with the requirement of any one in the field being familiar with the latest applications and their relevance to the practice of medicine. Learning a new language of "cost accounting and management control" is essential to incorporating clinical perspectives into resource-based decisions.

The mission statement for a healthcare organization should be readily displayed so patients can understand the focus of the organization—who are we, what do we want to be and how do we get there? How should we think about "competitive marketing" in light of our mission and our strengths and weaknesses? How does it all relate to our medical practice, clinic, hospital, or healthcare delivery system?

Working one's way through third-party payers, health plans, accountable care organizations (ACOs), the role of consulting firms, the pharmaceutical sector, law, ethics, and communication are predicated upon one's knowledge and understanding of current approaches to the practice of medicine in combination with healthcare management.

Strategic planning provides a road map as to where one is progressing over a defined period of time. It provides the basic tenets for expansion and growth delivery of quality care and a host of other aspects germane to survival in the current increasingly competitive healthcare environment. What about quality improvement, leadership, and communication? These are areas of concentration that allow for a focus on patients as consumers with the ability to address their wants and needs but also to deliver an integrated care approach across all settings of care.

Being privy to the patient experience is perhaps the most important aspect of healthcare delivery. We are all focused on "what's best for the patient," and we provide you as our audience with a modus operandi to make the encounter a more efficient and worthwhile experience.

The modern hospital-physician relationship is one other area that remains in evolution. The advent of the electronic medical record has indeed changed the face of the practice of medicine. We are all leaders no matter role we assume as part of the healthcare team, certainly in the eyes of our patients. That being said, we need to consider applied law and risk management to be quite germane to what we do day in and day out. We come full circle as we address topics that include ethics, entrepreneurship, and negotiation.

We have set the stage to provide you with the knowledge base and skill set to make you more successful from the perspective of healthcare management. As authors, we come from backgrounds as educators, clinicians, hospital administrators, organizational psychologists, and attorneys, with extensive experience both inside and outside of the classroom. Our overriding goal is to provide you with the insights to be a step ahead in the increasingly challenging world of healthcare and as a result to achieve competitive advantage for your organization. We hope you enjoy and benefit from our effort.

Joseph S. Sanfilippo, MD, MBA
Eric J. Bieber, MD, MSHCM
David Javitch, PhD
Richard B. Siegrist, Jr., MS, MBA, CPA

William Annable, MD
Chief Quality Officer and Director UH
    Quality Institute
University Hospitals Cleveland
Cleveland, Ohio

Eric J. Bieber, MD, MSHCM
President and Chief Executive Officer
Rochester Regional Health
Clinical Professor of Health Sciences
Rochester Institute of Technology
Rochester, New York

Maria Chandler, MD, MBA
President, Association of MD/MBA
    Programs (mdmbaprograms.org)
Director, MD/MBA Program, and
    Associate Clinical Professor of
    Pediatrics
Associate Clinical Professor, Paul
    Merage School of Business
Chief Medical Officer, The
    Children's Clinic
University of California, Irvine
Irvine, California

John V. Foley
Chief Information Officer
University Hospitals Cleveland
Cleveland, Ohio

Elizabeth Hammack Esq.
Associate General Counsel, University
    Hospitals Health System, Inc.
Cleveland, OH USA

David Javitch, PhD
President
Javitch Associates
Boston, Massachusetts

Linda MacCracken, MBA
Senior Principal
Innovation and Thought Leadership
Health and Public Service
Accenture
Adjunct Lecturer on Health Policy and
    Management
Harvard T.H. Chan School of
    Public Health
Boston, Massachusetts

Shruti Malik
Fellow
University of Pittsburgh School of
    Medicine
Pittsburgh, Pennsylvania

Jen Radin, MPH, MBA
Healthcare Provider National Human
   Capital Leader
Global Consulting Talent leader
Principal, Deloitte Consulting
International Women's Forum Fellow

Joseph S. Sanfilippo, MD, MBA
Professor of Obstetrics, Gynecology &
   Reproductive Sciences
University of Pittsburgh School
   of Medicine
Pittsburgh, Pennsylvania

**Richard B. Siegrist, Jr., MS,
MBA, CPA**
Director of Innovation and
   Entrepreneurship
Co-Director, Health Care
   Management Program
Harvard T.H. Chan School of
   Public Health
Boston, Massachusetts

Steven R. Smith, JD, MS
Dean Emeritus and Professor
California Western School of Law
San Diego, California

Cost Accounting

RICHARD B. SIEGRIST, JR.

KEY POINTS

- Most healthcare organizations use full cost when performing cost analysis. This approach looks at the direct costs plus a fair share of the overhead or indirect costs for a cost object, such as a product or a service.
- Differential costing identifies which costs are different from one set of circumstances to another set of circumstances. It is a superior costing approach for add/drop, expand/contract, make/buy, and other internal management decisions.
- Break-even analysis and contribution analysis are two common techniques for analyzing management decisions regarding differential costs. These techniques consider variable costs, which go up proportionately with volume, and fixed costs, which remain the same when volume changes.
- Making alternative choice decisions involves defining the problem, identifying likely alternatives, evaluating quantifiable factors, considering nonquantifiable or qualitative factors, and making a decision.

MANAGEMENT ACTIVITIES

We can view the management activities of all healthcare organizations, from the largest tertiary hospital system to the smallest health clinic, in three broad categories—strategic planning, management control, and operational control. Depending on the size and complexity of the organization, these management activities may be quite formal and involved or informal and ad hoc.

Although this chapter will focus on management control, it is important to understand the definitions of strategic planning and operational control to place management control into context. Professor Robert Anthony from Harvard Business School, the father of modern cost accounting, viewed the three management activities in terms of a pyramid (Figure 1.1), with strategic planning at the top, management control in the middle, and operational control at the bottom.

At the top of that pyramid, strategic planning is the process of (1) deciding on the goals for the organization in relation to its mission, (2) determining the level of resources necessary to attain those goals, and (3) defining the policies and procedures required to govern the acquisition and proper use of those resources.

Strategic planning is a process that involves senior management and support staff and typically looks over a 3- to 5-year period. It combines both creative and analytical thinking, involves a significant amount of judgment, and is difficult to appraise in terms of success until time has passed.

In contrast, at the bottom of the pyramid, operational control is the process of ensuring that specific operational, day-to-day tasks are carried out efficiently and effectively. Efficiency measures the relationship between inputs (labor, materials, and capital) and outputs (goods and services). An organization or department is more efficient if it uses fewer inputs to achieve the same output or generates a greater output with the same level of inputs.

Although efficiency does not measure how well the tasks are being accomplished, effectiveness does. A laboratory may be efficient at meeting labor standards for doing laboratory tests but produce a lot of false-positive results because of a lack of attention to quality. Effectiveness measures the relationship between outputs and the goals of the organization. Optimally, an organization or department should be both efficient and effective—meeting the labor standard for production while at the same time producing high-quality output that furthers the goals of the department and organization.

Figure 1.1
Management activity pyramid.

Operational control focuses on day-to-day tasks and involves a large number of people throughout the organization, typically at the supervisor or middle manager level. Because it relates to relatively routine activities and involves following procedures, it is comparatively easy to evaluate how well a job is being done and to do so using a limited amount of judgment or subjectivity.

Management control is the process by which managers ensure that the resources needed to attain the stated goals are obtained and used efficiently and effectively. It takes the goals as a given from strategic planning, and it applies the lens of efficiency and effectiveness from operational planning at the department level, rather than the task level. There are no hard and fast lines between strategic planning and management control or management control and operational control.

> Management control fits in between strategic planning and operational control. It involves managers, not just numbers and analytics.

More importantly, management control involves managers, not just numbers and analytics. Accordingly, concepts from behavioral economics and social psychology become quite relevant to management control in understanding how people behave as a result of the management structure and processes in place at an organization. The time horizon of management control is typically monthly and involves senior management and line managers throughout the entire organization. The thought process tends to be administrative and persuasive. It is less subjective than strategic planning and more straightforward in determining how well a job is being done.

An organization may do a good job of strategic planning and operational control, but without strong management control, it is unlikely to be successful. This chapter will explore what it takes to achieve success in management control.

Cost Accounting as the Foundation of Management Control

To understand management control, one needs to understand the basics of cost accounting and then examine an organization's management control structure and process. This understanding will enable healthcare professionals to be more effective in internal discussions with senior operational leadership and with the chief financial officer and others in the finance department.

To build a familiarity with cost accounting concepts and uses, the remainder of this chapter will explore the key topics of full costing, differential costing, and alternative choice decisions.

Full Costing—Uses and Misuses

When performing cost analysis for management decisions, most healthcare organizations use an approach called full costing. Full costing attempts to determine cost of a particular cost object, either in total or on a per unit basis. A cost object is the unit of output for which one wants to know the cost. That cost object may be very narrow, such as the cost of a complete blood count performed in the hematology laboratory, or much broader, such as the cost of treating a patient for congestive heart failure for an entire year.

Full cost is measured as a combination of the direct costs for the cost object plus a "fair share" of the overhead of the institution. Direct costs are directly traceable to or caused by the cost object, such as the chemicals and reagents used to perform a complete blood count. Direct costs may include labor expenses, supply costs, or specialized equipment used related to the cost object.

In contrast, indirect costs are not directly traceable to only one cost object and thus must be allocated to multiple cost objects. That allocation occurs using a reasonable allocation method such as square feet, salary dollars, or hours of service. Typical indirect costs in a healthcare institution include administration, finance, and information services. Although it is easy to set the goal of a "fair share" for the allocation of indirect costs, achieving it often becomes contentious in reality. Those department managers being allocated indirect costs often argue about the magnitude of the indirect cost and the allocation statistic, believing that their performance is being unfairly evaluated based on costs that are not under their control.

A healthcare organization typically allocates these indirect costs to other departments using a selected allocation basis and related statistics for each department using a step-down method. In the step-down approach, a department can allocate costs only to the departments below it in a hierarchical structure. Accordingly, back and forth or up and down allocations are not allowed in the step-down method.

To address this limitation, some organizations may use the reciprocal method, with simultaneous equations, which allows departments to allocate costs to one another. Because of the difficulty in explaining reciprocal allocations, most organizations rely on the simpler step-down approach.

A straightforward example of full costing using the step-down approach will help illustrate how full costs are calculated. Let us use a hypothetical medical practice, Bolton Medical Associates, to illustrate full costing and other concepts in this and subsequent chapters. As shown in Table 1.1, Bolton has six departments—three support departments for Building, Administration, and Information Services and three clinical departments for Internal Medicine, Pediatrics, and Sports Medicine.

The direct costs of these departments are broken down into salary and nonsalary components and total $3 million for the healthcare facility. To determine the full cost for a visit in each of the clinical departments, it is necessary to allocate the costs of the support departments using a reasonable allocation method for each support department. We will use square feet to allocate the building expenses, dollars of direct salary to allocate the administration cost, and number of staff to allocate the cost of information services.

TABLE 1.1 BOLTON MEDICAL ASSOCIATES COSTS

Department	Salary Costs ($)	Nonsalary Costs ($)	Total Direct ($)	Square Feet	Salary Dollars ($)	No. of Staff
Building Expenses	100,000	100,000	200,000			
Administration	300,000	50,000	350,000	1,000		
Information Services	180,000	150,000	330,000	1,000	180,000	
Internal Medicine	720,000	300,000	1,020,000	8,000	720,000	10
Pediatrics	360,000	176,000	536,000	6,000	360,000	6
Sports Medicine	360,000	204,000	564,000	4,000	360,000	4
Total	2,020,000	980,000	3,000,000	20,000	1,620,000	20

In a step-down approach, the order of allocation will make a difference numerically in the allocations. The general rule of thumb is to first allocate the department that uses the fewest services from other departments, then allocate the one that uses the next fewest services from other departments, and so on. In this example, in Table 1.2, the Building Expense department is allocated first, then Administration, and finally Information Services.

In the example, the Building Expenses Department is allocated to the remaining five departments based on square feet. Because Administration has 1,000 of the 20,000 square feet in the organization, it receives 5% (1,000/20,000) of the buildings expense of $200,000, or $20,000. Likewise, Internal Medicine receives 40% (8,000/20,000) of $200,000, or $80,000.

All the direct and previously allocated costs for a support department need to be allocated to other departments below it in the step-down sequence such that the department has no costs remaining. Because Administration has been allocated $10,000 from Buildings, its cost to be allocated is now $350,000 of direct plus the $10,000, or $360,000. Information Services, which is below Administration in the step-down, receives 11.1% ($180,000/$1,620,000) of $360,000 or $40,000. The same process is repeated for Information Services, with its costs to be allocated totaling $380,000 ($330,000 own direct plus $10,000 from Building plus $40,000 from Administration).

As shown in Table 1.3, at the end of the allocation process, all costs should reside in the clinical departments at Bolton Medical Associates as total full cost.

By incorporating number of visits for each clinical department at Bolton, it is now possible to calculate the full cost per visit for each, ranging from $79 per visit for Pediatrics to $152 per visit for Sports Medicine.

Full costs are useful for managers for specific purposes. First, full costing answers the question of what it cost last year for a chest x-ray or an Internal Medicine visit on a fully loaded basis. Second, it enables the institution to fulfill its reporting obligations to external agencies or regulatory groups such as to the Centers for Medicare and Medicaid Services or grantor agencies. Third, it provides appropriate cost information for financial statement preparation. Finally, full cost can be a useful input into pricing decisions.

Full costing is useful for answering the question "what did it cost" and for external reporting but not for most internal management decisions.

Full cost is not appropriate and can give highly misleading results for expand/contract, add/drop, make/buy, and other alternative choice decisions. Full cost is also problematic when used in evaluating the performance of departments and their managers.

The following examples regarding Bolton Medical Associates indicate the dangers of using full costing for certain management decisions:

Situation 1: It is expected that the volume for Sports Medicine visits will go up by 10% next year because of the facility's growing reputation. How much more

TABLE 1.2   BOLTON MEDICAL ASSOCIATES COSTS EXAMPLE

Department	Total Direct Costs ($)	Allocated Building ($)	Allocated Administration ($)	Allocated Information Services ($)	Total Full Cost ($)
Building Expenses	200,000	–200,000			0
Administration	350,000	10,000	–360,000		0
Information Services	330,000	10,000	40,000	–380,000	0
Internal Medicine	1,020,000	80,000	160,000	190,000	1,450,000
Pediatrics	536,000	60,000	80,000	114,000	790,000
Sports Medicine	564,000	40,000	80,000	76,000	760,000
Total	3,000,000	0	0	0	3,000,000

TABLE 1.3   BOLTON MEDICAL ASSOCIATES COSTS EXAMPLE

Department	Total Full Cost ($)	No. Visits	Full Cost per Visit ($)
Building Expenses	0		
Administration	0		
Information Services	0		
Internal Medicine	1,450,000	15,000	96.67
Pediatrics	790,000	10,000	79.00
Sports Medicine	760,000	5,000	152.00
Total	3,000,000	30,000	100.00

will the expected expenses be in Sports Medicine? Because the full cost per visit for Sports Medicine is $152, will it not be necessary to spend $152 for 500 new visits (10% of 5,000) or $76,000 more? No, because not all of the direct costs (salary and nonsalary) will go up proportionately to the visit increase and expenditures on Building Services, Administration, and Information Services will not likely increase at all. How much will expenditures go up then? We need to understand differential analysis to find out.

Situation 2: A local employer would like Bolton to offer wellness visits for its employees, but is only willing to pay $85 per Internal Medicine visit. Because the full cost for such a visit is $96.67, should the facility turn down the deal? Again, the right information to make that decision will not be available until the differential cost (instead of the full cost) is considered.

Differential Costing—The Right Approach for Most Management Decisions

Differential costing looks at what costs are different from one set of circumstances to another and should be the basis for most management decisions.

In differential costing, it is necessary to look at what costs would be different under one set of circumstances versus another set of circumstances. In other words, what would change from alternative A to alternative B to alternative C? Alternative A is often simply sticking with the status quo.

Under differential costing, it is important to understand how costs will behave. For these purposes, it is necessary to classify costs into four categories—variable, fixed, semivariable, and semifixed. As Figure 1.2 shows, variable costs vary proportionately based on volume. If volume goes up by 10%, variable costs in total will

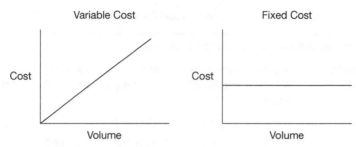

Figure 1.2
Variable costs varying on volume.

go up by 10%. Very importantly, variable cost per unit will not change. Medical supplies are a typical variable cost.

Fixed costs behave in the opposite way from variable costs. Within a relevant range, fixed costs remain the same regardless of volume. In other words, if volume goes up by 10%, fixed costs will not change in total. Fixed cost per unit will decline, but what is most relevant for the purposes of this discussion is that fixed costs in total *will not change*. Rent is a typical fixed cost.

There are two in-between types of cost—semivariable and semifixed. As shown in Figure 1.3, semivariable costs have a fixed component and a variable component. For analytical purposes, those two components are typically separated. A phone bill is an example of a semivariable cost—a fixed monthly fee for service plus a variable fee based on number of minutes exceeding the plan limit.

A semifixed cost is also referred to as a step cost. It is fixed for a range of volume but then jumps up to a new level when a volume threshold is exceeded. For example, an organization might need one supervisor at $80,000 per year until monthly customer volume exceeds 1,000, at which point two supervisors are needed.

It is worthwhile to take a closer look at Bolton Medical Associates, in Table 1.4, to better understand cost classification into variable versus fixed.

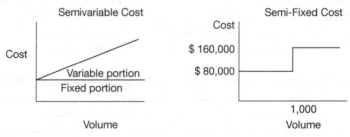

Figure 1.3
Semivariable costs with a fixed component and a variable component.

TABLE 1.4   BOLTON MEDICAL ASSOCIATES EXAMPLE 4

Bolton Medical Associates—Cost Classification

No. of Visits Account	30,000 No. of Staff	Salary per Person ($)	Total Amount ($)	Variable Costs ($)	Fixed Costs ($)
Physicians	4	150,000	600,000	0	600,000
Nurses	8	70,000	560,000	560,000	0
Medical assistants	4	40,000	160,000	160,000	0
Front desk staff	4	30,000	120,000	0	120,000
Total salary cost	20		1,440,000	720,000	720,000
Medical supplies			180,000	180,000	
Insurance			140,000		140,000
Office expenses			160,000		160,000
Other expenses			200,000		200,000
Nonsalary cost			680,000	180,000	500,000
Total direct cost			2,120,000	900,000	1,220,000
Indirect Costs			880,000		880,000
Total Cost			3,000,000	900,000	2,100,000

As indicated in Table 1.4, Bolton has 20 employees in total working in Internal Medicine, Pediatrics, and Sports Medicine. The salaries for the eight nurses and four medical assistants are considered variable because the departments adjust the staffing of those employees based on expected patient volume on a weekly or sometimes daily basis. In contrast, the four physicians and four front desk staff are considered fixed because their full-time services are required regardless of patient volume. Different organizations may have different approaches to what is considered variable versus fixed for personnel costs.

For nonsalary costs, medical supplies are classified as variable because they vary proportionally based on patient volume. Insurance, general office expenses, and other expenses are classified as fixed because they are not significantly influenced by fluctuations in patient volume. Again, there may be some judgment involved in this classification distinction.

Break-even Analysis

Now that the costs have been classified into variable and fixed categories, it is possible to use that information to make better management decisions than with full cost. Break-even analysis is a simple yet powerful tool to gain a general understanding of the financial situation facing an organization using this knowledge.

The break-even equation is:

$$px = a + bx$$

where **p** is price per unit, **x** is volume of units sold or provided, **a** is fixed cost in total, and **b** is variable cost per unit. The left side of the equation is revenue (**px**) and the right side is cost (**a + bx**). By solving the equation, we can determine how many units we need to sell or provide to break even.

To solve this equation for Bolton Medical Associates, it is first necessary to determine the value of **b**—variable cost per unit. We know that Bolton has classified $900,000 in costs as variable to provide 30,000 visits from Table 1.4. That results in a variable cost per unit or visit of $30 ($900,000/30,000 visits). This is a very important figure for differential costing because it says if there is one more average visit at Bolton, $30 more is spent. This is exactly how variable costs behave. In contrast, we would not expect to spend any more on fixed costs because they do not depend on volume.

Assuming an average price, **p**, for an average patient visit at Bolton Medical Associates is $98. It is now possible to solve the break-even equation for **x** (number of visits to break even) as follows:

$$px = a + bx$$

$$\$98x = \$2,100,000 \left(\text{our total fixed costs}\right) + \$30x$$

$$\$68x = \$2,100,000$$

x = 30,882.35, or rounding up, **30,883.**

In other words, if there are 30,833 visits, Bolton will break even and cover all its costs. The visit volume is currently 30,000; this is slightly below the break-even point by 883 visits, however, indicating that it is operating at a loss.

The break-even equation is most commonly used to solve for **x**, the break-even volume. But what if there is not the demand to increase volume? It is possible to alternatively determine the price at which Bolton Medical Associates would break even, assuming the volume (x) is 30,000 visits. In that case:

$$px = a + bx$$

$$p * 30,000 = \$2,100,000 + (\$30 * 30,000)$$

$$p = \$100$$

In other words, if it is possible to raise the price to $100 from $98 and not lose any current visits, Bolton would break even. Similarly, if we can reduce fixed costs in total by making some expense cuts or decrease the variable cost per unit by negotiating a better medical supply contract, the facility could also reach the break-even point. As we can see, the break-even equation is a simple but powerful equation that allows an initial understanding of the real economics of our business.

Contribution Margin Analysis

Contribution margin analysis is preferable to break-even analysis when evaluating multiple programs or services.

Contribution margin analysis allows us to develop a different kind of income statement for Bolton Medical Associates as a whole and for each of the three clinical departments. This income statement focuses on how costs behave and the associated contribution margins rather than financial accounting rules. It also avoids a limitation of the break-even analysis that all visits are treated the same when it is known that Internal Medicine, Pediatrics, and Sports Medicine visits are likely to have different prices and costs.

Table 1.5 is the contribution margin analysis for Bolton and its three clinical departments.

The statement in Table 1.6 presents four different contribution margins for use for different management decisions.

How can we interpret the contribution margin analysis results for Bolton? First, we can see that Sports Medicine visits are the most profitable on a per unit basis, with a variable contribution of $108 per visit versus $60 for both Internal Medicine and Pediatrics. If there are 100 more Sports Medicine visits, the profit should increase by $10,800 (100 visits at $108 apiece), assuming the fixed costs do not change.

Second, viewing the variable contribution margin shows that at Bolton, Internal Medicine has the largest at $900,000, followed by Pediatrics at $600,000 and Sports Medicine at $540,000. If the variable contribution margin for a department is negative, then that department should likely be closed down from a pure financial perspective because it is not even covering its variable or marginal costs.

Third, looking at the direct contribution margin at Bolton Medical Associates shows that again, all three departments have positive direct contribution margins, meaning that their revenues cover all their variable and fixed direct costs and each department contributes to covering allocated indirect costs. Internal Medicine has the highest direct contribution margin of $330,000, followed by Pediatrics at $264,000 and Sports Medicine at $226,000.

TABLE 1.5   BOLTON MEDICAL ASSOCIATES—CONTRIBUTION MARGIN
ANALYSIS

	Bolton Medical Associates	Internal Medicine	Pediatrics	Sports Medicine
Number of visits	30,000	15,000	10,000	5,000
Price per visit	$98.00	$90.00	$80.00	$158.00
Variable cost per visit	$30.00	$30.00	$20.00	$50.00
Variable contribution per visit	$68.00	$60.00	$60.00	$108.00
Revenues	$2,940,000	$1,350,000	$800,000	$790,000
Variable direct costs	900,000	450,000	200,000	250,000
Variable contribution	$2,040,000	$900,000	$600,000	$540,000
Fixed direct costs	$1,220,000	$570,000	$336,000	$314,000
Direct contribution	$820,000	$330,000	$264,000	$226,000
Indirect costs	880,000	430,000	254,000	196,000
Net margin	-$60,000	-$100,000	$10,000	$30,000

If a department's direct contribution margin is negative, then the facility may want to consider whether to discontinue that service if all the fixed direct costs could be eliminated. However, it may be best to expand the volume of that department if its variable contribution per unit is positive, because each addition unit sold would improve the overall direct contribution margin.

Finally, one can examine the net margin or bottom line after allocated indirect costs are subtracted. Bolton Medical Associates overall has a negative net margin of $60,000. Internal Medicine has a loss of $100,000, which is partly offset by slight profits in Pediatrics of $10,000 and Sports Medicine of $30,000.

What guidance should this information provide? The natural inclination is to think that the leaders of Bolton Medical Associates would be better off eliminating Internal Medicine because it is losing money while Pediatrics and Sports Medicine are making money. As we will shortly see, this approach would be counterproductive because the indirect costs for the organization would not likely decrease, whereas the contribution to cover those indirect costs made by Internal Medicine would disappear. This highlights the fallacy of full cost analysis upon which the net margin by department is based. Instead, the leaders should use differential analysis as represented by the variable contribution and direct contribution margins to understand what the impact would really be.

TABLE 1.6   CONTRIBUTION MARGINS

Margin Type	Calculation	Description	Uses
Variable contribution per unit	Revenue per unit—variable cost per unit	Marginal contribution to profit of one additional unit	Marginal contribution analysis
Variable contribution margin	Revenues—variable costs	Contribution remaining after variable costs to cover fixed direct and indirect costs	Differential analysis when fixed costs do not change
Direct contribution margin	Variable contribution margin— fixed direct costs	Contribution remaining after direct costs to cover indirect costs	Differential analysis when indirect costs do not change
Net margin or bottom line profit	Direct contribution margin—indirect costs	Net profit after covering all costs	Full cost analysis and overall profitability

Alternative Choice Decisions

In any alternative choice decision, it is important to consider the following five steps to make the best choice:

1. Define the problem.
2. Identify and compare the likely alternatives (usually including the status quo).
3. Evaluate the quantitative factors (how will costs and/or revenues change).
4. Evaluate the nonquantitative or qualitative factors.
5. Make a decision.

Defining the problem is a critical starting point for the analysis. How narrow or broad the definition determines the scope and accordingly what will be relevant for the analysis.

Any alternative choice decision should include five steps, starting with identifying the problem and ending with making a decision.

The second step of identifying alternatives involves choosing a reasonable number of realistic alternatives to compare. For better or worse, the status quo is the most frequently selected alternative so it should be explicitly considered in most situations.

For the third step, a common approach is to look at the specific differences between alternatives as follows:

Change in revenues (positive for increase, negative for decreases)
+/– Change in variable costs (positive for decreases, negative for increases)
+/– Change in fixed direct costs (positive for decreases, negative for increases)
+/– Change in indirect costs (positive for decreases, negative for increases)
= Net benefit/loss (positive for net benefit, negative for net loss)

This simple approach enables clinical and financial managers to analyze what impact a variety of changes would have on the organization.

The next step is to evaluate factors that cannot be quantified in financial terms or are qualitative in nature. This step may be the most important step in the analysis, especially if the quantitative difference among alternatives is relatively small.

The final step is to reach a decision. That decision may simply be staying with the status quo, but that should be recognized as the decision. Too frequently, organizations postpone decisions due to the lack of perfect information (e.g., more study needed), frequently missing future opportunities or responding too late to upcoming challenges.

Alternative choice decision-making clearly involves a number of quantitative and qualitative assumptions about what will happen if changes are made. These assumptions should be reasonable but do not have to be perfect to allow informed decisions to be made. Each assumption can be tested using sensitivity analysis as follows:

- Would a manager's decision change if the assumption were changed by 10%? If so, it would be necessary to investigate that assumption in more detail.
- Would a manager's decision change if the assumption were changed by 50%? If not, it would not be necessary to spend any more time fine-tuning that assumption.

Let us now apply alternative choice decision approach to whether we should continue offering Internal Medicine visits or simply shut down the department.

Change in revenues (15,000 visits × $90/visit)	–$1,350,000
Change in variable costs (15,000 visits × $30/visit)	$450,000
Change in fixed direct costs	$570,000
Change in indirect costs	0
Net change	–$330,000

As indicated, Bolton Medical Associates would be $330,000 worse off if Internal Medicine is shut. This result occurs because the indirect costs would not decrease for Bolton as a whole—they would simply be reallocated to Pediatrics and Sports Medicine if Internal Medicine closes. It is important to note that the $330,000 is the direct contribution margin for Internal Medicine from the previously shown Contribution Margin Analysis.

The decision to keep Internal Medicine open for financial reasons is even more strongly supported for nonfinancial or qualitative reasons. Bolton Medical Associates would likely lose its reputation as a full-service provider for families and consequently experience a drop in both Pediatric and Sports Medicine business if Internal Medicine were closed or scaled back.

CASE STUDY

As the Chief Financial Officer of Bolton Medical Associates, Ryan Broderick was reviewing a proposal from the mayor's office for his organization to provide back-up healthcare support for major outdoor sporting events on Saturdays during the upcoming year. The mayor's office projected that this arrangement would involve approximately 600 medical visits per year spread out over 20 Saturdays from May to September. The city was willing to pay an average reimbursement per visit of $80 and needed an answer by the end of the month.

Broderick estimated that to fulfill the contract, Bolton would need to open on Saturdays from 10 AM to 4 PM with a rotating staff of one physician, one nurse, one medical assistant, and one front office person. This would increase annual staffing costs by approximately $30,000. He knew they would also need to proportionately increase their cost for medical supplies.

As Broderick contemplated the contract, he wanted to answer the following questions.

Questions

- Would Bolton Medical Associates be better or worse off from the contract? By how much?
- Should Broderick be concerned about the $80 payment per visit when the normal average price per visit is $98?
- What were the key assumptions in Broderick's analysis? If they were off by a little, would it change his decision? If they were off by a substantial amount, would it change it?
- What nonfinancial considerations should he take into account?
- What decision should Broderick make?

SUGGESTED READING

Siegrist RB. Financial and operational analysis of non-operating room anesthesia: the wrong way versus the right way. *Anesthesiology Clin.* 2009;27:17–23.

Young DW. *Management Control in Nonprofit Organizations.* 9th ed. Chapters 1, 3, 4, 5. Stoneham, MA: Crimson Press; 2012.

2

Management Control Structure and Process

RICHARD B. SIEGRIST, JR.

KEY POINTS

- When evaluating the effectiveness of any organization, it is important to understand that organization's management control structure and management control process.
- A strong management control structure depends on having a sound organizational structure, well-defined responsibility centers, goal congruence, appropriate financial and nonfinancial incentives, meaningful transfer pricing, and recognition of the organization's key success factors.
- An organization also needs sound management control processes that function within the management control structure to be effective. Those essential management control processes are programming, budgeting, measurement, and reporting/variance analysis.

Now that we have a solid foundation in cost accounting and an appreciation of the limitations of full cost and the benefits of differential analysis, we can shift our attention to management control structure and process.

MANAGEMENT CONTROL STRUCTURE

When evaluating the effectiveness of any organization, it is important to understand that organization's management control structure. A strong management control structure depends on having a sound organizational structure, well-defined responsibility centers, goal congruence, appropriate financial and nonfinancial incentives, meaningful transfer pricing, and recognition of the organization's key success factors.

If any of these components are lacking or underdeveloped, the organization may experience dysfunctional behavior of management and staff, internal confusion, and lack of proper motivation, resulting in poor management decisions and substandard performance. Let us explore each of these important components in more detail.

Organizational Structure—More than Just an Organization Chart

An important initial step in understanding how an organization functions is to decipher its formal and informal organizational structure. Is it a centralized or decentralized organization? Who reports to whom? Are lines of authority clear or confused? Do matrix reporting relationships exist (i.e., one person reporting to two different people)? Do informal relationships occasionally or regularly supersede formal relationships?

Figure 2.1 and Figure 2.2 shows a centralized versus decentralized organizational structure both in general and for Bolton Medical Associates.

To analyze organization structure, first draw the organization chart listing departments, positions, and reporting relationships. Is it straightforward and clear who reports to whom? Do the reporting relationships make sense in regards to the organization's activities? Second, we are dealing with people, not just boxes on a chart, so it is critical to fill in who specifically is in each position

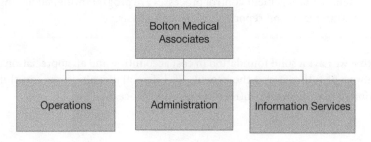

Figure 2.1
Centralized structure.

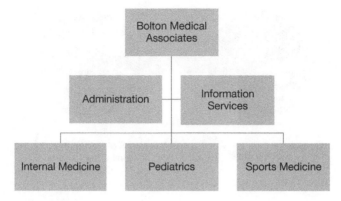

Figure 2.2
Decentralized structure.

---

and to understand each person's background and experience. Do the specific people fit well in their positions? Are there a number of vacant positions?

> Drawing the organization chart and identifying the people in the organizational boxes can provide important insights into how that organization functions.

Third, critically evaluate the structure. Does it make sense for this organization? Does it accurately reflect the way the organization works in reality? Do people in the organization feel that the structure is fair and effective in motivating people?

Responsibility Centers—Holding People Accountable for What They Can Control

For effective performance, it is important to hold managers responsible for what they can reasonably control. That control need not be absolute (and rarely is), but it should be to the level that managers feel that they are being measured fairly. In looking at the organizational structure, a responsibility center is an organizational unit headed by a manager who is responsible for the performance of that organization unit. Responsibility accounting measures the performance of managers and therefore influences the way managers behave.

> Responsibility centers are classified as expense, revenue, profit, or investment centers as a way to hold managers accountable for what they can control.

There are four common types of responsibility centers—expense, revenue, profit, and investment centers. In Figure 2.3, each responsibility center takes inputs (labor, material, and capital) and converts those inputs into outputs (tangible goods or intangible services).

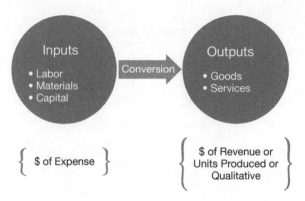

Figure 2.3
Inputs and outputs of responsibility centers.

For accounting purposes, experts measure inputs not in terms of hours of labor or units of materials, but as the cost of expense incurred. Similarly, it is preferable to measure outputs not in terms of units sold but as cost of revenue generated. In the absence of revenues, it is appropriate to rely on units produced or if the output is intangible such as the output of the president's office, qualitative evaluation.

If the manager of a responsibility center has reasonable control over and is held accountable for the expenses of that center, it can be considered an expense center. At Bolton Medical Associates, Information Services would likely be considered an expense center. Also, Internal Medicine, Pediatrics, and Sports Medicine are expense centers if primarily they are to be held accountable for the dollars they spend caring for their patients.

Likewise, if the manager is held primarily accountable for the revenue of that center, it can be considered to be a revenue center. The marketing department and the development office are often considered to be revenue centers. Even though they each have an expense budget that they need to adhere to, their focus is on generating new business for the organization or bringing in donations, respectively. At Bolton Medical Associates, Internal Medicine, Pediatrics, and Sports Medicine could be considered to be revenue centers if they are to focus primarily on the number of patients they attract and the related patient care revenues generated.

In a profit center, the manager is responsible for both the revenues generated and the expenses incurred for that center. This is typically a greater responsibility than just being an expense or a revenue center. The profit center concept combines both efficiency and effectiveness and makes decentralized organizations feasible. The concept applies to both for-profit and nonprofit organizations (where a goal is likely to generate sufficient surplus to fund future investments).

Common criteria for an effective profit center include:

- Reasonable degree of influence over revenues and expenses
- Perception of fairness by managers

- Absence of dysfunctional incentives or behavior by managers
- Existence of transfer prices to fairly value internal transactions
- Reasonable record-keeping costs such that benefits exceed costs

At Bolton Medical Associates, it is possible to choose to consider Internal Medicine, Pediatrics, and Sports Medicine as profit centers if their managers focus both on the number of patients they attract and the resources they expend to care for those patients.

Finally, if an organizational unit is to be held responsible not just for profit, but for profit in relation to the dollars of investment in that part of the business, then it would be considered an investment center. An investment center requires even more management sophistication than a profit center because it involves generating a sufficient return on investment to justify the level of investment in that organizational unit. In most cases, the organization is classified as a whole as an investment center. Bolton Medical Associates would be regarded as an investment center, with its performance evaluated as profit generated divided by dollars invested (profit/investment). In decentralized organizations that are larger than Bolton (e.g., a multihospital health system), there may be multiple investment centers (e.g., individual hospitals) rolling up into the overall organization.

As can be seen from the different options for how to classify Internal Medicine, Pediatrics, and Sports Medicine as responsibility centers (expense vs. revenue vs. profit), there is not necessarily one right choice. It depends on what the center's manager is held accountable for. However, there are wrong choices. If a manager is held accountable for things he or she cannot reasonably control or if a manager is not the right one in terms of level of knowledge or motivation, one must be aware of the potential consequences. For example, a "star" physician who is excellent at bringing in patients might be in charge of Sports Medicine. But if he or she does not have the basic management skills to manage expenses, Sports Medicine might be better treated as a revenue center. If we want it to be a profit center, someone else with broader skills might be a better person to put in charge.

Goal Congruence and Incentives

Under ideal circumstances, the goals for the organization set by senior management under the direction of the board of directors/trustees are clearly understood by people at all levels of the organization. This congruence is particularly critical in a decentralized organization. The lack of goal congruence can lead to organizational confusion, dysfunctional behavior by managers, and poor motivation of employees.

Two critical factors in achieving goal congruence are (1) transparency

> Incentives have an important influence on people's behavior, whether they are monetary or nonmonetary, formal or informal.

regarding the organization's goals and the rationale behind those goals and (2) appropriate incentives to achieve those goals at all levels within the organization.

People within any organization are motivated by a variety of incentives. Those incentives may be (1) monetary such as salary, commissions, or bonuses, or (2) nonmonetary such as promotion, perks, personal recognition, a feeling of accomplishment, or work autonomy. Research by such authors as Daniel Pink has indicated that nonmonetary incentives are often as or more important than monetary incentives once a basic level of financial compensation has been achieved.

Another aspect of incentives relates to whether they are formal or informal. Informal incentives are often much more difficult to identify without an in depth understanding of an organization, but they may explain why an organization is successful or experiencing problems.

For instance, Bolton Medical Associates could be experiencing problems with goal congruence and incentives for two reasons. Either the physicians running the departments are focused solely on generating a profit at the expense of delivering high-quality care or incentives are structured such that Internal Medicine and Sports Medicine are encouraged to compete rather than collaborate with each other.

Transfer Pricing—Encouraging Fair Internal Evaluation and Collaboration

In a decentralized organization where organizational units regularly interact with one another, transfer pricing is very important to ensure fair performance evaluation and to encourage appropriate collaboration. A transfer price is a price used to measure the value of goods or services furnished by a responsibility center to other responsibility centers within an organization.

> Transfer prices are critical when organizational units use each other's services. Market price is the "gold standard," but cost-based approaches are often used.

There are multiple options for setting transfer prices. The preferred transfer price is usually a market-based transfer price if a market price exists or can be reasonably estimated. This market price is sometimes adjusted downward to reflect selling costs saved or reduced internal transaction expenses by "buying" inside.

When market prices are not available, a cost-based transfer price is often used. This cost-based price can range from a high of full cost plus a profit margin as a normal price surrogate to a low of a variable cost for marginal cost pricing. Marginal cost pricing may be most appropriate if the organization has excess capacity. Other in-between options for a transfer price include full cost, direct cost plus a profit margin, or direct cost.

For example, consider a complete blood count. Some potential transfer prices may be:

Market price	$30.00 (from outside independent laboratory)
Market price—10% internal discount	$27.00
Full cost	$25.00
Full cost plus 25% markup	$31.25
Direct cost	$15.00
Direct cost plus 80% markup	$27.00
Variable direct cost	$9.00

There is no one "right" choice for transfer pricing. The key is that both parties believe the transfer price (1) is fair and (2) does not encourage managers to take actions that are in their department's best interest but not in the best interest of the organization as a whole.

Transfer prices are typically set by specific policy for anticipated internal transactions and by negotiation among the internal responsibility centers and senior management for nonstandard situations. If disputes occur, they are usually resolved in consultation with senior management. At the end of the process, an organization should have transfer prices that cover a vast majority of situations and are viewed as fair by those affected internally.

If Bolton Medical Associates designates Internal Medicine, Pediatrics, and Sports Medicine as profit centers, then setting transfer prices would be advisable to properly evaluate and motivate the managers of those departments. It would be reasonable to then set transfer prices for such services as laboratory tests (e.g., Internal Medicine runs the laboratory tests for Pediatrics patients) and consultations (an Internal Medicine physician asks a Sports Medicine physician for a consult on a particular patient during a regular visit). In the absence of transfer prices, one department would be incurring cost for another department without receiving any compensation and would therefore experience lower profitability.

Key Success Factors—Essential Tenets to Recognize and Nurture

Every organization has typically two to four factors about their organization that are critical to the organization's success. These factors are often referred to as key or critical success factors. They are not necessarily the same for every organization in a given industry or industry segment.

They may include outstanding customer service (e.g., L.L. Bean), elegant human design (e.g., Apple), exceptional supply chain management (e.g., Walmart), or continuous improvement ethos (e.g., Toyota). They are the things ranging from

Identifying the key success factors of an organization can help avoid problems that would likely occur if those success factors are threatened.

exciting to mundane that distinguish an organization's approach and philosophy. If these key success factors are threatened by ill-advised management decisions, this can lead to serious internal and external problems and even the organization's decline. Dysfunctional behavior, lack of motivation, and goal incongruence often arise when key success factors are put in jeopardy.

In healthcare organizations, such key success factors can include clinical excellence in "high-tech" treatments (e.g., open heart surgery, transplants, cancer care), outstanding patient-centered care, effective care coordination across the care continuum, in-depth management of cost and quality, or efficient operational management.

Bolton Medical Associates may pride itself on its excellent relationship with its patients that not only leads to greater patient loyalty but also higher patient health compliance. The team-based approach that Bolton encourages where a physician, nurse, and medical assistant work seamlessly together may be a key success factor. If something should disrupt the functioning of that team approach, Bolton may experience a loss of patients and declining health of its patient population as well as decreased revenues and profitability.

MANAGEMENT CONTROL PROCESS

Programming, budgeting, measurement, and reporting/variance analysis are essential management control processes.

An organization may have done a good job in setting up an effective management control structure by (1) having a well–thought out organization chart, (2) proper responsibility center designation, (3) reasonable goal congruence, (4) appropriate incentives, (5) defined transfer pricing, and (6) an understanding of its key success factors. However, if it does not have sound management control processes that function within that management control structure, it will not be as effective as it can be. Those essential management control processes are programming, budgeting, measurement, and reporting/variance analysis.

As shown in Figure 2.4, together they form a closed loop management system in terms of feedback and integration. In such as system, knowledge gained from budgeting may cause adjustments to programming, results from ongoing reporting and variance analysis may influence budgeting, and so on.

Programming

Programming is the process of deciding upon the type and size of the programs (planned courses of action) that are undertaken to achieve the organization's goals. Programming works within the overall strategic framework that is set

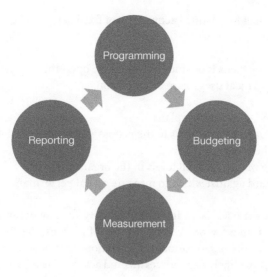

Figure 2.4
Closed loop management system.

during the strategic planning process. Programming encompasses both modifications to existing programs and consideration of new programs.

In Bolton Medical Associates, existing programs are Internal Medicine, Pediatrics, and Sports Medicine. They happen to correspond with the responsibility centers, but that is not always the case in an organization. Programming would include deciding whether a facility such as Bolton wants to expand an existing program such as Sports Medicine by adding a new physician or a new service such as pain management within that program.

Programming would also encompass deciding whether to add a new program such as Obstetrics-Gynecology or Surgery at Bolton Medical Associates. Organizational goals and strategy should help determine which program direction would make the most sense for the organization. An organization can suffer when programming decisions are made haphazardly, are based primarily on political considerations, or are not consistent with the organization's strategic direction or culture.

Budgeting

A budget is a plan expressed in monetary terms. The purpose of budgeting is to decide on the plan for the upcoming year based on previous programming decisions. There are three common types of budgets:

- Operating budget for revenues and expenses
- Cash budget for sources and uses of cash

- Capital budget for planned acquisition of fixed assets and capital investments

In this chapter, the focus is on understanding the operating budget. The operating budget has four critical uses for an organization:

- Making and coordinating plans
- Communicating those plans to the people who are responsible for carrying them out
- Motivating managers at all levels in the organization
- As a standard against which to measure actual performance

Budget preparation itself is an important activity for any organization. It make take anywhere from a few weeks to a number of months, depending on the size and complexity of the organization. Organizations that have an effective budgeting process are more likely to be successful and achieve the organization's goals on a consistent basis (Figure 2.5).

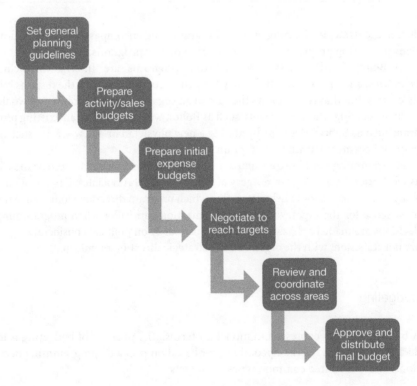

Figure 2.5
Common steps in an effective budget process.

There are three keys to an effective budget. First, the budget should
be a tight but attainable goal. If the
budget is too easy to meet, then the
organization will not be as successful as it could be and may be missing
important growth opportunities. If

> The three keys to a successful budget
> are (1) a tight but attainable goal, (2) com-
> mitment to and acceptance by all man-
> agement levels, and (3) regular use in
> performance measurement.

the budget is unrealistic, it will likely be a demotivating tool rather than one that
properly motivates managers and staff throughout the organization to perform.

Second, the budget process should result in commitment to and acceptance of
the final budget by managers at all levels of the organization. For this commitment and acceptance to occur, managers need to be very involved in the development of the budget and understand why certain budget decisions are being made
throughout the process. This budget transparency is an important component of a
properly balanced bottom-up and top-down budget approach. Finally, the budget
should be used as a tool for regular performance measurement in conjunction
with reporting and variance analysis as discussed later.

Measurement

The process of measurement involves determining what to measure, how to measure it, and what level of detail and frequency is most appropriate. Because measurement requires resources, an organization needs to balance the management
value gained from measurement versus the ongoing cost of measurement. The
most common areas for measurement include volume of activities, revenue generated, expense incurred, quality performance, and operational parameters.

Bolton Medical Associates would likely want to measure the following in those
measurement areas (Table 2.1).

TABLE 2.1   COMMON AREAS FOR MEASUREMENT
AND SUGGESTED METRICS

Volume/Activities	Revenues/ Expenses	Quality Metrics	Operational Metrics
By department	By department	Health status	Waiting time in office
By visit type	By visit type	Test improvement	Waiting time for appointment
By severity level	By severity level	Patient satisfaction	No show rate
By physician	By physician	Staff satisfaction	
By week/month	By week/month	Patient compliance	

Reporting and Variance Analysis

The purpose of reporting for an organization is to generate information for managers to understand performance against the organization's plan or budget. Reporting should be done on a regular and timely basis—typically, weekly, monthly, or quarterly depending on the size of the organization and the specific metrics for reporting.

Reports should be generated as soon as feasible after the close of the time period to give managers sufficient time to identify and react to any problems or opportunities. As a general rule, reports should be shared with managers as far down within the organization as feasible. Managers should not only receive reports regularly but also be empowered to act in addressing issues raised in the reports.

Variance analysis is an essential part of effective reporting. The purposes of variance reporting are to provide managers with the information to understand why revenues and expenses are different than expected and to identify potential problems early on so that corrective action can be taken expeditiously. Controllability and accountability are key aspects of variance reporting. An organization should hold managers accountable through variance reporting for revenues and expenses they can reasonably control, tying into the responsibility center concept discussed earlier.

There are two common types of variance analysis—traditional and flexible budget variance analysis. For traditional variance analysis, budgeted expenses are compared with actual expenses by line item (e.g., salaries, materials) and department (e.g., Information Services, Internal Medicine). Variances are shown on a monthly and year-to-date basis in absolute dollar terms and on a percent variance basis.

Table 2.2 is an example of traditional variance analysis for Internal Medicine at Bolton Medical Associates.

TABLE 2.2   INTERNAL MEDICINE—TRADITIONAL VARIANCE ANALYSIS

	Budget	Actual	Absolute Variance	Percent Variance
Visits	15,000	15,600	600	4.0%
Revenues	$1,350,000	$1,376,700	$26,700	2.0%
Direct costs				
Labor	$720,000	$753,822	−$33,822	−4.7%
Nonlabor	$300,000	$319,500	−$19,500	−6.5%
	$1,020,000	$1,073,322	−$53,322	−5.2%
Indirect costs	$430,000	$453,378	−$23,378	−5.4%
Net margin	−$100.000	−$150,000	−$50,000	

The shortcomings of traditional variance analysis include the lack of explicit consideration of the effect of volume (i.e., quantifying how changes in volume affect the cost) and limited guidance as to why the variance occurred. That raises several questions for Internal Medicine.

- How much of the $26,700 increase in revenues is from the 600 additional visits as opposed to a change in price per visit?
- How much of the $53,332 negative variance in direct costs is due to providing 4% more visits than expected?
- What portion of the $33,822 labor variance is due to the staff being less efficient than expected or wage rates being different than budgeted?
- What part of the $19,500 negative variance in nonlabor costs is due to the use of materials?

In this traditional variance analysis, it is possible only to guess.

The flexible budget variance approach helps address the shortcomings of traditional analysis and answer these specific questions. The flexible budget reflects what the expenses or revenues should have been given the actual volume of work performed. Only variable costs (affected by volume) are different in the flexible budget. Fixed costs by definition do not change. The flexible budget depends on the setting of per unit standards in a given department.

The advantages of the flexible budget approach are that it adjusts the budget when actual volume is different than budgeted volume, identifies potential causes of variances, and helps pinpoint responsibility and controllability. Under the flexible budget approach, commonly calculated revenue variances are:

- Volume (volume of activities different than budgeted)
- Price (price charged per type of activity different than budgeted)

The most prevalent expense or cost variances are:

- Volume (volume of activities different than budgeted)
- Efficiency (different amount of time spent than budgeted if for labor, different number of units used if for materials)
- Price (labor rate or materials price different than budgeted)
- Fixed direct/indirect costs (fixed costs different than budgeted)

The revenue and cost variances can be combined to look at comparable contribution/profit variances.

There are two related conventions or guidelines for variance calculation.

> Variance analysis is a powerful tool to understand whether you are different from budget due to volume, efficiency or price issues.

For revenues or contribution, actual − budget = variance. For costs, budget − actual = variance. Under those conventions, revenue or contribution higher than budget results in a positive variance while cost higher than budget results in a negative variance.

The formulas for calculation of revenue variances are as follows:

Volume variance = (Actual volume – Budgeted volume) × Budgeted price
Price variance = (Actual price – Budgeted price) × Actual volume

The formulas for calculation of cost or expense variances are as follows:

Volume variance = (Budgeted volume – Actual volume) × Budgeted variable cost per unit
Efficiency variance = (Budgeted efficiency – Actual efficiency) × Actual volume × Budgeted price
Price variance = (Budgeted price – Actual price) × Actual volume × Actual efficiency

Let us now apply those variance calculations to Internal Medicine at Bolton Medical Associates to see if we can gain a better understanding of why the profit is $50,000 worse than expected than from traditional variance analysis.

In Table 2.3, it is possible to first recast the variance analysis to be consistent with the contribution margin approach that separates variable and fixed costs and shows multiple contribution margins.

TABLE 2.3   INTERNAL MEDICINE—FLEXIBLE BUDGET
VARIANCE ANALYSIS

	Budget	Actual	Absolute Variance	Percent Variance
Visits	15,000	15,600	600	4.0%
Revenues	$1,350,000	$1,376,700	$26,700	2.0%
Variable direct costs				
Labor	$360,000	$393,822	–$33,822	–9.4%
Nonlabor	$90,000	$81,000	$9,000	10.0%
Variable contribution	$900,000	$901,878	$1,878	0.2%
Fixed direct costs				
Labor	$360,000	$360,000	0	0.0%
Nonlabor	$210,000	$238,500	–$28,500	–13.6%
Direct contribution	$330,000	$303,378	–$26,622	–8.1%
Indirect costs	$430,000	$453,378	–$23,378	–5.4%
Net margin	–$100,000	–$150,000	–$50,000	

TABLE 2.4   PRICE AND VARIABLE COSTS PER UNIT

	Budget	Actual	Absolute Variance	Percent Variance
Price per visit	$90.00	$88.25	−$1.75	−1.9%
Variable cost per visit	$30.00	$30.44	.44	1.5%
Variable labor hours/visit	0.80	0.85	−0.05	−6.2%
Variable labor price/hour	$30.00	$29.70	.30	1.0%
Variable materials cost/visit	$6.00	$5.19	.81	13.5%

To actually perform the variance calculations, it is necessary to obtain additional information about changes in the prices and variable costs on a per unit basis as shown in Table 2.4.

To understand why the revenue is $26,700 higher than budgeted, it is also necessary to separate that overall variance into a revenue volume variance and a revenue price variance (Table 2.5).

As indicated, the revenue was up by $54,000 because the visit volume increased by 600 or 4%, but that was partially offset by $27,300 due to the decline in the average visit price from $90 to $88.25. This breakout gives us more insight into what happened than just the $26,700 overall revenue variance.

Let us next analyze the $24,822 negative variance in variable direct costs (Table 2.6).

Accordingly, an $18,000 increase in variable direct costs would be expected due to the 600 additional visits (variable costs increase in proportion to volume by definition). However, Bolton Medical Associates spent $23,400 more than expected on labor because there were more hours per visit (0.85 hours per visit vs. 0.80). This labor inefficiency was partly offset by the favorable labor price variance of $3,978 because the labor rate per hour was less than expected ($29.70 vs. $30). Finally, there was a favorable material variance because fewer materials were used per visit than budgeted ($5.19 per visit vs. $6).

TABLE 2.5   REVENUE VARIANCE ANALYSIS

Revenue volume	$54,000	(Actual volume − Budgeted volume) × Budgeted price
		(15,600 visits − 15,000 visits) × $90 per visit
Revenue price	−$27,300	(Actual price − Budgeted price) × Actual volume
		($88.25 per visit − $90 per visit) × 15,600 visits
Total revenue variance	$26,700	

TABLE 2.6   VARIABLE COST VARIANCE ANALYSIS

Volume	−$18,000	(Budgeted volume − Actual volume) × Budgeted volume variable cost/unit (15,000 visits − 15,600 visits) × $30 per visit
Labor efficiency	−$23,400	(Budgeted efficiency − Actual efficiency) × Actual volume × Budgeted price (0.80 hours − 0.85 hours) × 15,600 visits × $30 per hour
Labor price	$3,978	(Budgeted price − Actual price) × Actual volume × Actual efficiency ($30/hour −$29.70/hour) × 15,600 visits × 0.85 hours
Materials variance	$12,600	(Budgeted cost/unit−Actual cost/unit) × Actual volume ($6 per visit − $5.19 per visit) × 15,600 visits
Total variable cost variance	−$24,822	

As a last step, we can look at variances in our fixed costs, both direct and indirect. These variances are simply a comparison of budgeted versus actual because they are not affected by volume (Table 2.7).

It is apparent that the fixed direct costs are $28,500 unfavorable to budget and the indirect costs that have been allocated are $23,378 higher than budgeted. For further analysis, the fixed direct cost variance could be separated by category (e.g., office supplies) and specific item (e.g., paper). And although it would be possible to further delineate the fixed indirect cost variance by allocating department (e.g., Building, Administration, Information Services), this would likely be of little value because the costs of these departments are not under Internal Medicine's control.

TABLE 2.7   FIXED COST VARIANCE ANALYSIS

Fixed direct	−$28,500	Budget fixed direct − Actual fixed direct $570,000 − $598,000
Fixed indirect	−$23,378	Budget fixed indirect − Actual fixed indirect $430,000 − $453,378
Total fixed cost variance	−$51,878	

In summary, the increase in the loss of $50,000 for Internal Medicine is in reality the result of a number of different factors, some of which are unfavorable (lower visit price, less efficient labor, higher fixed costs) and some of which are favorable (increase in visit volume, lower wage rate, lower materials cost). Different people within Internal Medicine may be responsible for addressing the different variances based on what they can reasonably influence or control. This flexible budget-based variance analysis has provided substantially more insight into what the problems are that Bolton Medical Associates may need to address to improve the profitability for Internal Medicine.

There are several important guidelines for effective application of variance analysis. First, recognizing that variance analysis does not provide the answers—it prompts one to ask the right questions of the responsible manager. Second, variances should be looked at over time—it may be a mistake to react too strongly to one month's results. Third, focusing on the largest absolute and percent variances, both positive and negative (e.g., management by exception) is a sound approach to investigating variances. Fourth, the quality of the standards underlying the variance analysis may be an important factor in the meaningfulness of the variances—if the standards are just rough estimates, the variance may be due to the inaccuracy of the standards rather than actual performance. Fifth, variance analysis should be a motivational tool to encourage managers to respond appropriately to problems before they become major. Finally, education of managers in understanding variance analysis is critical to the success of variance analysis.

In summary, the management control structure and process of an organization has a major impact on the success of that organization. Accordingly, the decisions made by senior management about organizational structure, responsibility centers, incentives, transfer pricing, programming, budgeting, measurement, and reporting should be carefully thought through and periodically reevaluated as conditions change.

CASE STUDY

Dr. John Klingler, Chief Executive Officer of Bolton Medical Associates, and Ryan Broderick, its Chief Financial Officer, were engaged in a heated discussion about how to properly compensate the physicians in charge of Internal Medicine, Pediatrics, and Sports Medicine. They had recently agreed to convert those departments from expense centers to profit centers and had chosen to set transfer prices based on the market price less an internal discount. However, they had not yet changed the compensation of the physician leaders from a straight salary.

Klingler was advocating an approach that compensated the physicians with a base salary plus a bonus that was based one-third on their department's profit, one-third on the overall organization's profit, and one-third on meeting quality and patient satisfaction metrics. Broderick agreed that a straight salary was no longer appropriate but wanted 80% of the bonus to be tied to the department's profit and 20% tied to overall profit, with nothing based on quality or patient satisfaction.

Broderick believed that quality was very hard to measure fairly, especially across departments, and that patient satisfaction results were easy to manipulate. Klingler countered that quality might be hard to measure, but their future depended on continually improving the patient experience they delivered from both clinical and nonclinical perspectives.

Questions

- Which compensation approach would you recommend? Why?
- Are there other alternatives that should be considered?
- Should nonfinancial incentives be included? If so, what kinds of nonfinancial incentives would you recommend?
- What are the downsides if the compensation approach is not seen as fair or has unintended consequences?

SUGGESTED READING

Pink DH. *Drive: The Surprising Truth About What Motivates Us.* Edinburgh, UK: Canongate Books; 2010.
Young DW. *Management Control in Nonprofit Organizations.* 9th ed. Chapters 6–12. Stoneham, MA: Crimson Press; 2012.

3

The Next Generation of Information Technology in the Healthcare Industry

JOHN V. FOLEY AND ERIC J. BIEBER

KEY POINTS

- The electronic medical record (EMR) has forever changed healthcare.
- The greatest value of the EMR lies in its ability to use data to provide valuable insights into health, wellness, and behaviors that can help us better engage patients.
- Technology should be an enabler of the organization mission.
- Establishing strong governance of technology and the associated programs is critical.
- Patient portals will become an increasingly important vehicle to engage patients.
- There will be a marked increase in "home-based" technologies to improve patient care.
- Patients expect real time access to their personal health information.
- Health information exchanges (HIEs) will allow providers to share important information that will not be dependent on the brand of EMR or employment model.
- The use of "big data" to drive clinical improvements is still in its infancy.

- Risk management and regulatory compliance are critical in the oversight of information technology (IT).
- IT will be a major expense to all healthcare organizations.
- Strong alignment to the project/change management group or to an operational effectiveness group is critical in implementing or optimizing IT systems.

This chapter introduces the reader to the challenges of modern healthcare IT and systems. This is not a discussion of which EMR to choose or how to implement these technologies. Nor is it a discussion of Meaningful Use measures that the government is incentivizing providers to meet. These issues are fleeting. Instead, the focus is on looking forward and discussing how to best develop technology and get people to move from the current state to what will be required in an information-rich healthcare environment.

The future of healthcare—and the business of healthcare—has never been more dependent upon technology than it is today. Technology will drive operations, interactions, and the future financial success of healthcare enterprises; it will be the foundation upon which the next generation of healthcare is built.

One need only look to other industries to see and understand the transformative power of technology. A good example of this is the financial industry, which has changed dramatically since its full adoption of technology. People no longer think of banks as the large marble-lined buildings with stainless steel vaults from past years but rather smaller community-based "outlets," online banking, and automatic teller machines. These electronic transactions have not only reduced costs but have created new revenue streams through business analytics, informatics, and new "personalized" financial services. Today, the online branch is the largest and most profitable branch of most banking businesses!

The emerging business model in the healthcare industry shows many parallels to banking. Large independent hospitals sprang up to serve communities, cities, and regions. Each hospital made independent investments in technology—primarily in a best-of-breed model that best served their clinical specialties. When these hospitals started to merge in the 1980s and 1990s, the majority of hospitals each maintained their independent and unique technologies, particularly the clinical systems. The health system enterprises that owned the hospitals were stuck with a "federation" of technologies that worked but did not integrate or interoperate easily. This resulted in operational inefficiencies, inconsistent data and quality reporting, and a limited ability to enhance patient outcomes across the enterprise.

The EMR has forever changed the course of the healthcare industry. The digitization of clinical information potentially allows clinicians to quickly view large portions of a patient's medical record, including medication usage, past medical and surgical history, test results, and visit notes from other caregivers. EMRs provide easy access and a consistent and repeatable view of clinical data. Digital clinical information can be shared across hospitals, interfaced among different applications, and consolidated in data warehouses. Most importantly, digitized information can be shared with the newest member of the care team—the patient and sometimes the patient's family.

As data are shared across the healthcare community, it is necessary to adhere to privacy and security regulations that include the Health Insurance Portability and Accountability Act (HIPAA), the Health Information Technology for Economic and Clinical Health (HITECH) Act, provisions of the American Recovery and Reinvestment Act (ARRA), Payment Card Industry guidelines, and various Food and Drug Administration statutes. Again, there are parallels with financial and retail business. The breach of personal financial information carries substantial fines and penalties for these industries. In healthcare, a breach of personal health information—given that it is even more "personal"—may receive more media attention and, in the end, have the possibility of economic consequences for the party that allowed the breach to occur.

The challenge in healthcare technology today is to make this data transparency happen with the same simple interfaces people expect and find in their lives as consumers. Patients use easy, yet sophisticated, online tools that can monitor their transactions and even predict their purchasing behaviors. The move to these next-generation systems and applications will not be easy for healthcare given the legacy systems and technologies that exist in the healthcare industry. These older systems were designed for "internal" use—by billing departments and more recently clinicians. The next-generation systems in healthcare must be patient/consumer-centric. In the future, the consumer will drive the information processes that they need from their care teams—whether from EMRs, billing systems, scheduling systems, secure messaging, online video visits, or social networks.

KEY COMPONENTS OF THE NEXT-GENERATION INFORMATION TECHNOLOGY MODEL

Today's healthcare enterprises can begin the journey to the future by realigning their technology strategies to match those of other industries that have found success in the consumer marketplace. Yet they must do this in the context of regulatory and business strategic drivers in the healthcare industry. Therefore, the technology goals must be aligned with the overall mission and strategy of the healthcare enterprise.

Organizational goals need to drive the technology strategies; technology is an enabler of the organization's mission. This principle implies that the organization should always include its technology leaders in the creation and development of organizational goals and strategies in order to provide better integration and alignment of technology. Conversely, strategic technology projects should include key business stakeholders as part of the project team governance and day-to-day work groups.

The alignment of business, clinical, and technology strategic priorities is not a simple task. The healing mission of the healthcare enterprise has been a strategic driver for decades. However, organizations are now dealing with the strategic implications of accountable care organizations (ACOs) and the need to expand the mission to include wellness and to view care as a continuum. The role that technology will play in these ongoing patient-consumer care continuum strategies will vary significantly based upon the decisions that each healthcare organization makes. Nevertheless, it seems apparent that the underlying theme of a patient/consumer-centric business model will be at the core for the majority of healthcare providers in the United States.

Once alignment exists, the organization can focus on the other key components of the next-generation healthcare technology strategy, including:

- Program governance
- Patient engagement
- Real-time access
- Coordination of care
- Predictive analytics
- Agile infrastructure
- Regulations
- Financial acumen
- Operational effectiveness and technical competence
- Change management

An overview of these strategic building blocks and their effect on next-generation healthcare enterprise technology strategies follows.

Information Technology Program Governance

The governance of technology and technology programs is a critical component of an enterprise technology strategy. This starts with appropriate policies and procedures and extends into business processes and practices. Disciplined program and project management will deliver end results more consistently and cost effectively. Involvement of the appropriate stakeholders should start very early in the process including patients and other consumers. Those closest to the opportunities and problems generally bring forward the best solutions. In addition, engaged leaders who are involved with the selection and oversight of key technology program initiatives have been proven to be most successful.

As the governance process matures, formal project charters and full business financial analyses begin to fall in place for all project requests. This creates alignment to the mission and strategy of the organization and will help ensure that the right projects are being worked on throughout the organization.

As the number of projects grow and the governance of those projects matures, managing the work efforts across the different domains allows for transparency to the rest of the organization as well as to the staff members participating in the work effort. Only projects that meet the criteria for organizational alignment and strategy should be in the technology project portfolio. Whether an operational process improvement project, or an upgrade to an existing application, clarity around the work effort, spending limits, and competing priorities are essential to all levels of leadership and to all stakeholders. Project management tools and metrics to measure progress and resource utilization allow the organization to manage the productivity of the workforce and reallocate resources as appropriate.

Patient Engagement

In the era of the ARRA, one of the primary drivers for healthcare enterprises today is *patient engagement*. The strategic implications of a patient engagement strategy in healthcare are extensive—primarily because the healthcare industry has never had to do anything like it before. Once again, healthcare can turn to other industries such as banking and retail to understand and adapt their strategies for consumerism, mobile applications, consumer loyalty, and social networks.

> Adapting patient engagement strategies reflects banking and retail consumer strategies.

Engagement starts with providing patients with "ease of use" interactions with their healthcare team. Online scheduling requests, bill payments, and secure online communication with physician offices instead of holding on the phone are simple ways to start this new relationship. Patient portals with integrated personal health records offer laboratory results and medication refills, and they also may have more complex online educational resources for disease-specific conditions. Online mobile tools, including telemedicine communication tools and chat capability with physician offices, are a natural extension of the physical office and align patients to their providers and regional health systems.

Medical devices that are wearable and track wellness activities (e.g., home-based weight, blood pressure, blood sugar, and other "distance" monitoring devices) are now capable of sending the measurements to home care offices, physicians, and clinics where the recording of the information is automatic and synchronized to the appropriate patient longitudinal record (even an EMR). The implications of such data capture is that healthcare technology systems must move away from the episodic to the whole patient record and be able to establish a "chain of trust" with the remote device monitoring vendors regardless of the platform.

As patients become more involved in and "connected" to their healthcare, patient engagement programs of next-generation health systems will evolve to include influencing and changing patient behavior via targeted education, purchasing, and even patient-consumer loyalty programs.

Real-time Access

In today's world, consumers are accustomed to personalized interactions and relationships with banks and retailers. Consumers expect immediate and real-time access to the tools that they require to meet their needs. In healthcare, this translates to meeting the patients' expectations for anytime/anywhere access to their personal health information—from medical records to financial information and from scheduling appointments to educational materials. Patients also want near real-time access to their care team—for simple transactions such as prescription refills and for more complex discussions with their physician via secure messaging or real-time video conferencing.

As EMRs become the standard for clinical documentation in the United States, they provide a digital mechanism for capturing, storing, and retrieving clinical information. Although the transition to EMRs must include scanned documents and historical records, the true value of an EMR lies in the discrete data that can be extracted and analyzed to provide insights into patient health, wellness, and behavior. Thus, real-time access to data benefits the healthcare team by providing immediate access to patient health parameters but also enables a broad view of the entire patient population for trending and research. Patient-consumers who are actively managing their health and their health data—the connected consumer—will also be able to leverage the real-time access to personal test results, physician notes, and longitudinal health records. If other consumer trends hold true for healthcare, it is expected that adoption by patient-consumers to embrace mobile applications, social media, and online access tools will be quick.

> EMRs provide the foundation for real-time access to data.

Coordination of Care

Historically, clinical care has been focused around acute episodic "sickness" events. Care was generally fragmented with primary care providers, specialists, and a cadre of other providers and entities playing various roles but with limited connectivity and coordination. With the advent of ACOs and a patient-centered focus, many organizations are attempting to bridge these gaps. In addition, there is now a focus on wellness and wellness-related activities. This focus provides a new point of patient contact to many healthcare organizations, but it is an additional area for which associated data streams must be managed. Another issue is the fact that very few organizations own and operate all of the pieces and parts of the continuum such as skilled nursing facilities, rehabilitation, long-term care, home care, assisted living, nursing homes, and hospice—to name a few. As we have pointed out, even if they are owned, these facilities tend to have disparate information and business systems.

The digitization of clinical records and medical information in discrete data format now allow care providers to share data more easily and quickly—both with each other and

> Data sharing facilitates broader use of EMR platforms, enabling a more complete view of patient health histories.

with their patients. The data sharing and transmission standards required by ARRA have accelerated the healthcare industry's ability to move data across EMR platforms. It is now much easier to transmit data securely in standard formats that can easily be imported and assimilated into a local EMR or personal health record than ever before.

The ARRA requirements that also demonstrate the ability to transmit these data in the state or regional HIE provide a community-wide view of a patient's health profile. This data-sharing opens the doors to more collaboration among the full care team. By crossing the cost and time barriers of custom-made interfaces for EMR integration, standard processes for transmitting summary of care documents, specific clinical results, or full medical records makes access to patient demographic and clinical information an integrated part of the patient visit and the physician-to-patient conversation. One might imagine an optimized environment where (1) information from an ambulance is immediately downloaded to the receiving emergency department's EMR, (2) information from a hospital is seamlessly sent from hospital care managers to a skilled nursing facility, or (3) care coordinators in an ACO are able to continuously follow a patient's progress through all transitions of care and then are able to communicate through the personal health record or other telemedicine devices to the patient at home. Through the appropriate integration, optimization, and interfacing of the various data streams, all of these opportunities are quite possible.

Predictive Analytics

Much of the healthcare data was created in silos to serve a singular purpose—for example, patient demographics, treatment codes, billing and insurance information, and physician notes. Data pools of this type create organizations that are "data-rich and information poor." It has been difficult for most hospitals and healthcare systems to deliver a rigorous

> Healthcare organizations have been creating financial and clinical data for many years.

cost-accounting process for clinical procedures because of the disjointed and disconnected systems for clinical documentation and financial accounting. Recently, healthcare organizations have realized that they need to aggregate these various data pools, combine them with other "outside" data sources, and extract new information and insights about their processes, their patients, and the delivery of healthcare.

The new mantra of value-based care delivery requires in-depth analysis of quality, clinical outcomes, operational efficiencies, and supply costs. To understand the total cost of care across the care continuum, providers are adding data sources from insurance companies and others to create a complete view of patient care and healthcare costs. All of these data sources need to be normalized and validated before creating an enterprise-wide data warehouse that can be used by the healthcare organization for population health management. It is becoming increasingly important to be able to analyze large populations of patients and not only identify those presently at high-risk but also to find those patients who will be at future increased risk. This analysis allows for earlier intervention with the potential for disease avoidance or minimization.

Large retail and banking institutions have learned to leverage their broad and deep data sources to forecast and predict consumer behavior. Healthcare is certainly on the same path, but it is lagging somewhat in functionality due to the immaturity of its data management processes. The use of "big data" and "metadata" to predict the need for clinical intervention is in its infancy. Healthcare organizations must execute strategies not only to house data to be used for clinical interventions, including data storage and organization, but also develop methods to interpret and then act on the information provided. Once these processes mature and healthcare organizations add data sources such as clinical trials, genetics, and disease-specific research outcomes, healthcare will see significant improvements in the *personalized* treatment of disease. This full view of the patient's longitudinal medical record and wellness profile will facilitate new models of care that customize pharmaceuticals, treatments, and health monitoring to maximize positive clinical outcomes and the patient-consumer experience. To this end, we are presently adding trained clinician-informaticists to teams to manage the information across the care continuum for various patient populations.

Agile Infrastructure

Next-generation healthcare systems will need to make substantial investments in core technologies to meet these new expectations.

The core infrastructure technologies in healthcare must advance to meet the new and evolving expectations of patient-consumers in the next generation healthcare model. The service levels, reliability, and resilience of the core data centers built for healthcare have been centered on the traditional hospital and physician users. These internal users are accustomed to the standard down time windows and occasional outages of their legacy clinical and business systems. The service and access expectations of the emerging patient-consumer user base will mirror their expectations of their online banking and retail relationships—always "on" and always available, anywhere and anytime.

The next-generation (healthcare systems) investments go beyond the hardware and software required to deliver and maintain a "consumer-grade" network. It also includes investments in new technology skills and competencies for online tools, user interfaces, mobile applications, and 24-hour customer support. As healthcare organizations establish a patient-centric model, these new skills and services will be a critical ingredient in achieving competitive advantages in the future.

REGULATION OF THE USE OF INFORMATION TECHNOLOGY IN HEALTHCARE DELIVERY

Technology strategy in healthcare must address a wide range of state and federal regulations and guidelines. For example, a comprehensive tech-

> Patient privacy and confidentiality must be maintained with utmost care.

nology strategy must consider International Classification of Disease–10 (ICD-10) requirements, HIPAA privacy and security, and the potential incentives—and penalties—for Meaningful Use (as defined by the content management system). Risk management and regulatory compliance require a substantial portion of the technical resources in any healthcare organization. As each organization defines its strategies and creates its priorities, the resources required to meet the related regulatory requirements of each strategy must be considered.

The patient-consumer model that provides "anytime/anywhere" access to health information for a patient-consumer creates substantial privacy and security issues for the technology team. Legal and compliance processes to allow patient-consumer access to medical records must be included as part of the technology design and operational workflow. Protection of personal financial information—particularly as part of an online patient financial management and Web-based bill payment processes—needs to be built into the technology platform. As new technologies for patient engagement expand into mobile devices, the security and privacy of all patient personal data will become a larger part of the ongoing regulatory requirements and risk management criteria. The technology team must be prepared to monitor and manage compliance to an increasing body of federal and state regulations and guidelines in an expanding "techno-verse" that includes a large number of patients.

Almost every aspect of healthcare delivery in the United States is subject to federal, state, and/or local regulations, with the use of IT being no exception. These regulations are the primary mechanism used by governments to incent or deter specific behaviors by healthcare providers. Therefore, to better understand the IT decisions made by healthcare providers, it is necessary to understand the framework of regulations that shape them.

TABLE 3.1   ADMINISTRATION OF HEALTH INSURANCE PORTABILITY AND ACCOUNTABILITY ACT RULES[a]

Administered by HHS	Administered by CMS
Privacy Rule	Transactions and code sets standards
Security Rule	Employer identifier standard
Enforcement Rule	National provider identified standard

[a]HIPAA Administrative Simplification Statute and Rules, http://www.hhs.gov/ocr/privacy/hipaa/administrative/index.html.

Health Insurance Portability and Accountability Act (HIPAA)

The primary regulation governing the security and privacy of electronically stored healthcare information is the Health Insurance Portability and Accountability (HIPAA) act of 1996. Title II of the HIPAA act required the Department of Health and Human Services (HHS) develop "provisions that required HHS to adopt national standards for electronic healthcare transactions and code sets, unique health identifiers, and security."[1]

The rules created to meet these requirements can be broadly separated into two categories: those which provide rules governing the use of and consequences related to the use of protected health information (PHI) and those which are primarily specifications for common identifiers to be used throughout the healthcare industry.

Rules governing the use of PHI are managed by the HHS, and the specification rules are managed by the Centers for Medicare and Medicaid Services (CMS) (Table 3.1).

As initially implemented, the HIPAA Privacy and Security rules outline the requirements that covered entities must meet to protect the confidentiality and integrity of the PHI that they store and process. (Table 3.2) Covered entities is one of the many new terms defined in HIPAA and encompasses health plans, healthcare clearinghouses, and healthcare providers that transmit health information in an electronic form.[2]

Health Information Technology for Economic and Clinical Health (HITECH) Act

The requirements originally defined in HIPAA have been revised and extended by a number of laws, including provisions of the HITECH Act, part of the ARRA

1. HIPAA Administrative Simplification Statute and Rules, http://www.hhs.gov/ocr/privacy/hipaa/administrative/index.html.

2. HIPAA § 160.103, http://www.hhs.gov/ocr/privacy/hipaa/administrative/privacyrule/adminsimpregtext.pdf.

TABLE 3.2   DESCRIPTION OF HEALTH INSURANCE PORTABILITY AND
ACCOUNTABILITY ACT RULES

Privacy Rule	"The HIPAA Privacy Rule establishes national standards to protect individuals' medical records and other personal health information and applies to health plans, health care clearinghouses, and those health care providers that conduct certain health care transactions electronically. The Rule requires appropriate safeguards to protect the privacy of personal health information, and sets limits and conditions on the uses and disclosures that may be made of such information without patient authorization. The Rule also gives patients rights over their health information, including rights to examine and obtain a copy of their health records, and to request corrections"[a]
Security Rule	"The HIPAA Security Rule establishes national standards to protect individuals' electronic personal health information that is created, received, used, or maintained by a covered entity. The Security Rule requires appropriate administrative, physical and technical safeguards to ensure the confidentiality, integrity, and security of electronic protected health information."[b]
Enforcement Rule	"The HIPAA Enforcement Rule contains provisions relating to compliance and investigations, the imposition of civil money penalties for violations of the HIPAA Administrative Simplification Rules, and procedures for hearings."[c]

[a]The Privacy Rule, http://www.hhs.gov/ocr/privacy/hipaa/administrative/privacyrule/index.html.

[b]The Security Rule, http://www.hhs.gov/ocr/privacy/hipaa/administrative/securityrule/index.html.

[c]The HIPAA Enforcement Rule, http://www.hhs.gov/ocr/privacy/hipaa/administrative/enforcementrule/index.html.

HIPAA § 160.103, http://www.hhs.gov/ocr/privacy/hipaa/administrative/privacyrule/adminsimpregtext.pdf.

act of 2009.[3] The provisions of the HITECH Act introduce new requirements that have necessitated changes to the Privacy, Security, and Enforcement rules, as well as the creation of a new Breach Notification rule (Table 3.3). The changes under HITECH focus on stricter standards for disclosure of PHI, detailed notification

3. In addition to changes to security and privacy regulations, the HITECH/ARRA Act includes the well-known program providing incentive payments for the adoption and meaningful use of EHRs by healthcare providers.

TABLE 3.3   BREACH NOTIFICATION RULE SUMMARY

Breach Notification Rule	"The HIPAA Breach Notification Rule, 45 CFR §§ 164.400-414, requires HIPAA covered entities and their business associates to provide notification following a breach of unsecured protected health information. Similar breach notification provisions implemented and enforced by the Federal Trade Commission (FTC), apply to vendors of personal health records and their third party service providers, pursuant to section 13407 of the HITECH Act."[a]

[a]Breach Notification Rule, http://www.hhs.gov/ocr/privacy/hipaa/administrative/breach-notificationrule/index.html.

requirements for breaches of PHI, and stronger enforcement procedures and penalties.

Notably, the HITECH Act also extends requirements to comply with the Privacy and Security rules—and the associated penalties for noncompliance—to the business associates of covered entities.

Of interest, HIPAA compliance is not a product, service, or certification but rather a combination of clinical and technology policies, procedures, and practices.[4] There is no discrete endpoint, and success is best judged integrating good security and privacy practices into an organization's culture and the continuous assessment of the effectiveness of those practices.

SECURE ACCESS TO PATIENT RECORDS

In addition to requiring covered entities to protect the PHI that they store and process, the Privacy Rule requires that healthcare providers have a mechanism to provide patients with on demand access to their own records. A number of methods are in common use for providing records access, including the delivery of an electronic record on physical media, access to a patient portal, and integration with a personal health record (PHR) provider.

Electronic Record

The first and most common access method is to give the patient a copy of their record directly on electronic media, such as a DVD or CD-ROM. This is analogous

4. HHS, HIPAA FAQs, http://www.hhs.gov/ocr/privacy/hipaa/faq/securityrule/2003.html.

to providing a paper copy of the record, and security protections similar to those for paper apply. For this method, the provider's duties are to ensure the record cannot be accidentally altered by the patient and the electronic format is generally accepted. HHS provides recommendations for file format in Adobe PDF or as an ASTM/HL7 continuity of care document (CCD). Providing the record as a PDF allows the patient to easily review the record using freely available Adobe software but presents difficulty when uploading the record into a destination EMR system. Providing the record in a CCD format allows for the record to be easily uploaded but limits the patient's ability to review their records prior to upload.

Once the electronic copy of the PHR has been transferred to the patient, a providers' duty to secure the record ends. Even so, some providers will digitally sign and encrypt the record as an added layer of protection. This safeguards the record from alteration and inadvertent disclosure in the event the media is lost or stolen. The downside is that the record must now be accompanied by a password for verification and access.

Patient Portal

The second access method for providing secure access to PMRs is to provide a secure patient portal or website. As with any Internet-facing system, appropriate security protections must be enabled. Both patients and regulators alike have certain minimum expectations when it comes to securing data on a publicly available website. For the underlying infrastructure, these protections typically include a segmented architecture that separates the application (Web) layer from the database layer by using firewalls, virtual local area networks, and intrusion detection. For data access, patient identity and authentication mechanisms are key. During initial enrollment to the portal, the patient's identity must be verified before access to his or her record is permitted. Once enrolled, secure password retrieval and reidentification system for lost credentials is a requirement. The majority of patients are infrequent users of patient portals, unlike social media websites; this makes patients more prone to forget or misplace their credentials.

Third-Party Personal Health Record

A third access method is for the provider to partner with a PHR vendor, such as Microsoft's HealthVault, to provide access. The advantage of this type of arrangement is the security of the record data. Once with the PHR vendor, the data becomes the patient's responsibility through a business associate agreement. The provider's security responsibilities are limited to the necessary due diligence to ensure the PHR vendor has adequate protection and the determination of the best method to securely (and timely) transfer patient record data to the PHR vendor.

Blue Button

As the market for the use of electronic health data continues to mature, consumers have and will continue to demand additional functionality such as the ability to selectively share portions of their healthcare data with third-party solution providers. Proof of concepts includes applications that allow parents to automatically chart their children's height and weight over time.[5] To facilitate this interconnectivity, the Office of the National Coordinator has introduced BlueButton+, providing a "blueprint for the structured and secure transmission of personal health data on behalf of an individual consumer."[6]

FINANCIAL ACUMEN

The IT department is a major expense of any healthcare organization. Effective management of the business side of IT is vital to an organization's success. The team managing the finances of the IT department must understand sound general accounting procedures and adhere to financial operating procedures.

One of the largest expense line items for any healthcare organization is the IT third-party contracts. Contract management includes negotiating the legal, business, and financial terms, and specific project deliverables per vendor. Contract management also includes oversight of the terms of the contract throughout the life cycle of the arrangement. An exquisitely written legal document does not add value to the organization if the terms of the agreement are not followed through or managed by either party. Projects being brought forward should meet specific criteria and have meaningful metrics and measurements that become visible throughout the organization.

Finally, the organization should assess the value and return on investment against the enterprise technology strategy. To maximize value, the technology strategic initiatives should be reviewed periodically and critiqued for operational and financial performance.

OPERATIONAL EFFECTIVENESS AND TECHNICAL COMPETENCE

Healthcare enterprise technology strategies need to include a proactive approach for managing both revenue and costs. Improvements in revenue cycle effectiveness

---

5. Growth-tastic, http://www.additiveanalytics.com/blog/engaging-patients-blue-button/.

6. ONC BlueButton+, http://www.healthit.gov/buzz-blog/health-innovation/introducing-blue- button/.

and operational efficiencies will continue to be strategic drivers for years to come. Better yet will be technologies that enable new models of care that lower the cost structure and/or create new sources of revenue. A number of organizations have formed departments of operational effectiveness. They combine the use of various performance improvement methodologies with critical evaluation of existing practices. Through these efforts, process optimization can be achieved with significant reductions in redundancies and associated expenses. Given the complexity of working with multiple databases across multiple entities, it is helpful to use such processes when creating the architecture for a modern IT organization. In addition, it is imperative to engage IT leaders to become part of the process for care model redesign. With engagement of IT resources comes a richer understanding of what it is that the organization is trying to accomplish. Undoubtedly, this input is invaluable in facilitating the dialogue but also in identifying additional opportunities.

IT skills and competencies is an often-missed component of technology strategy in healthcare. Many technologists in healthcare have grown old with their legacy systems. A modern consumer-centric model means that new technology skills and competencies will be required to succeed. This includes in-depth knowledge of consumer-centric systems for data capture, analysis, and integration into multiple workflows. Mobile application development and full "customer support" will be paramount. The skill sets and thus employees required to facilitate this new IT functionality are quite different than what was required to simply implement an EMR. This will require most organizations to consider a very different organizational chart for their IT departments. There will be a premium for employees who can function in this ever-evolving architecture where optimization and working in interdisciplinary environments will yield the most significant success. In addition, each organization must decide how to attract, develop, and retain people with these skills to best execute technology strategies of the future.

EFFECTIVE CHANGE MANAGEMENT

It is essential to understand the patient's perspective and expectations and deliver solutions that meet the needs of a changing healthcare environment. Equally as important, it is necessary to give thoughtful consideration to the impact of the change on caregivers as well as on the entire health system.

> As healthcare is transformed from a hospital-centric model to a patient-centric/consumer-centric model, emphasis on change management within a health system is imperative.

This focus on the "people side" of change is change management (i.e., policies, process, procedures). Change management uses a structured process to achieve the desired outcome and is most effective when it is launched at the beginning of a project and integrated into the project activities. The ability to meet business objectives directly correlates with change management effectiveness. This is especially true as it relates to IT and the implementation and optimization of systems. When change management is done well, people feel engaged in the change process and work collectively towards a common objective. Risk for change failure is minimized and speed to adoption is increased.

From an IT perspective, change management focuses equally on people, process, and technology. It is closely aligned with project management and embedded in the project life cycle. Successful change management includes identifying key stakeholders, assessing where things are today and where they should be in the future, building awareness about the change, and providing a clear picture of the benefits.

Considerations for applying successful change management include:

- Understanding the audience
- Knowing their expectations
- Gathering their input
- Involving them in the process
- Providing continual communication
- Reinforcing to sustain the change

As healthcare moves to ready access to personal medical information for patients, a healthcare organization must be prepared for patients taking a proactive role in their own healthcare, be able to respond to a potential increase in patient inquiries, and provide comparative data to help patients make informed choices. Effective organizations will transform systems, streamline processes, and coach leaders and individual contributors before the change.

Initiatives, such as launching a PHR, introducing an EMR platform, or transitioning from paper to electronic charts, require reeducation and behavioral change that can be as significant as the technology change. When planning for a change of this magnitude, consider all roles affected by the change in developing the organization's plan for training, support, and reinforcement. These plans should include a communication matrix, training documentation and delivery customized by role, a support model, and a plan to overcome resistance.

The implementation of a structured change management process requires visible executive sponsorship and support to promote the benefits of the change and foster adoption. Success of a project or initiative ultimately requires that individuals in the organization perform their jobs differently. This visible executive sponsorship establishes priority and motivates people to make the change. In addition, involving all roles in the change process provides a sense of ownership and accountability across the organization.

Change management and project management are both tools that support project benefit realization—project management is the "technical" side and change management is the "people" side. Unlike project management, the change management life cycle does not end after implementation. Each and every healthcare organization must embrace a patient-consumer model to not only best serve their communities and their patients but to survive in the next generation of healthcare. Healthcare must adopt a new perspective on technology—one in which the patient is at the center of the business model. Historically, the healthcare model was focused on hospitals—and more recently on physicians. The new model for healthcare is patient-centric, or, perhaps more appropriately, consumer-centric. Patients—both well and sick—are the consumers of the healthcare industry.

A consumer-centric model changes the game for healthcare. Federated/ independent systems that do not share data easily are not viable in this model. Physicians who cannot provide easy access to their patient records will compromise the continuity of care that patient-consumers expect. Health systems that cannot share full medical records across the community will be penalized with reduced reimbursements. The management of the patient across the continuum of care instead of a single episode becomes a necessity, not luxury.

The new consumer-centric model for healthcare will trend to the same practices and processes as the retail and banking industries—increased data standardization to improve quality, full integration and/or interoperability among systems for data sharing, predictive analytics and personalization, mobile applications for access anytime and anywhere, and social networks. In the long term, full quality and pricing transparency for patient-consumer "shoppers" should result.

As healthcare technology enters the new model of consumer health, the key is providing the information in such a way that engages the patient and their caregivers in the active participation of their care. Incomplete data or complicated medical information will not provide the same experience for the patient as presenting the information in a usable and easily consumable format. Patients will demand that their health information be fully transparent—readable, understandable, and completely accurate. Organizations must change and adapt their current technologies to leverage past investments and optimize new technology tools to reach the patients in newer more appropriate ways. Mobile devices and applications will become increasingly important as they have the capability of being the integration tools that move healthcare data from complex to easily usable by the average patient.

In the future, the patient-consumer becomes the center of the health technology strategy, and is the central focus of the applications, tools, workflow, and information processing of the future. Full transparency of the patient-consumer healthcare information will lead the industry to significant improvements in clinical outcomes and clinical quality. Just as technology has transformed banking and retail businesses, health IT will be the catalyst that helps deliver the next generation of healthcare.

CASE STUDY

You are the vice president of a newly created service line in urology. One of your initial tasks is to bring all of your physician practices up on an EMR. Prior to your arrival, an EMR had been chosen and several services lines have already been implemented. The physicians in the newly implemented areas are having some challenges with using the EMR, and your physicians are concerned about the impact this will have on them. Your physician staff ranges from newly graduated residents to several senior physicians (who are also politically important in your organization). Your service line partner, who is the chair of urology, is quite forward-thinking and believes that the EMR could actually be used to improve productivity and connectivity to patients. Unfortunately, there are others who feel quite differently. Your service line is somewhat complex, with multiple office settings and a number of nurse practitioners and physician assistants. You also have relationships with multiple independent urologists, who refer cases to your subspecialty physicians. Most of these independent physician groups have already started to use an EMR, but none have the same platform that you will be implementing.

Questions

- What will be your steps in setting up an implementation team?
- Who will you tap to become part of this interdisciplinary team?
- Several of the physicians do not know how to type and have limited comfort with using a computer—how will you lead them through this change?
- What thoughts do you have about "just in time training" for your staff versus the schedule as currently given to you, which has your staff training several months in advance of the "go live" date?
- If physician productivity or satisfaction drops after your system "go live" date, what tools would you employ to improve?
- The EMR your service line has picked has a robust personal health record. How might this be used to increase patient engagement and satisfaction in your specialty?
- What strategies will you use to stay connected to your independent physicians given their disparate EMRs and lack of current connectivity to your organization's EMRs, PHR, and so on?

SUGGESTED READING

Brennan PF. Personal health technology can improve outcomes. *Mod Healthcare*. 2014 (Feb 24);44:27.

Crotty BH, Mostaghimi A. Confidentiality in the digital age. *BMJ*. 2014;348:2943.

Hoppszallern S. Skimping on IT security is costly. *Hosp Health Netw*. 2014(2);88:24.

Savage N. Bioinformatics: big data versus the big C. *Nature*. 2014;509:S66–S67.

Sheikh A, Jha A, Cresswell K, Greaves F, Bates DW. Adoption of electronic health records in UK hospitals: lessons from the USA. *Lancet*. 2014;384:8–9.

Yasnoff WA, Sweeney L, Shortliffe EH. Putting health IT on the path to success. *JAMA*. 2013;309:989–990.

4

Leadership

DAVID JAVITCH

KEY POINTS

- Effective leadership and ineffective leadership must be distinguished.
- Identify and understand one's personal and professional values and how they have an impact on one's current behavior and future aspirations.
- Several important theories of leadership and new ways to improve one's own styles are:
  - The leadership challenge: five challenges that ask which behaviors one now uses and which, if adopted, would make one a superior leader
  - High-impact leadership behaviors: five heavily researched actions that lead the leader toward success
  - The work of leadership: six principles that guide one's behavior toward increased effectiveness
  - The differences between male and female leaders
- How to answer the serious question of "Why leaders fail, and what they could do about it?"

Leaders and potential leaders in the field of healthcare need to be particularly aware of how to build and constantly improve their leadership skills. This is particularly the case for providers in healthcare because new concepts in science and technology are discovered daily and the industry seems forever in a state of flux. Also, providers, working together with their patients to provide high-quality, cost-effective, timely, and successful care find the challenges very demanding.

In addition, healthcare is one of the most highly regulated industries. Accordingly, government officials (federal, state, and local), professional organizations, and the industry itself demand both legal, moral, and ethical guidelines for the many procedures they follow. Often, these guidelines, if ignored, are accompanied by significant penalties; thus, healthcare leaders need to be extraordinary.

But first, let us look at how *Harvard Business Publishing* in 2009 described the worst leaders. Do you see any of the leaders you have known, or currently work for, portrayed here? Do you see aspects of yourself here?

1. Lack energy and enthusiasm
2. Accept their own wrong or mediocre performance
3. Lack clear vision and direction
4. Have poor judgment
5. Do not collaborate
6. Do not follow the standards they set for others
7. Resist new ideas
8. Do not learn from mistakes
9. Lack interpersonal skills
10. Fail to develop others

Anything look familiar? If so, what will you do about it? If you are interested in minimizing or eradicating any or all of those descriptors, please keep reading.

Warren Bennis, a world-renowned management expert, once said: "Successful leadership is not about being tough or soft, sensitive, or assertive, but about a set of attributes. First and foremost is character."[1] In essence, he was referring to the makeup of an individual, at the formation level of a leader. That leads directly to the next paragraphs concerning values.

VALUE: THE RELATIVE WORTH, MERIT, OR IMPORTANCE OF SOMETHING

Thoughts, feelings, behavior's, attitudes … what is at the bottom—the basic motivating force behind these assessments? One can debate the answer with philosophers, professors, colleagues, and friends. But most people who are aware of their own motives will say that these attitudes, actions, and beliefs take place based on what they hold true in their lives, personally and professionally. Of course, this may differ from individual to individual.

At this point, the very beginning of the leadership chapter, take the time to reflect seriously on what you value as a leader. What are the factors that propelled you into healthcare? Do you still hold true to these concerns? Have you embraced others?

1. http://www.azquotes.com/author/1232-Warren_G_Bennis?p=2.

Do your daily tasks and interactions allow you to fulfill and gain satisfaction from these values? Do they keep you interested and involved in your career now? Are there values that you want to strive to attain in the near-term or long-term future? Or are you even aware of what your values are? To help refresh your mind and perhaps to encourage you to broaden your scope, check out Table 4.1, which captures many of the more common standards on which we base our lives. Underline those that reflect who you are now or want to be in the future. You can personalize this by further adding additional "value" words in the empty boxes.

As you read and learn from the following pages, think about your responses to this chart and identify what values fulfill, or could potentially fulfill, you in your current or future life position.

While doing so, remember that the art and science of leadership have been practiced and researched for centuries. The simplest and latest definition of leadership comes from Marcus and Dorn, who state that leadership simply is "getting the people to follow you." Kouzes and Posner provide a more detailed definition by saying that leadership is "the art of mobilizing others to want to struggle for shared aspirations." Both definitions demonstrate actions and skills that involve any individual motivating others. There are of course hundreds of ways that this can be accomplished.

Kouzes and Posner, for example, interviewed more than 100,000 people across six continents and asked them what characteristics or traits they thought described superior leaders. They came up with many. How many of the words that follow describe you—or your past or present leaders? Which characteristics do you wish were more descriptive of you or your leaders? Which ones do you already exhibit or aspire to attain? Are you honest, competent, forward-looking, inspirational, intelligent, fair-minded, broad-minded, courageous, straightforward, imaginative, dependable, caring, cooperative, or ambitious?

These words fit into a category that can be used to describe the "trait theory of leadership." Basically, theorists thought that if you possessed those traits in a leadership role, you would be a superior or successful leader. However, experience and further research called those conclusions into question. However, recently, the trait theory has again gained in popularity.

TABLE 4.1   WHAT ARE *YOUR* VALUES?

Helpful	Supportive	Caring	Self-confident	Loyal
Ambitious	Social	Fair	Adaptable	Principled
Devoted	Open to change	Experimenter	Tolerant	Cautious
Persuasive	Trusting	Flexible	Looks for options	Modest
Analytical	Methodical	Forceful	Reserved	Quick to act
Risk taker	Persevering	Competitive	Honest	Initiator
Compassionate	Broad-minded	Courageous	Imaginative	Dependable
Supportive	Caring	Cooperative	Mature	Competent
Inspiring				

At the same time, other studies revealed that those individuals who possessed these traits were "okay" leaders, but they were not necessarily "superior" leaders. In other words, some components in the trait index were missing. There had to be other factors in addition to the previously described traits that one had to possess to be successful.

THE LEADERSHIP CHALLENGE

In their research, Kouzes and Posner surveyed another aspect of leadership, and they determined that leaders who wanted to be successful needed to perform these five challenges constantly:

- Challenge the process.
- Inspire a shared vision.
- Enable others to act.
- Model the way.
- Encourage the heart.

Their pivotal thoughts serve as the basis for many subsequent theories and approaches to leadership. Furthermore, they posit that superior leaders, especially healthcare leaders who are almost constantly confronting changes, need to seek out opportunities to complete the following challenges.

Challenge 1: Challenge the Process

- Decrease mediocrity and encourage and train others to do the same, with an eye toward achieving superiority.
- Question and change the status quo.
- Grow and develop themselves and their organization.
- Innovate now.
- Improve people, policies, and procedures.
- Constantly be vigilant about questioning what no one else has questioned or what other people see as ordinary and acceptable.
- Go out and find something to fix.
- Take risks and learn from mistakes—your own as well as those of others.

Challenge 2: Inspire a Shared Vision

- Review your past, and then determine how the future can be different and how you will make that happen.

- Create a vision statement that describes the "then and there" of the future.
- Invite others to join you in understanding your views of a positive and exciting future.
- Discuss the hopes and dreams of yourself and others.
- Involve others in a spirited discussion of how they can actively participate in behaving in a manner that demonstrates their understanding of where you and they want to go and be in the short and long term.
- Develop interpersonal competencies.
- Speak and act positively and from the heart.
- Listen first—and often.

Challenge 3: Enable Others to Act

- You are a team; use the word "we" frequently. Minimize the use of the word "I."
- It is all about collaboration cooperation and trust—what can you do to instill all these?
- Create and work with an interactive and supportive team.
- Ensure that everyone participates and makes positive statements. This does not mean that you overlook, omit, or avoid asking questions or correcting teammates' behavior or comments as you seek to reach your goals.
- Educate your team by identifying both positive and negative behaviors of individuals while pointing out areas for growth and development. Do not avoid mentioning errors or omissions, because these also are opportunities for growth. But make sure that you do this in a manner that makes heroes of those who are doing well and does not make losers out of those who are not. Everyone can benefit and learn from the mistakes of others.
- Focus on gains, not losses.
- Above all, be as positive as possible.

Challenge 4: Model the Way

- "Walk the talk" and encourage everyone else to do the same; ensure that you are the example you want others to emulate. (Recall one definition of leadership—"getting people to follow you.")
- Ask whether your behaviors and attitudes reflect your values and the values of your organization.
- Look in the mirror for reasons other than to put on your makeup or to shave. Who is staring back at you? Are you the person that you think

you are? Are you the person that you want to be? Are you the person you want other people to think you are? Are you the person that others want to lead them?

- Be active and dramatic when demonstrating to others the types of behaviors and attitudes that you want them to exhibit.
- Increase interpersonal interactions by inviting employees to breakfast or lunch. Informally describe your work life, and within strict appropriate boundaries, your personal life.
- Describe personal and shared values at team meetings, informal gatherings, and organizational meetings.

Challenge 5: Encourage the Heart

- Recognize each individual's contribution and efforts to the success of every project.
- Demonstrate and teach everyone that recognition is one of the most important motivators of most people in most industries, especially in healthcare, where employees rarely get the recognition that they deserve.
- Find an avenue to publicize the accomplishments of each individual, especially in challenging situations; use such techniques as voice mail, e-mail bulletin boards, newsletters, and team meetings.
- Offer feedback, especially positive feedback, as soon as, and as often as, you see someone doing something correctly. Go out of your way to find examples that involve patient care, because this is why many people are in the business of healthcare.
- Be the best coach possible to encourage people on the way toward superior performance and job and patient satisfaction.
- Celebrate individual and team accomplishments, birthdays, and anniversaries. It does not take long to provide cake, muffins, coffee, or other healthy alternatives to honor these types of events. These efforts go a long way to creating a positive esprit de corps. The results can be outstanding!

HIGH-IMPACT LEADERSHIP BEHAVIORS

The Institute for Healthcare Improvement (IHI) is an internationally renowned leader in innovative research, models for change, best practices, education, and optimal healthcare delivery systems. In their latest research and together with many significant industry experts, IHI has concluded that there are five behaviors that propel leaders toward having a high impact on their organizations:

1. Person-centeredness: be consistently person-centered in word and deed.
2. Front-line engagement: be a regular authentic presence at the front line and a visible champion of improvement.
3. Relentless focus: remain focused on the vision and the strategy.
4. Transparency: require transparency about results, progress, aims, and defects.
5. "Boundarilessness": encourage and practice systems thinking and collaboration across boundaries.

Person-Centeredness: Be Consistently Person-Centered in Word and Deed

Person-centeredness is the sine qua non of professionalism. The most effective healthcare leaders are person-centered in word and deed, seeking opportunities to interact with patients and families frequently. A leader can demonstrate person-centeredness with the following actions:

- Routinely participating in rounds in the organization—whether in a medical clinic, hospital, or community service organization—to talk with patients and families
- Consistently inviting and supporting patient and family participation at board, leadership, and team improvement meetings
- Discussing results in terms of persons and communities, not only diseases and dollars
- Declaring harm prevention a personal and organizational priority

Front-Line Engagement: Be a Regular, Visible Presence at the Front Line and a Visible Champion of Improvement

- The most effective leaders build trust and acquire and establish an understanding of the work at the front line of care by regularly meeting with colleagues who deliver care at the bedside, in the clinic, or in the community, and by exhibiting a genuine interest in the work performed. Behaviors such as asking questions, sharing concerns, engaging in problem-solving and improvement projects, and transparently discussing results (both successes and failures) help create leadership authenticity. A leader's authentic engagement and presence at the front line of care helps motivate multidisciplinary teams, especially in the context of modeling improvement-oriented thinking and the latest techniques and methods.

- Leadership engagement with front-line staff provides the opportunity for leaders to articulate how work at the point of care aligns with strategy, thus building good will and promoting a culture of teamwork and patient-centeredness. Leadership engagement promotes a sense of accomplishment, pride, and joy in the workers who directly care for patients and those who support their care.

Relentless Focus: Remain Focused on the Vision and the Strategy

- Talk about the vision every day, clearly articulating the measurable and unambiguous improvement and a means by which the results can be accomplished. For example, to reinforce the organization's current high-priority efforts, leaders may start every meeting with, "Remember, right now we are focused on three key safety initiatives and reducing a wasted effort."
- Align leaders' weekly schedules with high-priority initiatives in the organization.
- Designate resources to high-priority efforts, and do not divert resources to projects that are not aligned with the organization's strategic plan.
- Review the results of the most critical initiatives weekly, removing barriers to progress.
- Appoint the most effective leaders to high-priority initiatives and identify high-potential leaders in training.

Transparency: Require Transparency About Results, Progress, Aims, and Defects

- Transparency is a powerful catalyst for organizational change and learning. It entails sharing data that demonstrates both positive results and the facts, as well as reveals opportunities for improvement. Leaders need to be open and firm about the organization's commitment to—and expectations for—transparency and a path to action for eliminating defects.
- Delivered use of transparency for transformation enables accountability and trust to develop, and it promotes self-study and learning. Active transparency begets humility, and humility begets trust, the currency of leadership. The most successful healthcare organizations and leaders collect the most meaningful data on the most important patient care issues and then relentlessly work to improve them. A leader's transparency has many salutary effects; transparency helps to:
  - Build the will to improve care
  - Shape the culture into one of openness, with attention to eliminating defects

- Raise improvement capability through access to real-time data
- Track the progress of outcomes such that midcourse corrections are possible
- Engage partners and empower teams across boundaries
- Provide patients and community members with opportunities to participate in improvement and motivate change

"Boundarilessness": Encourage and Practice Systems Thinking and Collaboration Across Boundaries

- The concept of "boundarilessness" bridges two closely connected leadership behaviors. The first is the genuine, action-generating receptivity and openness to ideas or mental "boundarilessness." It can be applied to an active search beyond one's immediate confines for best practices when approaching problems. It is a model for successful engagement across boundaries, fostered by greater social capital, an attribute of a learning organization. Leaders who play a key role in modeling and leading engagement across boundaries should establish the expectation for both the adoption and active diffusion of best practices and learning. Mental "boundarilessness" is tightly coupled with innovation and displayed by behaviors that emphasize curiosity—asking open-ended questions, encouraging others to seek and try new ideas, encouraging and promoting diversity, and encouraging nontraditional approaches to problem solving.
- The second type of "boundarilessness" is reflected in the leader's willingness to cross traditional boundaries, both internal and external, in the pursuit of best results. With an increasing proportion of care aimed at persons with chronic conditions, care delivery organizations of all kinds will need to work together and with social service organizations to coordinate care across the continuum and deliver person-centered care. Their shared aim is seamless, coordinated care that answers the question, "What matters to me?" for the people receiving care. Leadership across organizational boundaries requires new actions and relationships.
- How do leaders demonstrate "boundarilessness"?
  - They ask open-ended questions.
  - They visit improvement teams, work units, and other organizations.
  - They harvest ideas from within the organization and from other leaders and organizations.
  - They see shared aims and advocate for win-win scenarios with physician practices and other community service providers.
  - They share resources.
  - They utilize systems they gained to frame problems and challenges for those they lead.

When boundaries are removed, good will builds around shared aims and a shared vision emerges; a culture of openness becomes possible; and new capabilities, ideas, and resources become available.[2]

THE WORK OF LEADERSHIP

Change occurs daily and is unavoidable in almost every phase of life. In the workplace, employees seem to be the recipients of its consequences. Some of the more common changes occur in employees' standard of living, productivity, job stability, and of course, morale. In the world of work, many employees regard stability and a lack of change as very important as those factors provide them with a sense of security, comfort, and predictability. That stability often escapes them when change occurs.

At the same time, employees want and expect their leaders to state and restate organizational values as well as the company vision, mission, and goals. To know where they stand, employees also want to know that the rules, policies, and procedures undergo few, if any, changes, so that the status quo is maintained.

If there are negative consequences to life's inevitable changes, many employees look to leaders to make the adjustments. The latter seem to remove themselves from the responsibility or challenge to devise new or adaptive methods to cope.

Many leaders like the idea of stability as well, and they use the same "tried and true" styles that they learned long ago. Some examples of that thinking may include the idea that "if I keep working hard enough or enforce a standard frequently enough the outcome will be sufficient, and that will be acceptable." Or using a top-down approach, they implement some sort of change that invariably may not be successful.

Recall that in an earlier section, Kouzes and Posner encouraged leaders to take risks and model the way for others to do the same. However, in the fast-changing dynamic of today's healthcare environment, for example, maintaining the same position means that you are going to fall behind. Staying ahead of the pack, remaining competitive, and simply surviving must involve learning new roles, responsibilities, and installing innovative policies that at first neither employers nor employees want to embrace.

Heifetz and Laurie, cutting-edge thinkers and practitioners, encourage leaders to take a new adaptive leadership role to address changes; pressures; and new visions, missions, or goals. Organizations cannot solve current or future problems with the same old tools as they did in the past; therefore, it is inevitable that new ways, new thinking, and new approaches will force change.

---

2. Excerpted with permission from Swenson S, Pugh M, McMullan C, Kabacenell A. High-Impact Leadership: Improve Care, Improve the Health of Populations, and Reduce Costs. Institute for Healthcare Improvement white paper. Cambridge, MA: Institute for Healthcare Improvement, 2013.

Therefore, Heifetz and Laurie devised six principles that effective leaders could follow and implement to shape change, maintain success and advance. These principles are designed to help leaders and employees adapt and cope with the world around them.

1. **Get on the balcony.** Distance yourself to some degree from the immediacy of rapidly unfolding events so that you are in a position to gain some perspective.
2. **Identify the adaptive challenge.** Periodically do a "sweep" of the organization to evaluate the goals, roles, policies, procedures, values, attitudes, conflicts, and past successes and failures to diagnose the problems or issues that need to be confronted.
3. **Regulate distress.** Because change can often lead to distress, you need to take the temperature of the organization to ensure that the distress is not overwhelming. This can be done by (1) encouraging a discussion of change and allowing for a manageable amount of stress, and (2) providing direction and helping to shape norms while coping with internal and external challenges.
4. **Maintain disciplined attention.** Note the pleasure-pain principle: people go toward things that give them pleasure and avoid things that cause them pain. In organizations, the leader and others may want to avoid addressing certain people, issues, factors, and conflicts that seem negative, counterproductive, time-consuming, or simply obstructionist. Such avoidance can cause future problems.
5. **Get the work back to the people.** It is very easy for many of us to want to be very directive and solve the issues. However, adaptive leaders will encourage the employees to address these challenges without seeming as if they are avoiding them.
6. **Protect voices of leadership from below.** In many organizations, individuals who criticize or want to suggest an alternative are occasionally criticized, ignored, or deemed troublemakers. Adaptive leaders must listen to these people and allow others to hear their concerns as well.

Successful adaptive leaders embrace these six principles to build an even more effective and skilled organization consisting of individuals who feel safe, protected, valued, and listened to. Furthermore, they have confidence in their leaders, who wants to take them on a journey, even into the unknown.

THE DIFFERENCES BETWEEN MALE AND FEMALE LEADERS

Theorists and practitioners have long wondered and researched whether men or women make "better" leaders. Actually, many aspiring women are asking whether they can be as successful in leadership positions as men. The so-called "glass ceiling" that to whatever degree has stymied female goals in reaching "the top" is being broken more and more in recent years (e.g., female Supreme Court justices, presidents of large and important corporations, presidents of universities, US Secretaries of State, prime ministers of countries).

In Robbins' latest work on organizational behavior, he reinforces the following conclusions that have been stated or at least inferred many times in the past: there are no major differences between successful male leaders and female leaders. However,

- Men tend to be more directive, whereas women tend to be more democratic.
- Men tend to emphasize on command and control, whereas women tend to encourage participation.
- Men tend to rely on formal authority, whereas women tend to share power in information to enhance follow worse self-worth.
- Women tend to lead more through inclusion of others than do men.

Emphasis is on the word "tend." There are plenty of exceptions that almost anyone can think of where women are more directive than men, men are more inclusive than women, and vice versa. Thus, this report out must only be used as a general descriptive of male versus female leaders.

WHY DO LEADERS FAIL?

To answer this very complex, multifaceted question, consider the following factors:

1. Definition of failure and success. This is the most basic and crucial issue that underpins the response to this all-encompassing, critical question. Is your response based in financial terms, such as income stream, general revenue, costs of services, return on investment, payer mix, bonds, or other obligations? Or are you considering organizational behavioral issues such as patient satisfaction, adverse events, quality, employee and patient complaints, or lawsuits? And what is the nature of the environment? What kind of organization are you leading—public or private, large or small, complex or single hierarchy and structure? Is the organization located in a metropolitan, suburban, or rural area? What is the level of competition from other healthcare providers?
2. Type of organization. Is it a small or large physician practice, a clinic and outpatient facility, a hospital, or an assisted-living center (some or all of which may be vertically or horizontally integrated)?
3. Funding. Is the organization the recipient of or dependent upon grants or private and/or public payers? What is the financial stability

of the organization, and how is it prepared for current and future unavoidable changes?

4. Your role. Is this clearly specified in terms of your expectations and those of others to whom you report and interact? Where are you in the hierarchy? Do you have a number of trusted colleagues with whom you can rely on or delegate responsibilities and authority? What is your span of control in terms of finances and budget? What are the breadth and depth of your resources? Are your responsibilities clearly defined? How many employees are there?

5. Dynamics. How would you describe the effectiveness of the relationships between you and your subordinates? What are the pressures on you? For example, do you need to perform tasks within a certain time frame? Are you expected to continually perform at a superior level? And where do these pressures come from in the organization (self or others)? Again, where are you in the hierarchy to make these positive and productive?

6. Goals. Whose are you fulfilling—your own, those of your boss, the board of directors, the organization, or others? And most importantly, do you agree with them and actively work to fulfill the goals?

7. Value. Have you identified which ones bring you the most satisfaction in your daily work? Are these values aligned with your activities, attitudes, views, and daily behaviors?

As you can see, a complete, well-thought out answer to the question, "Why do leaders fail?" must take into consideration a whole host of factors. Pinpointing one answer is not that easy. A serious response involves addressing the previous seven factors. By doing so, you will arrive at the best response to the question of success and failure. Intertwining those factors with the theories principles and some of the other factors mentioned in this chapter will help you come to a more solid answer. And most importantly, by carefully examining the many components listed and discussed here, you will know for yourself how to avoid failure and move toward success.

THE CASE OF HENRY

Henry has been the president of a large network of 2 major hospitals and 10 healthcare clinics in the midwestern United States for the past 14 years. His senior management staff consists of 15 people, both medical and nonmedical. Based on his long years of experience with them, he trusts them and delegates a great many issues to them. That lets him focus on paying attention to getting the job done.

Henry's critics say he has been doing things the same old way for many years now. He responds by saying that what worked in the past will work in the future. When employees, including heads of units or chairs of departments, approach him with questions or challenging problems, his standard technique is to throw the issues back onto them to resolve. The result is that they resolve most of the issues by themselves, which is his goal. He sees this as a growth opportunity for these people. Yet some complain that Henry has no time for them or does not care about them—and he is just too busy to respond to their issues.

When leading a senior staff meeting, Henry is very direct and forthright—*no* fooling around with him. His philosophy is that the business of running hospitals and clinics is to make money and take care of sick people. Accordingly, he takes few risks. When Henry takes a position on an issue, he can be very articulate and quite persuasive when he outlines his thoughts with his staff. Sometimes, some staff are concerned that he does not allow for more discussion before reaching a decision.

When people do speak up, however, Henry seems to lack empathy for the difficulties the staff must endure to resolve certain problems. Furthermore, he gives the distinct impression that he does not like it when staff disagree with him. When he does listen to opinions that differ from his, his typical response is to adopt a more coercive style to get his staff to embrace his point of view.

As a result, morale goes up and down. But there are other factors that also contribute to the roller-coaster staff morale. First, the hospital campus is too spread out, hampering face-to-face communication. The three buildings on campus are far enough apart that it is too difficult to drop by just to talk to a colleague or to scurry over to another office building to resolve an emergency. Overall, employees, even senior management, do not seem happy in their jobs. Some say that revenues could be better, and there seems to be a lack of energy in the clinics.

In the past few months, conflicts have arisen between some of the senior managers. A silo effect appears to be in place, and there is not a great deal of cooperation between departments. Henry is rarely seen making rounds or even meeting informally with employees at various levels in the hospitals or the clinics because he is much too busy.

Soon it will be time for performance appraisals. That period is usually a time of high anxiety as well. Most people score in the average range, and compliments are rare, with few promotions given. Although people feel fortunate to have their jobs, they grumble about the low wages they are receiving, especially given the high cost of living near a big city. Many people know that Henry wants high productivity and concern for patient care, but they really do not know where he is headed. Henry does not understand why staff are upset with him.

Compounding all of this, the Board of Trustees and the Regional Administration hold Henry in high regard. Moreover, he has a very favorable relationship with them, all of whom see him as an effective leader. His clinics are the few in the healthcare sector that are operating in the black.

Questions

- Henry considers himself to be an effective leader. Would you agree? Why or why not?
- What potential problems do you see looming for Henry of which he may not be aware?
- What advice and counsel would you give to Henry and his senior management team to increase organizational satisfaction and success?
- Do you believe Henry to be an effective or ineffective leader? Why?

SUGGESTED READING

Heifitz RA, Laurie DL. The work of leadership. Best of HBR, Reprint R0111K, *Harv Bus Rev.* December 2001.

Kouzes J, Posner B. *The Leadership Challenge: How to Make Extraordinary Things Happen in Organizations.* 5th ed. San Francisco, CA: Jossey-Bass; 2012.

Robbins, SP, Judge, TA. *Organizational Behavior.* 12th ed. Upper Saddle River, NJ: Pearson Education, Inc; 2007.

Swenson S, Pugh M, McMullan C, Kabacenell A. *High-Impact Leadership: Improve Care, Improve the Health of Populations, and Reduce Costs.* Institute for Healthcare Improvement white paper. Cambridge, MA: Institute for Healthcare Improvement; 2013.

5

Ethics and the Business of the Healthcare Professional

STEVEN R. SMITH AND JOSEPH S. SANFILIPPO

KEY POINTS

- Professional codes of ethics are commonly adopted by private organizations as statements of the profession itself regarding the obligations of its members to the public and to one another.
- Codes are also adopted as part of the licensing statutes.
- Violations of ethical principles may, among other things, result in civil liability, licensure discipline, loss of hospital privileges, and loss of professional standing.
- Ethical concerns in the health area have been confidentiality (including the Health Insurance Portability and Accountability Act [HIPAA]), autonomy, protecting children and the elderly from abuse, and avoiding dual relationships.
- Adhering to good ethical principles and sound business practices is an essential part of any good healthcare organization.

ETHICS—WHY WORRY ABOUT IT?

In the early days of medicine, it was clear that the great power for good health-care had also contained the threat of harm. All professions have an ethical commitment, and the Hippocratic Oath reflects approximately 2,500 years of formal ethical commitment in the healthcare professions. An excellent resource for dozens of ethical principles for professions and associations is at http://ethics.iit. edu/library/professional-trade-associations.

This chapter defines ethics broadly. There are formal codes of ethics for all professions, and for the most part these are enforceable rules, as described in the next section. In addition, professionals also have aspirational ethical principles. Examples are "everyone who needs medical services should receive them" and the Hippocratic Oath's provision, "I will preserve the purity of my life and my arts." There are often additional ethical inclinations that have not become a part of even aspirational codes but are increasingly accepted as something the profession should be doing. For example, a profession might decide that as part of its professional service it has an "obligation" to explain to the public the health risks of overeating.

The "ethics" discussed in this chapter are not necessarily the same thing as "moral standards." They may be—it would be both unethical and immoral to kill a patient. As shall be described in a moment, there may be legal consequences to violating ethical rules, but although law and ethics are related, they are not always the same thing. Indeed, breaching some ethical principles, particularly aspirational principles, may not be violations of the law.

Business ethics is a term commonly used to mean good, honest business practices—matters that are covered throughout this book. When used this way, it has a different meaning than *professional ethics*, where there is a generally accepted and enforceable code of ethics. Business ethics may also be used to such legal requirements as the Sarbanes-Oxley law. And ethics is sometimes meant to refer to the formal ethical statements of some professions (e.g., certified public accountants). A variety of ethical statements adopted by businesses is available at http://ethics. iit.edu/library/business-organizations.

> The formal codes of ethics with the force of law are generally contained in state licensing laws.

Most commonly, a state code is based on a national model code of ethics adopted by a professional group. The trend in modern times has been to streamline these statutory codes of ethics by removing aspirational provisions, leaving the enforceable provisions. A word of caution—although licensing statutes may include what purports to be ethical standards, these may not be all of a state's ethical requirements. Some obligations are scattered throughout state statutes in provisions that allow license discipline (e.g., abuse reporting).

States have general constitutional authority to adopt laws to protect the health, safety, and welfare of citizens. Ethical provisions of licensing statutes are adopted as part of this authority. Ethical dilemmas will always be a concern for clinicians. Patient safety and quality of care must always remain of paramount importance.

PROFESSIONAL ETHICS

There are many reasons professionals should know, understand, and abide by the ethical standards of both private professional organizations and those imbedded in state law. Both the minimum standards they describe and the aspirational standards represent important commitments of the profession as a whole. Professionals receive special legal privileges through licensing, and part of the bargain in return is that the profession will adhere to standards that protect the public.

In the long run, honoring and abiding by ethical principles is good business. Professionals and professional organizations that adhere to high standards ultimately are likely to be reflected in the regard for which the public and the rest of the profession hold them. Another reason for paying attention to ethical requirements is that the failure to do so may have very unpleasant consequences. These will be discussed in a moment.

From a historical perspective, the Federation of State Medical Boards was established in 1912. Guidelines were subsequently codified into the "Essentials of a Modern Medical Practice" in 1956. State legislatures are also responsible for the definition of laws regarding professional misconduct. The spectrum of penalties legislatures may authorize state medical boards to impose include:

- Reprimand or censure that becomes part of public record
- Administrative fines
- Restitution, for which the healthcare professional is required to "repay money" improperly earned
- Probation regarding licensing
- Limitation or restriction placed upon the individual with regard to his or her ability to practice in his or her area of expertise
- Suspension from practicing
- Voluntary license suspension
- Denial of renewal of medical license
- Revocation of license and thus inability to practice

Specific medical societies also monitor professional, ethical conduct. They are charged with overview of ethical conduct of their membership. Their activity is separate and apart from state medical boards. The American Medical Association's Code of Ethics provides guidelines related to a variety of topics, including confidentiality, allocation of medical resources, conflicts of interest, and patient autonomy.

Consequences of Violations

The violation of professional code(s) of ethics may have serious consequences. The range of sanctions were noted earlier. The consequence generally arises only after formal charges have been brought and some form of hearing conducted. In criminal cases, the charges must be proved by the prosecution beyond a reasonable doubt. In civil cases and disciplinary proceedings, the level of proof required is much lower—usually a preponderance of the evidence or, in a few instances, the intermediate standard of "clear and convincing evidence."

Although there may be federal consequences (e.g., Medicare provider eligibility) flowing from finding of state ethical violations, most of the law regarding ethics comes from the state and state laws regarding ethics violations vary. Although states have similar principles of ethics, the processes they use, how they receive complaints from the public, and the standards they apply are not identical.

What the list of consequences described previously does not take into account is the nonlegal ramifications of licensure discipline or even of a charge of violation of ethics. There may be reputational and public relations problems. Traditionally, all but the most serious claims of ethical violations have been confidential. That confidentiality has been criticized, at least when discipline is imposed, because of the understandable sense that the public has a right to know when a professional is not maintaining the public trust. The confidentiality surrounding ethical complaints is beginning to change.

LICENSURE DISCIPLINE

The professional license is awarded by the state, and it may be removed or limited by the state. Or the state may impose sanctions. Licensing boards, and disciplinary processes, are substantially in the hands of the licensed professionals in most states. Public concern about this process has led to representatives of the public (not the licensed professional or his or her families) being added to the boards.

> The disciplinary process generally begins with a complaint being filed by a member of the public or another professional.

Sometimes the misconduct of a professional results from a news article or referral by a state agency. The disciplinary body of the licensing authority (here called "the board") generally conducts a preliminary investigation, and if it appears that there is merit to the claim, it will proceed by asking the professional to respond or by filing a formal complaint. The board will investigate the matter further, and often with the assistance of the state's office of attorney general, it will ultimately conduct a hearing at which it will receive evidence. Then the professional will have an opportunity to defend against the charges, present witnesses, and the like. A prosecutor is appointed to present the case against the professional. This is not a formal trial with a jury but a hearing with an administrative law judge/hearing officer or the members of the board. Sometimes the board acts as an appellate body to a hearing officer. A professional who is disciplined may appeal to the courts, although the courts will usually defer to the judgment of the board if it has followed its own procedures. It is common for professionals and the board to reach a negotiated agreement rather than going to a formal hearing.

The board may find in the professional's favor and determine that no violation of the code has been proved. If it finds a violation, it may impose a range of sanctions, as noted earlier in the chapter, from a reprimand (sometimes a private reprimand) to license suspension or even permanent licensure revocation. Boards may also order restitution (e.g., returning money taken from a patient) or rehabilitation services (e.g., entering a substance abuse program).

The formal action by a board in one state is likely to result in boards in other states in which the professional is licensed to determine whether they too should take action. Following an adverse board decision, it would not be unusual for hospitals granting privileges, employers, and private organizations to also consider taking action.

Civil Liability

The violation of a code of ethics does not automatically lead to civil liability. There may, for example, be no damages resulting from the violation. Violating ethics codes, however, generally means that a healthcare professional has not acted reasonably under the circumstances; this suggests that there has been negligence that can subject the practitioner to liability. Beyond the technicalities of this civil liability, violations of ethical duties look very bad to juries and judges. Careful adherence to ethical obligations is one way to avoid unnecessary liability risks.

Criminal Liability

Violation of codes is seldom a criminal offense. However, the same conduct that results in a violation of ethical obligations may also be criminal. For example, in some states it is a crime for some healthcare professionals to have sexual relationships with patients. That is very likely to be an ethical violation as well. But it is not a crime because it is an ethical violation; it is a crime because there is a statute that makes it a crime. Therefore, the criminal sanctions may be imposed apart from any discipline related to violation of the code of ethics.

Medicare and Medicaid Eligibility

The ability of a healthcare practitioner to qualify as a participant in federal reimbursement programs may be affected by ethical violations. Particularly where there is formal state board action against a professional, Centers for Medicare and Medicaid Services and other governmental bodies may open an investigation or consider precluding the professional from these programs. Private insurance plans and panels may also review any adverse actions of state boards.

Problem Physician Reporting

Significant license sanctions must be reported by states to the National Practitioner Data Bank. Because other state boards, hospitals, and certain others may query this database, the report itself may cause difficulty for the physician who is reported. Other state and federal reporting systems have been established or are being considered.

HOSPITAL AND PRACTICE PRIVILEGES
Ethical violations will play some role in any consideration of a professional for
hospital employment or privileges. This is particularly the case where there is formal board action. In these instances, like most of those above, the professional
will have an opportunity to explain the violation and why it should not preclude
employment or privileges. But that can be a steep hill to climb if the violation is
recent or serious.

PROFESSIONAL ORGANIZATIONS
Some professional organizations maintain independent ethics processes. Those
organizations follow up after actions by state boards. They may also receive
complaints from the public, which the professional organization will independently investigate, and may impose sanctions (e.g., removing membership in
the organization). The American Psychological Association and some specialty
boards have such processes. State and local associations may also have such
procedures.

RESOLVING ETHICAL DILEMMAS

Understanding and Avoiding Ethics Problems

It goes without saying, but we will say it anyway, that professionals must know
and stay current with the ethics of their professional boards, associations, and
organizations. Ignorance of these rules is not an excuse, and it is important that
all ethical requirements be reviewed annually.
Continuing education courses may also help
in staying current.

Many ethical issues are clear-cut.

When ethical issues are less clear, however, there may be genuine dilemmas in determining the proper course of action. There are a number of ways
to receive ethics assistance. There are written guides, including websites, that
set out the codes and provide commentaries. Many states and professional
organizations have offices that may be contacted for formal or informal
advice. Esteemed colleagues may, in many circumstances be able to provide
thoughtful advice (with appropriate steps taken to ensure appropriate patient
confidentiality).

These suggestions are meant to apply *before* an ethical lapse has occurred. They
are unlikely to be privileged, so *after* an ethical violation that may be serious it
is better for professionals to contact an attorney who represents them—in which
case an attorney-client privilege does exist. (More about privileges later in this
chapter.) Confession may be good for the soul, but it may also be very bad for protecting information unless it is privileged.

Grievances

As part of dispute resolution mechanisms regarding ethics or similar matters is the formal grievance procedures and informal or ad hoc procedures that some organizations develop. This section discusses issues related to a variety of grievance procedures.

Dissatisfied patients may well pursue a formal "grievance process." Individual patients may elect just to grieve against healthcare providers, assertively confront the physician, or seek medicolegal routes of retribution. Disgruntled patients can "spread the word' and affect patient referral patterns.

Grievances fall into a wide range of areas. Here are a few examples:

- Failure to fulfill expectations for examination and treatment
- Failure to promptly diagnose
- Rudeness
- Producing excessive pain or practicing beyond the area of expertise
- Inappropriate behavior related to billing

One study conducted in North Carolina noted that 45% of the grievances were not associated with breach of practice standards. In 17% of the filed grievances, the solution was physician apology, adjusting the bill, or completing insurance forms. Also of interest is that the majority of grievances were filed by younger women and associated with newly encountered physicians, which in retrospect reflected poor communication or delayed diagnosis. Interestingly, academicians are brought into litigation less often that private practitioners, 36% versus 64% respectively (Halperin; see Suggested Reading),

Patients with grievances may also contact state medical boards or medical society complaints, Better Business Bureaus, governmental consumer affairs, attorney generals' offices, or consumer action reporters. Once the medical society or board receives a complaint, a grievance committee proceeds with screening, review, physician education, and communication with the patient. Following filing of the complaint, the patient is asked to sign a release of records for review by the committee. Determination may be made that the physician did not act improperly and thus the claim is terminated. Depending upon the circumstance, further referral may be made to state medical board, law enforcement authorities, and so on. Every effort is made to mediate and solve the dispute.

In the state of California, information for patients is provided online at a website entitled "Got a Complaint?." The patient/client is provided with a step-by-step procedure to file a complaint. The option of discussing such with the medical society in the county of physician practice is provided, and a mediation committee can be arranged. The site tells a patient what to do if the healthcare provider is not a California Medical Society member. If a patient complaint concerns a hospital, it is suggested that the patient contact the "patient complaint coordinator." A sample letter is provided at www.anapsid.org/cnd/activisim/calmedcomplaint.html.

From the practitioner's perspective, once a grievance or medical malpractice suit is filed, the practitioner's perspective on the practice of medicine may change. A swing to a more defensive approach is common. Defensive medicine is focused on avoiding malpractice liability more than appropriate based solely on a patient "risk-benefit" analysis. The provider may experience a sense of shame which can result in "observable changes in practice behavior" (Cunningham and Wilson; see Suggested Reading). From the 30,000-foot perspective, complaints regarding medical practice, as well as adverse outcomes, may well have a hidden benefit of improving delivery of better healthcare to society. Consequences of these patient-related occurrences affect on the physician-patient relationship. There may be:

- Personal anger and depression
- Less enjoyment regarding the practice of medicine
- Guilt and shame
- Additional referrals, often not necessarily indicated, as well as additional tests
- A reduction in trust, goodwill, and commitment toward patients
- Concern for self-confidence

Counseling services have become available for healthcare practitioners to meet the emotional, stress-related needs of providers. In some instances, trained physicians serve as mentors for colleagues and focus on the events, analysis, and the physician-patient relationship. Taking the time to review the circumstances of a complaint or adverse event may well allow the healthcare providers' personal feelings to be considered and addressed.

AREAS OF SPECIAL ETHICS CONCERN TO HEALTHCARE

Healthcare has specific areas of ethical concern. These vary, of course, within the health professions, but there are many common issues, and this section addresses these.

Do No Harm

For centuries, the watchword for medical ethics has been, "First, do no harm." It is frequently cited in modern codes of health ethics. But in its pure form, it does not give much specific guidance. Sometimes, despite the best possible care, harm does result, not intentionally or because of carelessness, but because medicine is not an exact science. And, of course, what "harm" means may depend on the values of the patient and the time and place where care is delivered.

Many of the specific provisions in codes of ethics are intended to apply reasonable interpretations to the "do no harm" principle in the context of this time and this place—protecting confidentiality, autonomy, welfare and so on.

Confidentiality

All health professionals have protecting patient privacy as a central ethical principle. But privacy and confidentiality are not absolute and as shall be seen, there are many exceptions. The following discussion will first consider some general privacy and confidentiality issues and then look at HIPAA and its amendments—a very hot topic in all of healthcare. (Additional information regarding HIPAA is provided in Chapter 3.)

Three related concepts may be confusing. "Privacy" is a generic term referring to individual interest in keeping some information private. "Confidentiality" refers to the obligations of professionals and some organizations to maintain the secrets of patients and their treatment. "Testimonial privilege" or simply "privilege" is a federal or state rule that allows patients to refuse to allow disclosure of certain information in court (or similar proceedings). Confidentiality or privilege belong to the patient. However, both of these are protected by the professions—it is ordinarily the patient's decision of whether to disclose, not the professional's.

As a general principle, healthcare information is private and can be disclosed only with the permission of the patient, or consistent with certain other legal exceptions. There are many legal protections for privacy, and breaches of privacy can have significant consequences, including ethics violations, possible civil liability, and a variety of regulatory sanctions.

All states and the federal government have a number of laws that protect the confidentiality of health treatment. Some of these are broad statements of confidentiality. Others are specific to a condition or type of treatment (e.g., HIV status or drug/alcohol treatment). These laws apply to healthcare organizations as well as to individual practitioners.

No health information has complete protection—there are many exceptions to confidentiality. The most common is "waiver"—that is, the patient has agreed to the release of the information. The release may be, for example, to an insurance company for payment. The release is only to the extent the patient directs. Thus, the consent to the release to an insurance carrier does not permit the professional to give the information to the newspapers. State laws may also permit or require the release of information to protect the public, as is true with abuse reporting laws and in the case of a dangerous patient.

There is some confusion about the authority of healthcare professionals to release information to others who should have the information for treatment. Almost all privacy rules, including HIPAA, permit the transfer of information from one provider to another where it is important for treatment. The exception is where the patient expressly declines to permit such transfers.

Special issues of privacy arise in court or other legal proceedings. Testimonial privileges provide exceptions to the general rule that courts may require the presentation of all of the information they need to decide cases. Physician-patient and psychotherapist-patient privileges are recognized by almost every state and the federal courts. These privileges generally apply to information from medial practice or psychotherapy that is disclosed confidentially. There are many exceptions to these privileges. This is another area in which state laws vary in terms of the extent of the privileges and the exceptions to them. By and large, however, there are exceptions when the information is not confidential, the patient has waived the privilege or has raised medical issues in litigation, or there is a compelling social interest in having the information (e.g., abuse reporting).

The fact that information is not covered by a privilege or that there is an exception to the privilege does *not* mean that the professional is released from the general obligation to maintain the confidentiality of the information. That obligation exists apart from the privilege.

Healthcare organizations should have specific protocols, consistent with the laws of their jurisdictions, to implement the requirements of confidentiality. That has always been important, but it has become even more critical with the advent of the "HIPAA era." HIPAA is such an important part of the protection of confidentiality that we will turn to an extensive discussion of it.

Health Insurance Portability and Accountability Act (HIPAA)

The primary purpose of HIPAA is to provide protection of patient health information without unduly interfering with medical processes and legitimate uses of medical information. (See Chapter 3.) HIPAA particularly addresses concern about the risks associated with electronic records and electronic transmission. HIPAA and its amendments (most notably the Health Information Technology for Economic and Clinical Health [HITECH] Act) focus on the security and privacy of medical information. The Security Rule relates to technical mechanisms for encrypting and otherwise protecting health information. The Privacy Rule addresses the use and disclosure of "protected health information" by organizations that are "covered entities." It is impossible to cover the entire range of legal obligations under HIPAA, but the following discussion notes some of the highlights of the law.

> Four kinds of covered entities must safeguard patient health information: health plans, healthcare clearinghouses, healthcare providers, and business associates.

"Health plans" include individual and group plans that provide or pay the cost of medical care. A "healthcare clearinghouse" includes billing services, repricing companies, community health management information systems, and value-added networks and switches. A "healthcare provider" is an entity that transmits any health information in electronic form, which includes a medical chart, claims, benefit eligibility inquiries, and referral authorization requests.

"Business associates" are not providers of medical information but create, receive, maintain and store the protected health information on behalf of a covered entity. Healthcare entities must have confidentiality agreements with their business associates and may be liable for violations by the business associates.

All "individually identifiable health information" held or transmitted by a covered entity or its business associate in any form or media (e.g., reports, letters, e-mails, text messages, audio files, and medical device data) is protected health information (PHI). Because individuals "own" their PHIs, ordinarily they choose whether to share information.

A covered entity must make reasonable efforts to use, disclose, and request only the minimum amount of PHI needed to accomplish the intended purpose of the use, disclosure, or request. This is called "minimal necessary requirement." For internal uses, a covered entity must develop and implement policies and procedures that restrict access and uses of PHI based on the specific roles of the members of their workforce. These policies and procedures must identify the persons, or classes of persons, in the workforce who need access to PHI to carry out their duties.

A covered entity must disclose PHI to individuals (or their personal representatives) when they request access. In other words, under HIPAA, patients ordinarily have the right to see their own records. When the Department of Health and Human Services (HHS) is undertaking a compliance investigation or review or action, a covered entity must cooperate in providing the access to health information.

A covered entity is permitted to use and disclose protected health information, often without an individual's specific consent, for the following purposes or situations:

- For the treatment, payment, and healthcare operations activities of another covered entity involving either quality or competency assurance activities or fraud and abuse detection and compliance activities, if both covered entities have or had a relationship with the individual and the protected health information pertains to the relationship
- For the placement of patient contact information on the facility directory, with assent from the patient. In addition, similar disclosure of PHI directly relevant to that person's involvement in the individual's care or payment for care may be made to the individual's family, relatives, or friends, or to other persons whom the individual identifies.
- When necessary in the public interest, including judicial and administrative proceedings and law enforcement purposes regarding victims of abuse, neglect, or domestic violence
- For research (in limited circumstances), some public health purposes, and necessary healthcare operations (where the patient will not be unnecessarily identified)

Note that these are the exceptions. The rule is that covered entities must have the specific consent of patients to transfer health information. Marketing and fundraising purposes are especially good examples of areas in which patient consent is necessary to disclose health information.

A HIPAA-covered entity must develop and implement written privacy policies and procedures that are consistent with the Privacy Rule and train all workforce members on its privacy policies and procedures. It must also designate a privacy official responsible for developing and implementing its privacy policies and procedures as well as a contact person or contact office responsible for receiving complaints and providing individuals with information on its privacy practices. A patient must receive specific and fairly detailed notices of his or her rights under HIPAA. A covered entity must have procedures for individuals to complain about its compliance with its privacy policies and procedures.

A covered entity may not retaliate against a person for exercising rights provided by the Privacy Rule, for assisting in an investigation by HHS or another appropriate authority, or for opposing an act or practice that the person believes in good faith violates the Privacy Rule. It may not require an individual to waive any right under the Privacy Rule as a condition for obtaining treatment, payment, and enrollment or benefits eligibility.

There are special rules that cover "Psychotherapy Notes," which are mental health records kept separate from the regular patient records that analyze or document therapy. These need not be disclosed to the patient nor may they ordinarily be transferred to insurance companies to obtain payment for services.

HITECH increased the obligations under the Privacy Rule. (Also see Chapter 3.) It most notably imposed obligations in the event of an inadvertent breach of security—as, for example, what happens when a thumb drive with health information is lost. Patients must be informed of the accidental disclosure, and in some instances information must be posted on the institution's website and federal agencies informed of the disclosure. In addition, a patient may request a list of every release of personal health information for the past five years.

The Office for Civil Rights of the HHS is responsible for administering and enforcing these standards and may conduct complaint investigations and compliance reviews. There is a tiered civil penalty structure that ranges from $100 to $50,000 or more per violation. Significant criminal penalties have been added for serious or intentional misconduct. For example, imprisonment of up to 10 years is possible if the wrongful conduct involves the intent to sell, transfer, or use identifiable health information for commercial advantage, personal gain, or malicious harm.

One particularly important aspect of HIPAA is that it does not preempt state laws. That is, the federal law does not displace state laws to the extent that they provide greater protection of health information. Most states now have such laws.

Autonomy

Autonomy, the right of the patient to make critical decisions regarding care, has been a central value in modern healthcare ethics. From the US Constitution (e.g., the right to choose abortion) to a variety of statutory protections (consenting to treatment) autonomy has a special place in health law. Informed consent is a major mechanism to protect individual autonomy.

INFORMED CONSENT

The principle of informed consent is that every person should determine whether to accept medical intervention, and that, to make a sound decision, certain information is important to have. "Intervention" means not only treatment but also diagnostic processes and pharmaceuticals. Among the questions in applying this doctrine have been what information is enough and what exceptions are there to the informed consent requirement. Many of the rules of informed consent have developed in the common law, but states have modified these rules by statute. What follows are the general principles, with the understanding that there are individual state adjustments.

Regarding the information that a patient should receive, the purpose of informed consent is to give the patient information so that he or she can make important decisions. So the basic idea is to provide the information the patient would need to know to make a good (for the patient) decision. There are four types of information that should be included: a clear statement of the proposed treatment (or other intervention), its risks and benefits, the alternatives that are available, and the consequences of doing nothing. Much debate has focused on the "risks" portion of this formulation, and there are several legal rules. Rather than focusing on the technicalities of these rules, the better approach is the practical one of what the person needs to know to make a decision.

There are generally two exceptions to the informed consent requirement. One is easy to understand, and the other is a little tricky. The first exception is the "emergency situation" in which there is no opportunity for the patient (or a substitute decision-maker) to consent. The quintessential example is the patient who arrives in the emergency department unconscious and without any family. Here the law assumes consent to reasonable treatment necessary to preserve life and health. That is easy.

The second one is the "therapeutic exception." Where it would be harmful to inform a patient of a particular risk because even explaining the risk puts the patient's health in jeopardy, it may be proper to withhold the information. It is, however, best to discuss it with the family if possible. Suppose a patient really needs to undergo a diagnostic procedure but is highly suggestible to the point that even mentioning that there is a 0.1% chance of a reaction will most likely produce a negative reaction/response in the patient. It may be appropriate to avoid disclosing that risk. This is a very, very limited exception, and it should seldom be used. It does not apply, for example, when the difficulty is that having heard of the risk, the patient would decline the treatment. When it is used, it should be clearly documented in the chart.

There is currently a strong preference for informed consent being in writing. It certainly makes it easier to prove that consent was given. But oral informed consent is at least technically permitted in many states. Most healthcare institutions have some protocols to ensure that consent is obtained. Often, however, these are ages old and outdated. The forms and processes for obtaining informed consent should be reviewed annually.

Although the absence of informed consent may lead to liability, such liability is unusual without something more. The "more" may be especially egregious conduct by healthcare professionals, careless care, or a procedure to which the patient never consented.

More than meeting the legal requirements, informed consent is an excellent opportunity to have a meaningful conversation with the patient about their care. The participation of the patient in this decision-making appears to have clinical and risk management benefits that should not be lost by just going through the motions.

REFUSAL OF TREATMENT

The concept of consenting to treatment implies that there is a right to refuse treatment. Part of informed consent—the fourth element—is that the patient should be told of the consequences of refusing the proposed procedure. A patient who declines a Pap smear, for example, should be informed of the risks associated with that decision and it should be documented in the record.

In short, healthcare institutions should have clear processes to honor patient refusals but to do so in a way that ensures that it is an informed refusal, is respected without retaliation, and is well documented in the institution's records.

END-OF-LIFE DECISIONS

A special kind of refusal is one that will result in the death of the patient sooner than would occur with treatment. Do-not-resuscitate orders, removing ventilation, and withholding extraordinary treatment are examples. All states have rules regarding the circumstances when such actions may be taken and the documentation that should accompany the decision and its implementation. For competent adults there is a constitutional right to refuse life-sustaining treatments. For adults who are not competent (notably unconscious), states may require that their wishes or directives be fairly clear before life-sustaining treatment is removed, and state process vary somewhat for incompetent adults.

A few states allow physicians to prescribe, for a patient terminal condition, pharmaceuticals that will cause the death of the patient. In those states there are many statutory limitations on the use of what is commonly called "physician-assisted suicide." This is presently a small minority of states, although it is being considered by several other states.

CHILDREN AND ADOLESCENTS

The law has traditionally given parents the decision-making authority for children. Indeed, for a long time, children were essentially property of their parents. Although this status has changed, the decision-making and information rights of parents is mostly still in place. It has, however, been modified for "emancipated minors"—essentially those permanently living without parental care or supervision. Also, "mature minors" have increasingly been given the right to make basic decisions.

There was a trend in states to specify areas in which minors may seek medical attention without parental involvement. Examples include treatment for sexually transmitted diseases, substance abuse, and birth control. Because these are largely a matter of state law, there are variations throughout the nation. The more recent trend may be reversing, but minors still generally have the right to consent to treatment in these areas. The right of parents to obtain information about the treatment, however, is sometimes less clear and often in doubt.

The areas of abortion and permanent sterilization have created considerable difficulty. Basically, states may require some form of parental consent or at least information about abortion requests, so long as they allow minors to have a "judicial bypass" to go to court to obtain consent without the parents' involvement. Permanent sterilization is, absent truly extraordinary circumstances, not acceptable for minors.

Human Subjects

There are many ethical limitations on the use of human subjects in medical research. These are reviewed in the chapter on applied business law (see Chapter 6). The short version is that the use of human subjects should be undertaken only after Institutional Review Board approval. Institutions should have processes in place to ensure that rogue research is not possible.

In some respects, patients who are "teaching" subjects have some of the same risks as those who are research subjects. Although there is debate about the details, increasingly it is common to have policies requiring patients to be told of the educational status of the practitioners providing treatment. Most teaching facilities make sure that the consent forms include information about those providing care.

Conflicts of Interest and Dual Relationships

Some specialties are particularly sensitive to the ethical problems of dual relationships. Notably, mental health specialties generally prohibit or limit them. An ultimate dual relationship is sexual involvement of professional and patient, and prohibitions on such involvement is, of course, not limited to any particular specialty. Less intense relationships, including business relationships, however, may well depend on both the specialty and the nature of the business arrangement.

Uncooperative and Difficult Patients

Providers may be faced with uncooperative patients, who refuse to abide by medical recommendations despite the efforts of the healthcare team to educate them regarding the consequences. Here clinicians must make a decision: whether to (1) honor patients' autonomy with regard to care and allow lack of compliance with treatment recommendations despite potential adverse outcomes; as time permits, (2) suggest a second opinion; or in the case of patient incompetence, (3) seek legal action to provide proper medical care. Of course, another option in many circumstances is to dismiss the patient (ask the patient to find another physician). This must be done very carefully, however, to avoid "abandoning" the patient.

Pharmaceutical Industry and Patients

Another ethical hot point relates to the pharmaceutical industry (and medical devices in some cases). For example, acceptance of incentives from pharmaceutical representatives is one area that is controversial and borders on the unethical. Acceptance of free samples of a new drug may come with many "strings attached." Specifically, in many academic centers, a physician must be responsible for each sample received and its distribution. The majority of physicians surveyed have agreed that samples are ethically proper, and 53% of those surveyed believed it is ethically proper to accept a well-paid consultantship from a company for which the physician is a "high-volume prescriber." An additional survey noted that 33% of physicians thought their decision to prescribe a drug was influenced by availability of samples. Healthcare providers continue to acquire knowledge of new drugs primarily from journal articles, continuing medical education, and colleagues as opposed to pharmaceutical representatives. Individuals in private practice are more likely than academicians to interact with industry representatives. The American Medical Association continues to discuss these issues with the Pharmaceutical Research and Manufacturers of America, focusing on ethical interactions with healthcare providers.

Clinical-Ethical Conflicts

Allied health professionals must of course provide care in an ethical manner. Twelve types of clinical-ethical conflict have been touted to be "common" among nursing and physician providers.

- Disagreement about care decisions or treatment options
- Others not respecting a patient's wishes
- Patient not receiving quality end-of-life care
- Patient's or family's behavior preventing safe or quality care for self or others
- Patient and/or family not having informed consent or full disclosure
- Not knowing the "right thing to do"
- System deficit or deficiency preventing quality care
- Nurse or physician values conflicting with patient values or lifestyle choices
- Possible or perceived deficiencies in care resulting from nurse or physician level of competency
- Disagreement with national clinical practice guidelines
- Estimating the odds of survival and futility of treatment
- Balancing merit of survival with disability in an infant or child

The entire healthcare team can experience ethical conflict when patients and/or families feel they did not receive informed consent or full disclosure. Neglecting to provide "all the information" can result in ethical conflict. Mentally disabled individuals fall into this category, and their families are concerned about not receiving sufficient information.

The ethical challenge of limited services availability at a particular location in comparison to provision of care at a major medical center can result in ethical dilemmas. A Jehovah's Witness patient and the need for blood transfusion can set the stage for ethical concerns on the part of the healthcare team. Physician competency as viewed by the eyes of the nursing staff on more than one occasion sets the stage for ethical concerns for patient care. The chain of command is of paramount importance and willingness to proceed with such, having the patient's best interests in mind.

A WORD ABOUT BUSINESS ETHICS

Most of this chapter has focused on the ethics of health practitioners and organizations. As is noted earlier, the law imposes many obligations that define a kind of business ethic. For all intents and purposes the law requires that businesses, even nonprofits, have ethics-like policies regarding whistleblowers and conflicts of interest, and it encourages clear statements of confidentiality, good employment practices, and so on. Nothing precludes medical professional corporations from having their own codes of ethical practice. They can—and should. Many do.

Healthcare organizations particularly should develop and publish their own ethical principles, and be guided by and enforce them. Such codes may include the organization's commitment to the highest levels of honesty and integrity; safety and health of its patients; obligations of confidentiality to patients, their families, and the organization; welfare and respect of employees; public health of the community generally; and other elements (such as research), if that is part of the mission of the organization.

Business leaders can serve their organizations well by having the business (1) promulgate such a code of ethics if none exists or (2) review and update it if one exists but has fallen into neglect. Once it is adopted, it needs to become part of the soul of the organization. That means discussing what it means, making it part of personnel evaluations and enforcing it—from the top to the bottom of the organization. Solid business ethics practiced by healthcare professionals can pay big dividends in the long run.

THE ETHICS OF MISTAKES

Most ethical principles are aimed at avoiding mistakes of omission and commission. Mistakes occur in all organizations, so it is worth considering how an organization ought to respond to its own mistakes. The chapter on risk management (see Chapter 17) suggests practical ways that organizations might reduce their legal and regulatory risks for errors. But beyond that, organizations might think about how they should, given their values, respond when things go wrong. This chapter closes with a few suggestions to healthcare workers in responding ethically to mistakes.

- Own up to the mistake. Recognize it. Apologize for it. Fortunately, the law increasingly makes this an attractive option.
- Learn from it. Why did it happen? How can it be prevented from ever happening again?
- Never cover it up. Never, ever, ever, ever! Do not change records, do not lie about it, and do not pretend it did not happen.
- Report it when obligated by law or good practice to do so.
- Express genuine concern and sympathy for individuals who may have been harmed by it.
- Consider what obligation there may be to assist those who were harmed.

"A man without ethics" Albert Camus noted, "is a wild beast loosed upon this world." Ethical principles are more than rules. They express the commitment and values of the profession. Commitment to the letter as well as the word of ethics, therefore, is among the hallmarks of the true professional.

CASE STUDY

You are asked to comment on a colleague whom you have known for many years. Dr. X is a physician who has been in practice for more than 20 years and has always been well respected in the community. His career has included serving as residency program director for a large community hospital. He has spent a good deal of his career in academics, his research has been quoted in prestigious journals, and he has always been in essence a role model for physicians in training. During the past 6 months, a number of complaints have been brought to you and the chairman of the community hospital where he now works. The concern is his temper; he cannot control it! Nurses have stopped you in the hallway and asked "what's with Dr. X, we are noticing quite a change in his 'attitude'." The way he handles patients and residents in the program is also a concern. Independently, the department chair has called you to her office to discuss Dr. X's behavior and the threat of a lawsuit that was brought to her (the chair's) attention.

Questions

- What are the best next steps?
- Should Dr. X be permitted to continue to practice medicine?
- Should he be banned from the teaching program?
- Should the state medical licensing board be notified?
- Should you ignore it all, feeling his home life is probably the cause of his behavior?
- Should you confront him just you and him? (No chairman present.)
- Is this case reality?

SUGGESTED READING

Cunningham W, Wilson H. Republished original viewpoint: complains, shame and defensive medicine. *Postgrad Med J*. 2011;87:837–840.

Farrow V, Leddy M, Lawrence H, Schulkin J. Ethical concerns and career satisfaction in Obstetrics and Gynecology: a review of recent findings from the collaborative ambulatory research network. *Obstet Gynecol Surg*. 2011;66:572–579.

Gaudine A, LeFort S, Lamb M, Thorne L. Clinical ethical conflicts of nurses and physicians. *Nurs Ethics*. 2011;18:9–19.

Halperin E. Grievances against physicians. *West J Med*. 2000;173(4):235–238.

Seidman S. Professional misconduct and ethics. *Clin Perinatol*. 2007;34:461–471.

6

Applied Business Law

STEVEN R. SMITH AND JOSEPH S. SANFILIPPO

KEY POINTS

- Traditionally, much of healthcare-related law is at the state level, including authority to practice, liability, and consent.
- Overall primary sources of law include statutes, regulations, administrative hearings, and cases, which may originate from federal, state, county, city, and special districts. Also, private authorities develop "quasi-law" or "near law," which has some legal recognition.
- Medicare and the Affordable Care Act (ACA) have focused on national level intervention regarding delivery of healthcare and will result in greater legal involvement in the healthcare system.
- Basic legal principles include contracts, torts, business organizations, securities law, agency and vicarious liability, employment, antitrust, intellectual property, reporting, and debt collection.
- The generic definition of medical malpractice is "a negligent professional error that causes harm."
- Not every bad outcome is negligence, and, for that matter, not every mistake is negligence—only mistakes that are unreasonable under the circumstances are subject to liability.
- "Fraud and abuse" includes a wide range of activities, including self-referral, kickbacks, and the presentation for payment of false claims.
- Health-related businesses are "law-intensive" enterprises.

Government regulation of business in general has become increasingly detailed and complicated. The most common purposes of business law have been, broadly stated, (1) to protect consumers, investors, and workers, and (2) to promote fair competition.

The increase in the legal regulation of healthcare entities has been nothing short of massive in the past half century. The purposes have mostly been to protect patients (and the public) to ensure minimum quality, prevent quackery and fraud, and require some minimum access to essential care. The fact that healthcare spending in the United States accounts for approximately 18% of the gross domestic product makes it big business, and that alone means it will produce a lot of legal issues. Arguably, however, the real change during this time has come from the government as purchaser of health services.

From a relatively small player as a purchaser of health services in 1960 (before Medicare and Medicaid), all forms of government health spending accounts for about 50% of health spending. This includes Medicare, Medicaid, federal employees' care, the Veterans Administration, as well as a variety of state and local programs. With the implementation of many parts of the ACA, that percentage will undoubtedly increase significantly. Any larger purchaser of services is likely to exercise control to reduce its costs and control its suppliers, and governments have done exactly that with health services, resulting in very extensive regulation of the healthcare system.

Beyond the economic importance of healthcare, the law reflects the fundamental values that healthcare touches, and the great emotional, religious, and political significance that people attach to many of these questions. From abortion to removal of life-sustaining treatment to medical marijuana, there are great conflicts of views and values, and those conflicts play out in legal regulation of health entities.

This chapter will review the major categories of business law that apply to healthcare entities. It will offer a primer on business law generally, then look at a number of applications of the law relevant to healthcare organizations. Next it will look at areas of special current concern to many healthcare entities, and conclude with some advice about avoiding legal problems. In many ways, this chapter is a companion to Chapter 5, on ethics, and Chapter 17, on risk management. Together they are intended to provide a sense of the legal milieu in which healthcare leaders must operate. The legal issues touched on are often very complicated because the sources of law are numerous and not always consistent. Furthermore, many laws that affect healthcare organizations change frequently. (These issues appear in the next section.)

Several book chapters could not provide someone with the training to then undertake even simply surgery, and the chapters here do not prepare readers to plunge into health management secure in the knowledge that they understand and are prepared to deal with relevant business law. The chapters are intended only to provide an overview and some sense of the areas in which legal issues may arise. In most circumstances, basic honesty and moral principles suggest what the law is—it is no surprise that the law generally makes it illegal to steal or cheat people. But not all legal principles are so intuitive or obvious. For example, can a female patient see her own medical records when it contains the physicians' own thoughts about her (the patient's) dishonesty? May a physician accept a computer from a hospital to implement electronic medical records (EMRs)?

A central theme of these specific chapters is this: it is essential for healthcare managers to have ongoing access to reliable legal expertise. In addition to resolving problems as they arise, this expertise should be used for counseling and for preventive law—to avoid problems.

SOURCES OF LAW

The complexity of the source of law is illustrated in Table 6.1. This complexity in part relates to the federal system of government—both the federal government and each of the states are able to adopt laws related to many of the areas that affect health law. In the area of health information privacy, for example, there are several important federal laws (including the Health Insurance Portability and Accountability Act [HIPAA], which is discussed in detail in the chapter on ethics; see Chapter 5), but all states have laws regarding the same health information. It is further complicated by the fact that within states there are generally counties, cities, and special agencies (e.g., health or hospital districts) that have authority to create laws. In the area of health information privacy, it would not be unusual for a county or city, as well as a health district, to have some regulations concerning patient information laws, at least to hospitals it controls.

> A challenge in understanding "the law" regarding any question is that there seldom is a single source of law.

Much of the law related to healthcare has traditionally been primarily state law. For example, medical malpractice, licensing of professionals and healthcare facilities, and consent to treatment have mostly been state issues. Fortunately, there are general principles that most states follow. In some areas, however, the differences are quite substantial, or there are subtleties of importance. An example is abortions; some states have tried to limit access to abortion to the extent permitted by the US Constitution, whereas in other states there are few limitations on abortion. An example of the subtleties is child abuse–reporting statutes. All states have such statutes, but they vary concerning who is required to report such abuse. In some states, "anyone" knowing or suspecting abuse must report it; in other states only listed professionals who are caring or responsible for the child must report it.

Another complication is the way in which laws from one level of government interact with another level. For example, suppose a state law prohibits minors from obtaining birth control pills without their parents' consent. Does that violate a federal constitutional right? If so, which law prevails? (In this case, the difficult

TABLE 6.1   SOURCES OF LAW INTERNATIONAL LAW AS A SOURCE OF LAW[a]

	Constitutions	Statutes	Regulations	Administrative Hearings	Executive Orders	Court Decisions
Federal	X	X	X	X	X	X
State	X	X	X	X	X	X
County	Charter	X	X	X	X	X
City	Charter	Ordinances	X	X	X	X
Special districts	Charter	Rules and standards	Interpretations	Committees	Executive decisions	—
Quasi-legal	Charter and bylaws	Standards	Interpretations	Committees	Interpretations	Governing body decisions
International law	General law of nations and humanity	Treaties	Rules of customary international law	Persuasive effect of other laws		

[a]X indicates that this level of government generally produces this type of law.

answer is that the state law might violate the federal constitution if there are not some exceptions, and the US Constitution would prevail.)

In health law, there is also what is considered "near law" or "quasi-law"— principles adopted not by government authorities but by private authorities, which have very substantial legal recognition. A particularly good example is the Joint Commission. It is a private, nonprofit organization, but it is recognized by many private and governmental organizations as the accreditation body for reimbursement of services. Thus, its rules have the practical effect of law. In some ways, even the bylaws and regulations of individual hospitals are "quasi-law" in that they set enforceable standards that carry considerable legal weight with courts and regulatory agencies.

Another problem in knowing "the law" is that there seldom is a single source of law, even within a jurisdiction. Constitutions, statutes, and regulations are all a part of defining what the law is. Similar to regulations are "executive orders" by the US president, state governors, or city mayors. A significant source of law is administrative hearings (by an agency itself or by an administrative law judge). These administrative hearings are not specifically adopting regulations at the federal or state levels, but rather they are applying statutes and regulations to a specific case or circumstance.

> A significant source of law is court decisions. Federal and state courts play major roles in applying the constitutions, statutes, and regulations.

The most common role of the courts is interpreting the statutes and regulations. Sometimes courts must determine which of the conflicting laws apply to a given situation. In a few cases, the courts must determine whether a statute or regulation is constitutional. In each of these decisions, the courts are determining what the law really is. In the case of the Supreme Court, Justice Jackson famously noted that the Supreme Court is final because it is infallible, but is infallible "only because we are final." Infallible or not, the Court does change its mind from time to time and overturns an earlier decision of its own.

International law deserves a brief mention, although it is not nearly as important as the federal, state, and local laws under discussion. International law can have a meaningful impact on the law in the United States by establishing principles to which US law must conform. In the area of research involving humans, international law established the principles on which US law is based. In other areas, treaty obligations require the application of certain legal rules. Recognition of the patent rights of foreign pharmaceuticals is an example. Or, US legal institutions may be influenced by the legal principles generally accepted by other countries. The US Supreme Court, for example, looked at the law of other countries in holding that it is unconstitutional to execute minors for murder.

Table 6.1 summarizes the sources of law. On the vertical axis are the most important levels or jurisdictions of lawgivers. For the most part, these are listed in order of supremacy. That is, the higher the jurisdiction is on the list, the more likely it is to trump the lower jurisdictions. Federal law, for example, is generally supreme to state law where there is a conflict. That is not an absolute statement, however, because the federal government is a jurisdiction of limited authority and federal law supersedes state or local law only if the federal government is acting pursuant to a power granted it in the constitution. International law is not really of the same character as the others and is thus noted in a separate part of the table.

In Table 6.1, the horizontal axis describes the kinds of legal documents or rules that may exist. For the most part, the list is arranged with the most authoritative to the left and the least to the right. The clear exception is "case law." Case law ("Court Decisions" in the table) is generally just interpreting and applying documents—constitutions, statutes, and so on. But that authority, including the power to invalidate the laws and regulations, makes "Court Decisions" among the most authoritative forms of law. "Executive Orders" is a peculiar group of directives of the president or a governor (or mayor) telling executive departments what to do. These laws can have substantial importance, but in most jurisdictions they also have considerable limits in terms of authority.

Finally, a confession is warranted. We often cannot tell what the law really is. Nobody knows—no lawyer, no judge, no lawmaker. The law frequently has ambiguity in it because the words used are unclear, there are contradictions between provisions of the law, or the validity of the law is unclear. Suppose the constitutionality of a law is challenged but the court has not ruled (this was the very circumstance when the validity of the ACA was challenged). During that time we do not know what the law is. Or the law may be "in process." Suppose a statute allows an agency to adopt regulations, but the agency has not yet finalized the regulations—that creates uncertainty about what the law is about to be. A final example: the law frequently requires "reasonable" efforts, and reasonable depends on a host of factors that makes it difficult to know just what is required until courts have had a chance to decide a number of cases to put some meaning into "reasonable." That was the case with the Americans with Disabilities Act; it required "reasonable accommodations" for those with disabilities.

It is this ambiguity, along with the fact that many kinds of law change frequently and the complexity of the interaction of federal and state laws, that accounts for the "art" in determining what the law is. Fortunately, however, most of the basic legal principles remain reasonably stable and are similar from state to state. Now this discussion will consider some of those basic principles.

BASIC LEGAL PRINCIPLES

Contracts

Contract law is at the very heart of basic business law because contracts are the way in which people and organizations can conduct business with one another and make agreements that are reliably enforceable in the future. It is axiomatic that there are three elements to contracts:

- Offer
- Acceptance
- Consideration

The absence of any one of these means that there is not a contract.

Contracts are voluntary agreements (not imposed by society but undertaken by the participants), in which the participants promise to undertake or do (or not to do) something. A simple example is A saying, "I promise to sell and deliver to you, B, 100 syringes tomorrow if you will pay me $100 later today." To which B responds, "I agree." A made an offer, and B accepted it. Thus, there is an agreement. Both A and B have promised to do something and each has given up something (the syringes or the $100). You may have noticed an ambiguity lurking in this simple example. Just what do they mean by "100 syringes?" This discussion we will come back to in a moment. In the meantime, note that to create a contract the offer has to be accepted before it is withdrawn.

Now for a complication in contract law. Suppose A had said, "I will promise to bring you 100 syringes tomorrow." To which B responds, "Great. I accept." Is there a contract? Probably not, at least not without some additional facts. There is clearly an agreement to supply the syringes, but there is no consideration. B has not promised to do anything or to give up anything, and A has received no benefit. The reasons for requiring consideration are in part historical, as well as a desire to avoid having to determining when promise-like statements were intended to be enforceable. Courts do not care much about the actual value of the consideration, only that there is some.

There are few exceptions to the consideration requirement. One example is when a party has reasonably relied on a promise to his or her detriment. In the example, if B an hour later turned down a later offer from C to sell 100 syringes for $50, because he was reasonably relying on A to bring the syringes and A could have anticipated that reliance, that should be enough to count as "detrimental reliance" and make A's promise a contract.

The core of a contract is a "meeting of the minds" of the party—a common understanding of what they are agreeing to. In the example, the objects of the contract were 100 syringes and $100. The dollar figure seems pretty clear, but what about the syringes? The size, sterility, quality, and condition of the syringes are unstated, and A and B could have very different specifics in mind. In modern times, courts will try to fill in ambiguous terms in contracts where, for example, it is possible to do so based on prior dealings of the parties (A and B made this deal several times before) and/or standards in the area ("syringe" means only one thing in a particular region).

The "breach" of contract by one party when it fails to fulfill all of its obligations may subject that party to civil liability.

The damages for a breach of contract are intended to return the injured party to the contract where that party would have been had the contract been performed. This often means what the cost is of "covering" or purchasing the goods or services elsewhere. Returning to the syringe example, suppose A failed to supply the syringes and B had to buy them from C instead at a cost of $150 plus $25 shipping costs. (Assume for this example that B was not expected to pay for the syringes until they were delivered.) B's damages would be the $50 + $25, or $75. That is, B had expected to pay $100 (including delivery) for the syringes and instead had to pay C $150 + $25 = $175. The difference is the $75 of damages. If, however, B had obtained the syringes for $50 + $25 shipping, B may have suffered *no* legally recognizable damages because he expected to pay $100, but the syringes only cost $75. (In

> One common misunderstanding is that contracts must be in writing to be enforceable.

these examples, we assume that B was able to change to another supplier without expending any real time or effort.)

To prevent fraud, a few types of contracts must be in writing (e.g., those contracts that cannot be performed within a year, are for the sale of goods more than $500, or are for the sale of land—but this varies and there are exceptions to these exceptions). Oral contracts, even if technically permissible, however, may be difficult to enforce because of the unreliability of human memory and the difficulty of proving that there was a contract or what its terms were.

There is broad right to contract, even to enter into foolish ones. But the courts will not enforce contracts that are contrary to public policy. A contract of slavery, for example, would be unenforceable. Nor would a contract to sell human organs be enforceable. Contracts that are so unfair or one-sided as to be unconscionable are also not enforceable. A hospital that required a patient with appendicitis to sign a contract promising to pay $1 million for the surgery is an example of such a contract.

Those who enter into a contract are generally held to the terms of the contract whether or not they are aware of them. For example, clicking "I agree" to the contract terms of service on a website or signing a rental car contract usually means (absent unconscionability) that the consumer is held to the terms whether or not he or she has read them. This is an especially important lesson for professionals who may be entering into complex contracts related to their practice—they will probably be held to the terms whether or not they understand them.

Torts

"Tort" is a generic term that applies to a bundle of civil wrongs that result in injury to someone. Although torts receive much attention, in fact in terms of cases filed, tort cases are a small percentage of all civil cases compared with all contract and business cases. (Torts are a civil wrong, but the same misconduct can result in both civil and criminal liability.) The three major categories of torts are intentional torts, negligence, and strict liability. This discussion will consider all three, but negligence is by far the most common tort claim in the area of healthcare.

Intentional torts occur when the defendant has, without legal justification, performed an act intended to invade the legally protected interest of another—usually it is harmful or offensive. Intentional torts include battery (touching), assault (putting someone in fear of a battery), false imprisonment (wrongful confinement), and intentional infliction of emotional distress (outrageous conduct that causes significant emotional distress). These torts require more than carelessness; they require an intentional interference with an important legal interest.

Intentional torts occasionally arise in the healthcare area. For example, a surgeon who performs unwanted surgery for a patient's own good may have committed battery. A psychiatrist who, without legal justification, locks up a patient "for the patient's own good" may have committed false imprisonment.

Strict liability is most commonly found in products liability where a defect in a product causes injuries. There are different rules that somewhat limit strict liability for many of the products that are specific to healthcare entities (notably, pharmaceuticals and medical devices). But health organizations use and sell some products that may be subject to strict liability. Decisions of the US Supreme Court have demonstrated that products liability is still a concern with brand name pharmaceuticals (but less so for nondefective medical devices and generic drugs). Employment relations, particularly workers compensation, is another area in which a form of strict liability exists for health entities.

Negligence is the "big tort." The essential elements of negligence are traditionally described as:

- Duty
- Breach of the duty
- Causation (proximate cause)
- Injury

Unlike contract duties, tort duties are imposed by society, usually because someone is engaging in an activity. For example, when someone is driving a car, society imposes a duty that it be done with reasonable prudence. Similarly, when someone practices medicine, there is a duty to do that with reasonable care. Seldom is a duty imposed just for living. Thus, an ordinary person walking on a beach does not have a duty to rescue (e.g., to throw a life preserver) to a stranger drowning a few feet away. Of course, if the person is hired as a lifeguard or the custodian of the drowning child, that would be a different matter. There is a moral duty, perhaps, but (unless there are additional facts) there is no legal duty. Healthcare personnel have specific duties, but they do not have duties to everyone in society all of the time—a point which we will return later.

Where there is a duty, the general statement of it is that a person is obligated to act as a reasonably careful person would act under the circumstances. A breach occurs when someone fails to act reasonably either by doing something (speed-ing) or failing to do something (keeping one's eyes on the road). That breach of the duty does not create liability, however, unless there are two other elements: an injury (to a person owed the duty) and a causal connection between the injury and the breach. An injury is economic or physical harm; pain, suffering, or emotional harm; or harm to property.

Causation has two components. The first is "but for causation," meaning that the injury would not have occurred "but for" the negligence of the defendant. For example, D (defendant) hits P (plaintiff) with his car, breaking P's leg. In the process of treating P, physicians determine that P has lung cancer. D is legally responsible for P's broken leg but not for the lung cancer, because the car accident did not cause it.

The second component is "proximate cause" or "legal cause," a somewhat murky concept consisting of foreseeability and directness of the causal events. It really means that there is a sensibly close link between the negligence and the injury. Suppose as a result of speeding by the driver of a car, D, the car reaches a spot in the forest just at the moment a tree falls, thereby injuring passenger P. There may be "but for" causation (but for the negligence of driving too fast, the car would not have been there when the tree fell), but there is not legal causation because there really is not a legal connection between the speeding and being hit by the tree.

The discussion will consider the specifics of negligence as they relate to mal-practice, or professional liability, subsequently.

Business Organizations

Businesses (professional practices) may be put together using a variety of organiza-tional structures. Each has its own set of legal strengths and problems. This section outlines the major organizational structures; the most common ones are corpo-rations and partnerships. Corporations are chartered by the government (usually state governments) and subject to the rules of the state in which they are incorpo-rated. They may, of course, do business anywhere—not just in that state. Delaware is a particularly popular state for incorporation of larger companies because of the absence of a corporate tax and several attractive rules regulating corporations.

A critical aspect of corporations is that they are legal entities, with separate identities from those who own them. Shares in them can usually be sold or traded from person to person. The shareholders are the owners, but the corporation has a separate existence. Shareholders can lose their investment, but otherwise they are not personally responsible for the liabilities of the corporation. If, for example, a corporation owes $100,000 but has only $1,000 of assets, the shareholders are not responsible for the $99,000 difference. Corporations are taxed as entities. They are taxed on their income by the federal government and by many states, and if they distribute after-tax profits (dividends) to their owners, those owners pay individual taxes on the dividends.

Partnerships usually do not *require* the formation formalities (incorporation) that corporations require. They are easily formed. A model state law describes the formation process this way: "The association of two or more persons to carry on as co-owners of a business for profit forms a partnership, whether or not the persons intend to form a partnership." Despite the ease of their creation and their informality, they should be undertaken with caution, as will be seen. Indeed, many partnerships are created with great formality.

Partnerships can be very informal organizations, or, by contract, can have complex structures and governance. Unlike in corporations, the identity of the partnership and individual partners are combined. Partnerships entail joint ownership and control of the enterprise, and essentially the partnership depends on the continued membership of all of the partners. The disadvantage of the partnership is that the liabilities of the partnership may flow through to the partners themselves. In the previous example, where there is $100,000 of liability and $1,000 of assets, in a partnership, the partners personally may be responsible for paying the remaining $99,000. On the other hand, partnerships have a tax advantage; they are not taxed as separate entities. Rather, the profits of a partnership flow through to the partners, and only those partners are responsible for the tax.

The attractive element of the corporate structure is the limited liability, whereas an attractive element of partnerships is the tax advantage. Over the years, there has been some blurring of these distinctions. For example, the Internal Revenue Service (IRS) has recognized subchapter S corporations (the reference is to a part of the Internal Revenue Code); it permits small closely held corporations to be treated as partnerships for tax purposes. Most states now recognize limited liability partnerships (LLPs), which allow some professionals to have partnerships that somewhat limit the liability of the partners, although not completely. These are matters of state law, and there are differences among states as to who can form LLPs and how far the limitations on liability extend.

Caution! "Limited liability partnerships" and "limited partnerships" are *not* the same thing and are not related. The limited partnership is an organization in which some (often most) of the partners (1) do not have the right to play an active role in running or managing the activities of the partnership, (2) may enter or leave the partnership without causing the partnership to dissolve or be reorganized, and (3) do not have responsibilities for the liabilities of the partnership. This may be a way for someone to invest in a partnership without having to be actively involved with the management (in these partnerships the general partner or partners may have personal liability for the debts of the business, but the limited partners do not).

Both for-profit and nonprofit (or not-for-profit) organizations are important in the health field. Nonprofit organizations may be unincorporated associations or nonprofit corporations. Only small or very temporary nonprofit organizations should continue without incorporation. Although an unincorporated association has many advantages of simplicity, it has the disadvantage of potential personal liability and the opportunity for confusion associated with its very informal structure. As with for-profit corporations, nonprofit corporations are chartered by the state. Unlike for-profit organizations, however, there are not shareholders who own and personally gain from them. They can be very large organizations with lots of assets—hospitals, for example, are often very wealthy nonprofits.

Nonprofit groups cannot be organized for the financial benefit of individuals. The state attorneys general have special obligations for nonprofit corporations—to see that they operate in the public interest. Regrettably, these obligations are most often observed in the breach, and there traditionally has been limited state supervision of nonprofit organizations.

Many, but not all, nonprofit organizations apply through the IRS to receive tax-exempt, 501(c)(3), status (again, a reference to the Internal Revenue Code). This permits organizations to avoid most taxes, although they still must pay taxes on "unrelated business income." Importantly, it also provides tax deductions for charitable contributions they receive from individuals and businesses. (States generally also allow tax deductions when granted by the IRS.) In this way, taxpayers are indirectly subsidizing these nonprofit organizations. This is under the theory that the public is receiving considerable benefits from the work of the health, educational, religious, or other charitable work. The US Congress and the IRS have increasingly taken the position that larger nonprofit groups must justify this public subsidy. The 990 tax return for nonprofit groups has become a lengthy, detailed report on the activities and financing of 501(c)(3) organizations. For hospitals, the 990 is augmented by Schedule H, which is an effort to detail the community benefits and free care that 501(c)(3) hospitals provide.

The IRS has also increased its scrutiny of executive compensation for 501(c)(3) organizations. The "intermediate sanctions" rules require that nonprofit boards of directors justify the salaries of executives. The failure to do so may result in tax penalties to the organization and to executives receiving excess compensation. Hospitals and other health organizations have been some of the targets of the intermediate sanctions investigations, in part because hospital and healthcare systems may have some of the highest paid nonprofit executives.

The clear trend has been for nonprofit organizations to receive closer examination by the IRS. Perhaps the taxman is stepping in where the attorneys general have been timid.

Securities Laws

The ability to sell shares of corporations allows for investors to trade parts of corporations. It also allows "con men" to exploit those markets. The economic crash of 1929 led to a series of laws that have been intended to limit a wide range of securities frauds. The sale and marketing of securities is now tightly controlled, primarily by the US Securities and Exchange Commission, but also by states through such laws as the "blue sky" laws. The creation of new financial instruments, the entry of a variety of financial institutions into the securities business (including banks), and the endless creativity of the likes of Bernie Madoff and the Enron executives has resulted in a series of increasingly complex securities regulations. Notable examples of these laws include Sarbanes-Oxley (dealing with accounting, disclosure, and management standards for public companies) and Dodd-Frank (dealing with financial and banking institutions).

Most of these regulations would seem to have little or no relevance to nonprofit organizations or their employees. And most days, that is true. But for the very large sector of healthcare professionals who work in some way with the commercial world, sensitivity to the securities laws is warranted. A sale of a divided interest in a commercial enterprise (a start-up company, healthcare facility, funding for a new app) should cause a red flag that legal advice may be needed. It is not always intuitively obvious when state or federal laws may require specific disclosures or notice.

Insider Information

One area deserves special attention: insider information. The securities laws preclude trading based on insider information, which is significant nonpublic information that is used or disclosed in violation of some duty of trust. One example of health-related illegal insider trading is a researcher who saw the preliminary positive (or negative) results of Phase III testing of a drug and then bought (or sold) shares of the pharmaceutical company. Another example is psychiatrist who sold stock in a particular company after learning from a patient that the patient was under stress as a result of his spouse's long hours in the company, which was suddenly losing money. And another example is the department chair in a medical school who bought shares in a public company after the chair received information from the annual report of a faculty member about a great new DNA testing device the faculty member was evaluating for that company. In each of these examples, it is assumed that the information had not yet been made public.

Any publically traded company should have strong rules regarding insider trading. But as these examples illustrate, insider trading can come from outside the officers and employees themselves, and it can include anyone who trades on nonpublic information in a way that is a violation of a duty of trust.

Agency and Vicarious Liability

Another fundamental business law concept is that of agency and the related doctrine of vicarious liability. Agency basically is the ability of people and organizations (principals) to appoint others (agents) to work on the principal's behalf. Agents carry the authority of the principal and can also bind the principal to contracts and other legal obligations. Organizations have no true persona, of course, and cannot work except through agents. Employees, partners, assistants, and the like are all actually agents. Agents can be other persons or other organizations. Agency relationships are at the very heart of business, including healthcare businesses.

The relationship between a principal and agent is essentially contractual, although the terms of the contract are too often not explicit. For example, principals may limit the authority of agents to handling only specific tasks. The compensation the agent will receive is also generally a matter of contract. Many agency relationships are so common that the law has a set of rules that govern the relationship, and the principal and agent may change only some of those rules. The employment contract or relationship is a good example. The terms of employment are sometimes only vaguely stated, and in the absence of such an agreement, the employment contract is often terminable at will (without specific cause). On the other hand, parties cannot, by contract, change other terms of the employment relationship that are set by law (e.g., the prohibition on discrimination on the basis of gender or age, or the wage and hour rules).

Agents are fiduciaries. This means that they legally owe principals the duty of loyalty, care, and obedience. They legally have to do what they are told. They must exercise reasonable care in doing it. They must work in the interest of the principal and avoid conflicts of interest. If, as a result of breaching these duties the principal is harmed, the agent may be legally responsible. (This rule is modified by law in some employment relationships.) Principals have duties to agents of paying compensation, reimbursing expenses as agreed and providing the essential information necessary to do the agreed-upon tasks. Agencies may be terminated as agreed or otherwise by either party under reasonable circumstances.

Of special importance is the relationship between agents and principals on one hand and third parties on the other. The whole purpose of agency is to allow the agent to act for the principal. So the acts of the agent are naturally attributed to the principal. Contracts signed on behalf of the principal are the responsibility of the principal (of course, if the agent did not disclose he or she was acting for the principal, the agent may also be obligated to the third party). In addition, the principal may be civilly liable for the torts of the agent, at least within the scope of the agency. This brings us to vicarious responsibility (Table 6.2).

Respondeat superior = the master should answer

Vicarious responsibility, or *respondeat superior*, is the concept that the "master should answer" for the harms of the servant. The rule applies to all kinds of agency relationships, including employment and partnerships (which is one of the things that make partnerships legally risky). If a physician employs a nurse and directs the nurse to give an injection, and the nurse does that negligently, thereby harming the patient, the physician may be held vicariously liable for that negligence. This is true even though the physician told the nurse to be careful or not to give the injection in the right arm, which is where the nurse gave it.

TABLE 6.2   APPLIED LAW DEFINITIONS AND ACRONYMS

Tort	One party asserts that the wrongful conduct of another has caused harm
Res judicata	"The thing is decided," which cites previous court decisions with respect to the matter in question
Stare decisis	"Let the decision stand," which means that when a lawsuit involving an identical or similar situation is filed, it should be resolved in a manner that reflects the initial decision
CMS	Centers for Medicare and Medical Services (formerly Health Care Financing Administration): a principal operating component of the Department of Health and Human Services. It oversees Medicare and Medicaid programs
FCOA	Federal Council on Aging: composed of 15 members who deal primarily with the elderly. It provides recommendations to the President, the Secretary, the Commissioner, and Congress with respect to federal policies regarding the elderly
NIA	National Institute on Aging: a segment of the National Institutes of Health designed for the "conduct and support" of biomedical, social, and behavioral research and training related to the aging process and specifically related diseases. The priorities of the NIA include Alzheimer's disease, understanding aging, frailty, disability and rehabilitation, health and effective functioning, long-term care for older people, special older populations, and training and career development as applied to the aged

Anything that the agent does within the "scope" of the agency or employment is likely the responsibility of the principal. At some point,

The law draws a distinction between agents and independent contractors.

however, an agent may so diverge from the scope of work that the principal is no longer responsible. The nurse in the preceding example who agrees, outside of the office, to sell a patient a used lawnmower is beyond the scope of employment, and unless there are additional facts the physician is unlikely to be liable for that transaction.

Unlike agents, those who engage independent contractors usually are not vicariously liable for their negligence. The traditional building contractor who does a remodeling project is a good example of the independent contractor. It is not just that someone is a contractor but that the contractor is "independent." Beyond issues of liability, independent contractors are not treated as employees for tax purposes, so the contracting party is not responsible for reporting, collecting and paying employment taxes, including Social Security. Rather, use of an independent contractor involves the purchase of a good or service.

The essential difference between agents and independent contractors is the right of the "principal" to control or direct the activities of the contractor. It is not whether the right to control is exercised, only that it exists. So, an employer who fails to control an employee does not thereby make the person an independent contractor. The line between an independent contractor and agent is based on a number of factual elements and, therefore, is fine and sometimes uncertain. The more clear-cut the independence is, the stronger the case for being an independent contractor.

There are many independent contractors in healthcare. In a physician-hospital relationship between a private physician who has hospital privileges and the hospital, the physician has traditionally been viewed as an independent contractor. In some cases, however, the concept of "ostensible" or "apparent" agency may result in these independent contractors being treated as agents. Many hospitals, for example, contract with physicians' groups as independent contractors for emergency department or anesthesia services. The physicians are not employees of the hospital. Those physicians may practice with limited control at the hospital and bill the patients separately for their services. To the public, however, it may certainly look as if they are employees or part of the hospital. They "apparently" are agents. Some courts have found this sufficient to impose vicarious liability on the hospital for the actions of the physicians.

Employment Laws

This discussion has noted that the employment relationship is at its core an agency contract but that it is now surrounded with many laws that define the relationship. A complex web of state and federal laws affect most aspects of employment. For the most part, these laws apply across the economy and are not specifically directed to healthcare. The wage and hour laws; prohibitions on discrimination based on gender, race, sexual orientation, and age; and Employee Retirement Income Security Act (ERISA) and other laws dealing with fringe benefits are examples. Such other employment laws of general applicability as the Occupational Health and Safety Act have special aspects related to health organizations. And some aspects of employment law, including the Bloodborne Pathogens Act, are directed specifically at healthcare.

Labor law is now commonly used to refer to federal and state laws concerning employee labor relations, including labor unions. Most healthcare workers have the same rights as other employees to unionize, although there are special rules related to government workers. In the case of state workers, the right to form unions, go on strike, and negotiate about working conditions is generally controlled jointly by the federal government and the state. These laws vary considerably from state to state.

No entity that hires employees can afford to ignore the thicket of employment laws. There are many helpful guides for complying with the law, particularly for small business. But employment laws tend to be complex, with many technical requirements. And there are often substantial consequences for failing to meet the requirements of the law. It is an area in which most employers will find that specialized assistance is required in establishing the proper compliance mechanisms.

Antitrust Laws

For more than a century, the antitrust laws have made illegal a wide variety of combinations and activities that significantly limit competition. Federal laws, notably the Sherman, Federal Trade Commission, and Clayton Acts, are the most significant basis for antitrust enforcement, but many states also have "mini-Sherman" or other antitrust laws. The federal government, through the Justice Department and Federal Trade Commission, is the primary government enforcer of antitrust laws, but states and individuals who are harmed by anticompetitive activities may sue as well. As an incentive to those harmed by these activities to take the frequently very complicated cases to court, a victorious plaintiff may receive treble (three times the actual) damages.

The antitrust laws essentially prohibit contracts, combinations, and conspiracies "in restraint of trade or commerce." The statutes are broadly stated and that has given courts, as well as government agencies, considerable latitude in interpreting the statutes. In addition to proceeding against past violations of the law, the antitrust laws permit challenges to proposed mergers when the harm to competition from the merger would be greater than its benefits. For example, the US Justice Department essentially blocked the merger of American Telephone and Telegraph (AT&T) and T-Mobile—competitors in the wireless market—because of the anticompetitive effects it would have on that market. In addition, the government can seek to break up large companies—as happened early with Standard Oil and much later with AT&T. Violation of antitrust laws may bring civil damages, civil penalties and, in extreme cases (e.g., price fixing), criminal penalties. In addition, the courts are given broad equitable remedies. They may, for example, order that companies stop anticompetitive activities or that monopolistic companies be broken up.

There are many activities prohibited by the antitrust laws. Some, known as *per se violations*, are so obviously harmful to competition

> The rule of reason review in antitrust is essentially a totality of the circumstances.

that the very fact that they occurred is an antitrust violation. The primary examples of per se violations are price fixing, bid rigging, and market splitting or allocation (potential competitors agree not to compete against each other in certain locations, product lines, or customers). Most antitrust cases, however, apply the "rule of reason" test.

At its most basic level, it is a cost-benefit analysis of a practice or combination that harms free competition. As an example, private accreditation of hospitals has anticompetitive effects—it is likely to drive up costs and limit competition. But, within limits, the effect of accreditation can be of greater public benefit than public harm. Thus, the improved safety and quality of care offsets the anticompetitive effects and accreditation may be reasonable. Of course, if one purpose of accreditation is to set prices (perhaps a minimum fee schedule for surgeries), then the conclusion of the rule of reason might well cut the other way, and an antitrust violation could be found. Rule of reason cases are commonly very difficult and complex to pursue.

There are a number of exceptions to the antitrust laws. State action, union activities, and insurance regulated by the states are examples of those exemptions. (Baseball, but not other professional sports, has been exempted by the US Supreme Court, but that is another story.)

Antitrust laws apply to health entities in several ways. In the 2012–2013 term of the US Supreme Court, for example, the Court determined that antitrust laws may prohibit hospitals, even public hospitals, from merging if it would harm competition significantly. During the same term, the Court also decided that agreements between brand name drug–making and generic drug–making pharmaceutical companies to delay introduction of generic drugs (known as "reverse payments" or "pay for delay") may violate the antitrust laws.

Intellectual Property Laws

The US Constitution gives Congress the power to enact laws to protect and encourage innovation. The patent laws and copyright laws are the core of that protection. In the health fields, patent laws are particularly important as they relate to pharmaceuticals, and this section will focus primarily on patents. First is a quick diversion to trademarks and copyright.

Trademarks are also considered intellectual property. The Patent and Trademark Office defines a trademark as "any word, name, symbol, device, or any combination, used or intended to be used to identify and distinguish the goods/services of one seller or provider from those of others." These receive formal protection through registration with that office, as well as common law protection even if not registered. Major healthcare organizations frequently have registered trademarks (®) to protect their public identity. Trademarks can last indefinitely as long as they are actively used and protected.

People commonly think of copyright protection for written works—this book for example. But copyright also applies to a wide range of creative activity, including photographs, music, audio recordings, videos, even architecture—and the list goes on. Although there are common law and unregistered copyrights that can legitimately claim copyright (e.g., with the ©), greater protection comes from registering the work with the Copyright Office. Copyrights exist for 70 years after the death of the author. For corporate "authors," they last the shorter of 95 years from publication or 120 years from creation. Only the expression of idea, not the ideas themselves, can be copyrighted.

Patents apply to a wide range of inventions, including machines, methods of manufacture, articles that are manufactured, new materials, and sometimes new uses (related to pharmaceuticals). The patent is the exclusive right to use the invention, or to license it to others, during the term of the patent. Laws of nature, abstract ideas, and literary works (which may be copyrighted) are examples of things that cannot be patented. Patents generally extend for 20 years from the filing of the patent application, although design patents last for 14 years. In addition, under some circumstances there are extensions of terms for some pharmaceutical patents because of regulatory lag or to promote "orphan" drugs.

The patent office reviews applications for patents. Unlike the filing of a copyright, which generally is not reviewed, patents are issued only after review and approval by the patent office. Although it is possible to register a copyright without much help, it is foolhardy to pursue any patent issue without expert advice and assistance. (The patent office maintains a very helpful website that explains the patent process, mostly in lay terms, at http://www.uspto.gov/inventors/patents.jsp.) The office notes that to receive a patent, the invention must be the following:

- Novel
- Nonobvious
- Adequately described or enabled (for one of ordinary skill in the art to make and use the invention)
- Claimed by the inventor in clear and definite terms

Patents are essential to the very existence of the pharmaceutical and medical device industries. But not everything new that happens in health is patentable. New surgical techniques using standard equipment are generally not patentable, for example. And, in 2013, the US Supreme Court ruled that segments of naturally occurring DNA cannot be patented, essentially because they occur naturally and are products of nature. However, DNA fragments that are manipulated by humans (and do not, therefore appear in nature) are patentable.

Reporting Laws

All states have laws requiring the reporting of known or suspected child abuse and neglect. These laws generally define abuse as including physical, emotional, or sexual abuse. These laws vary considerably among the states regarding who is required to report. Healthcare professionals, including physicians and nurses, along with teachers and law enforcement officers, are among those required to make such reports. Some states mandate reporting only if the professional is in some way responsible for the care of the child, and others require "anyone" knowing or suspecting abuse to report it.

Such abuse usually must be reported to a child protective services agency. The failure to report as required may result in civil and even criminal liability, and it may be the cause for licensure discipline. On the other hand, reporting in good faith usually carries immunity from liability.

States also require the reporting of various forms of adult abuse, particularly elder abuse. As with child abuse, these laws include medical professionals as among those required to make reports. The laws generally identify a social services agency to which reports must be made. Even where states do not mandate reporting, they frequently permit or encourage it and provide a form of immunity for those who do so in good faith.

A number of other reporting statutes affect healthcare providers. In most states, for example, gunshot wounds, sexually transmitted diseases, and certain infectious diseases must be reported to the state. The list of infectious diseases that require some kind of reporting may include several dozen conditions.

Reporting of "problem physicians" to the National Practitioner Data Bank is also required in some circumstances. This federal depository of liability and disciplinary actions against physicians may be queried by licensing authorities and a few other groups. Among the events that must be reported are significant malpractice payments, restrictions or suspensions of privileges (of more than 30 days), license discipline, Medicare/Medicaid exclusion, and professional society discipline.

All of the reporting requirements deserve the attention of both individual practitioners and healthcare organizations. These are laws that change frequently. If there are not standard protocols for reporting, including who is responsible for making the report and what records are made of the fact a report has been made, it is all too easy for the required reporting to slip between the cracks or be forgotten. Beyond the technical legal requirements, these reports are generally required because there is an important health matter involved, either to an individual or the general public. The failure to make the report may, therefore, put people at risk unnecessarily.

Debt Collection

The federal Fair Debt Collection Practices Act provides substantial limitations on some of the more aggressive debt collection practices, including debt that results from medical care. For example, things debt collectors may not do (there is a long list) include falsely represent that they operate or work for a credit reporting company, publish the names of people who do pay their debts (except to credit reporting agencies), repeatedly use the phone to annoy the debtor, and use a false company name. A number of states have similar, or even more stringent, limitations on debt collection practices for certain debts.

Debt collection issues must seem like a strange entry in this cavalcade of important laws. It is here for three reasons. First, healthcare entities are very big sources of debt collection efforts. The degree to which that will change under health reform remains to be seen. Second, there has been substantial public dissatisfaction with medical debt collection processes to the extent that Healthcare Financial Management Association and the Association of Credit and Collection Professionals in 2013 developed best practices for collecting medical debt. Third, some malpractice experts believe that mishandled or overly aggressive debt collection invites malpractice claims.

Licensing and Credentialing

Both for its individual practitioners and its organizations, healthcare is among the most intensely licensed and credentialed enterprises. The law, or "quasi-law," of licensing and licensing discipline, accreditation, certification, specialty credentialing, and the like are a major part of the law of healthcare entities. "Quasi-law" refers to the fact that much of this activity is at least technically voluntary, although practically required, or is conducted by private organizations. Licensing issues are discussed in the chapter on ethics. (See Chapter 5.)

Litigation and Dispute Resolution

The default dispute resolution mechanism has traditionally been litigation. Unless parties work out problems themselves or have agreed to an alternative mechanism for resolving disputes, one of the parties can file suit to resolve the dispute. Civil litigation frequently begins with a "demand letter" in which the plaintiff indicates what the defendant must do to avoid a lawsuit. The formal process begins with the plaintiff filing a civil complaint, which may be amended as the process moves along. The defendant formally answers the complaint. There may be preliminary motions, but discovery is likely to proceed. Each side demands documents and records from the other and takes the sworn oral depositions to find the facts of the case. After this, a trial date is set. There are likely to be motions to dismiss the case, and the judge will likely push for settlement. If the case goes to trial, it may be heard by the jury as the "finder of fact." Or if the parties agree, it may be tried by the judge (a bench trial). At trial, the plaintiff generally has the obligation of proving each of the elements of the tort or contract "by a preponderance of the evidence." The jury may find for the plaintiff, in which case the trier of fact must assess the damages due the plaintiff, or for the defendant. If the jury is deadlocked, the case may be retried. Appeals to higher courts are possible regarding the outcome, rulings and findings of the trial level. There are special rules in most states concerning medical malpractice claims.

Cases involving federal issues may be filed in federal courts. Federal courts may also hear cases (known as "diversity of citizenship" or simply "diversity" cases) in which the plaintiff and defendant are from different states and the amount in dispute is more than $75,000. Cases involving state law, except for the diversity of citizenship cases, are generally tried in state court. More than 95% of civil cases that are actually filed are settled without a trial. Thus, negotiated settlement, or abandonment of claim, is the outcome of most all cases.

Litigation is a particularly problematic form of resolving disputes in the health area. It often involves a dispute among people who will need to, or at least should, work together in the future. Hard feelings often develop, even among parties who are supposed to be on the same side of the litigation. Litigation is a kind of battle that is not likely to produce good feelings among the participants. It can also be lengthy, dragging on for months or years, and it can be expensive in terms of funding for attorneys, time for preparation and deposition, and emotional tension.

> Arbitration has become a common alternative to litigation.

Binding arbitration clauses in contracts are nearly ubiquitous. Arbitration has many advantages compared with litigation: it is faster, less expensive, and less public. The Federal Arbitration Act has promoted arbitration, and the federal courts, particularly the Supreme Court, have interpreted the act in ways that very much strengthen arbitration. If someone agrees to arbitration, that person is almost certainly going to be bound by that agreement if a dispute arises. But there are also some disadvantages to arbitration. With rare exceptions, there is no appeal from the decision of the arbitrator or arbitrators. Except in fairly extreme circumstances, this creates uncertainty in how legal rights will be enforced. Who appoints the arbitrator is also important—if one party has the right to select the arbitrator, arbitrators on that panel may be particularly oriented to the interests of the side making future appointments. In one study of consumer arbitration, consumers lost to companies more than 99% of the time. It is also now possible to use arbitration to avoid such things as class action lawsuits in which many people with small injuries can seek redress. The finality of an agreement to arbitrate is something that should be taken seriously. Nonetheless, there are real advantages to fair arbitration compared with trials where time, expense, and publicity are matters of concern.

Mediation is another form of alternative dispute resolution. It is a nonbinding process of negotiation in which a neutral third party tries to bring the parties to a settlement. It has the advantage of being even more informal and involves coming to a resolution to which the parties must agree in order for the dispute to be resolved. It can also be relatively fast and inexpensive and can be undertaken while a lawsuit or other dispute mechanism is moving forward. Many of the lawsuits that are settled are as a result of mediation, either by an outside party or by the judge.

Managers in the healthcare area should consider the consequences of dispute mechanisms carefully. Few people enter into arrangement expecting a dispute to arise, so they often ignore this important step.

LEGAL ISSUES SPECIFIC TO HEALTHCARE

Healthcare professionals and organizations are subject to hundreds of laws and legal principles that are specific to them. This section considers several examples of the more important of these laws.

Medical Malpractice

"Medical" malpractice, of course, is unique to health law, but malpractice principles are *not* unique. Malpractice is found in many professions (e.g., law and accountancy), and some of the same general legal principles apply. But medical malpractice has some special aspects.

"Medical malpractice" is frequently used as a generic term to refer to any professional error or other activity t hat gives rise to liability. For example, it could apply to intentional torts, where a researcher, to assess alarm effects on different personality types, falsely tells subjects that a close relative has died. There can even be malpractice (or malpractice-like) cases based in contract law. It is unusual, but healthcare professionals may guarantee a result and be sued in contract for breach of warranty. But overwhelmingly, malpractice means professional negligence as defined subsequently, by a healthcare provider.

The chapter on risk management also considers malpractice issues (see Chapter 17), but a few general words are appropriate here. Negligence, as previously stated, requires duty, breach, causation, and injury. Applied to medical professional liability, that translates as follows.

"Duty" is ordinarily described as the obligation to act as a reasonably careful practitioner would act under the circumstances. The "breach" is simply failing to practice with that degree of care.

Not every bad outcome is negligence, and, for that matter, not every mistake is negligence—only mistakes that are unreasonable under the

---
Not every bad outcome in medicine is negligence.

---

circumstances are subject to liability. That almost always means that the mistake is one that the profession itself would consider to be inappropriate or bad practice. For example, giving a drug to a patient that causes a serious allergic reaction may be a mistake, but it is not necessarily negligent. Usually failing to check about drug allergies, however, would be a negligent mistake. However, assume that the mistake occurred when a person was brought to an emergency department unconscious and alone, and the drug was administered to increase the blood pressure of a hypotensive patient. "Under the circumstances"—part of how we defined duty and breach—includes the emergency circumstances that required action and the fact that there was no way to determine allergic reactions.

One important limitation on duty is that the duty of medical professionals is generally to their patients—and infrequently to third parties or the public in general. This is in keeping with the general principle of American law that there is no duty to rescue someone for whom a person has no responsibility. Because the duty usually arises when there is a professional relationship, it is critical to know when that relationship exists.

Remember that causation and injury are also required for liability. A negligent mistake that does not cause injury would not result in liability.

Damages in malpractice cases include economic damages. For example, past and future medical costs, lost wages, and income are economic damages. "Damages" also may also include noneconomic damages, particularly pain and suffering. All of these damages are intended to put the plaintiff back in the position the plaintiff would have been in if it were not for the negligence, at least insofar as money can do that. They are meant to "compensate" the plaintiff for the injuries. "Punitive damages" are unusual in malpractice cases. Punitive damages are a way of punishing the defendant for particularly bad conduct.

A hospital or other health organization may be responsible, under vicarious liability, for the acts of its employees, including professional employees. In addition, the failure of these organizations to exercise reasonable care in the selection and supervision of nonemployee contractors (e.g., physicians given hospital privileges) may result in liability for the organizations.

Malpractice law is primarily a matter of state law. Malpractice practice and procedure vary from state to state. Many states have undertaken "malpractice reform," which is intended to limit the number or cost of medical malpractice cases, and thereby have reduced malpractice insurance costs to physicians. A "cap" on noneconomic damages (e.g., at $250,000) has probably been effective in reducing malpractice costs. Other more procedural reforms (e.g., limiting the expert witnesses who can testify in malpractice cases) do not appear to have had as much of a lasting impact. These laws are hotly debated in terms of their fairness to injured parties and social consequences. Because they are matters of state law, by definition, they vary widely from state to state.

Pharmaceutical Issues

Pharmaceuticals are highly regulated by federal law. We will consider three classes of pharmaceuticals: prescription drugs, over-the-counter (OTC) drugs, and nutraceuticals.

The patent on prescription drugs gives a pharmaceutical company the exclusive rights to market or license the compound for 20 years or so (the term may be extended in some cases). When the patent has expired, companies may manufacture and sell the generic compound. These simple

---

Prescription drugs are usually covered by one or more patents, at least initially.

sentences belie the very complex series of the US Patent Office and Food and Drug Administration (FDA) regulations that apply to the patenting and licensing of brand name and generic drugs.

Before the drug can be marketed, however, the company must demonstrate to the FDA that it is "safe and effective." That generally includes animal studies and then a series of studies in human subjects. In human subjects there are three formal phases of testing, with an increasing number of subjects in each phase. There is also a fourth postapproval phase. Phase I usually involves giving the drug to healthy volunteers to determine its safety. Phase II is designed to obtain initial human data on the efficacy of the drug for its intended purpose, establish proper dosage levels, and continue to assess safety. Phase III usually includes a fairly large number of subjects to more precisely assess efficacy, dosage and uses, and safety. "Safe" and "effective" are relative terms. Effective generally means that the medicine has been demonstrated to have significant medical effect, beyond that of a placebo. "Safe" essentially comes down to the fact that the benefits of the drug reasonably outweigh its risks.

Based on these studies, the drug sponsor presents evidence to the FDA endeavoring to obtain a license for the compound. The FDA may approve, reject, or request additional information and more studies. When approved, the company may distribute the drug. "Phase IV" involves ongoing monitoring of adverse events and problems with the drug as well as appropriate uses. It is in this area of postmarketing monitoring that there is additional focus. The experience with COX-2 inhibitors (Vioxx became the most infamous) drew significant attention to the need for this monitoring.

The FDA is responsible for ensuring the continued safety of the manufacture of approved drugs and that they remain unadulterated. There is a balance between protecting the public from harmful compounds that are inadequately tested and harming the public from keeping helpful compounds off the market too long. The FDA's regulatory pendulum swings a bit between these goals. The FDA also prohibits the "misbranding" of the drug—and that includes the package insert. The FDA must approve this branding, which includes indications as well as warnings, contraindications, and instructions. Uses of the medicine for something other than the indications—"off-label" use—is an area in which comprehensive regulation breaks down some.

Once a medicine is approved for use, physicians can prescribe it not only for approved indications but also for off-label uses. For example, a drug approved for one form of cancer might be used by physicians for other cancers—or even for conditions unrelated to cancer. Of course, an off-label use may be malpractice if not based on a reasonable judgment of the physician. For some compounds, the off-label uses exceed the indicated uses. This is true for some cancer drugs and some antibiotics. Some years ago, chloramphenicol (Chloromycetin), an antibiotic approved for a narrow group of infections, was commonly prescribed as a general broad-spectrum antibiotic, resulting in serious injuries (aplastic anemia) in a number of people. Drug companies that promote pharmaceuticals for off-label uses for prescription in government-funded programs may violate the False Claims Act.

OTC drugs are those generally required to be safe and effective without a physician being involved. Originally, OTC drugs were not required to affirmatively prove safety and efficacy, and a number of these older drugs are essentially "grandfathered" into the OTC status. OTC drugs may be pulled from the market, however, if the FDA determines that they are dangerous. In addition, the FDA has the authority to regulate the manufacture of these compounds to avoid adulteration.

Nutraceuticals are an exception to the claim of intense federal control; they are only modestly controlled. Essentially dietary supplements and similar compounds, nutraceuticals are generally treated as foods under US law. Except for clear pharmaceutical claims or impurities, they are subject to limited regulation. Claims that they cure disease or have medical qualities may bring FDA scrutiny, but nutraceuticals are more like the "wild west" than controlled products.

The issue of pharmaceutical liability involves a complex interaction between federal and state law. The mismanufacture or adulteration of drugs may result in liability. A thorny issue has been whether the FDA's approval of a drug or device precludes state liability for the drug itself or the warnings in the labeling (package insert). The US Supreme Court has decided a number of cases involving this question, and a summary follows. There may be liability for brand name prescription drugs that do not include appropriate warnings. The companies that manufacture them have the responsibility to gather and maintain and update (with FDA approval) information about the drugs they manufacture. However, generic drug manufacturers are not liable for inadequate warnings because they are required by law to use the warnings (package inserts) that are approved by the FDA for the brand name drug. Note, however, that Congress and the FDA are considering a number changes in these laws.

Medical devices are also regulated by the FDA. There are three levels or types of devices (for devices) that are registered. One class that has particular risks associated with it (Class III devices), for example, requires substantial FDA premarketing review and clearance. The Supreme Court determined that federal statutes provide significant legal protection for device manufacturers against personal injury liability for devices reviewed and approved by the FDA. This protection does not apply, however, to defects in manufacture, in which case the manufacturer may be liable. The protection does not apply to malpractice for improper installation or use of the device.

Medicare and Medicaid

This topic could easily require a multivolume set to begin to cover. The law related to these programs is nothing short of massive. This section will discuss only a few of these issues. Other sections in this and other chapters will consider a few additional topics that are closely associated with Medicare or Medicaid, including fraud and abuse, HIPAA, EMTALA, and EMRs. (See Chapters 3 and 15.)

In Medicare, the discussion views several programs—inpatient hospital care (Part A), physician care (Part B), Medicare Advantage (Part C), and a pharmaceutical benefit (Part D). These programs, however, are relatively uniform throughout the country.

Because Medicaid is a federal-state partnership, there are considerable variations among the states. These differences are becoming greater with the opt-in–opt-out of ACA Medicaid expansion.

Some practitioners sigh, "Medicare and Medicaid—can't live with it and can't live without it." Medicare encompasses such a large portion of the healthcare delivered that it is difficult for most providers not to participate in that program. Medicaid has the advantage to providers of reimbursing care for patients who might not be able to pay for themselves. It is becoming more important with the ACA. It can substantially reduce "bad debt" accounts. On the other hand, reimbursement for Medicare is not generous. And Medicaid is even less generous in reimbursing care and may not even cover the cost of providing the care. Both programs require substantial bookkeeping, and there are a lot of regulations about participating in the programs.

Healthcare entities are not required to participate in these programs, and it is possible to participate in one program, say Medicare, and not the other (Medicaid). Deciding whether to participate is not a decision to be taken lightly. Several features of the programs, in addition to the rather low reimbursement rate, will be significant. One example is "balance billing."

Medicare and Medicaid laws require that entities that participate in these programs may not "balance bill." That is, they do not bill the patient for part of the price (other than program copays). For example, if a physician determines that his or her charge for an uncomplicated appendectomy is $3,000, and if Medicare pays $1,000 for the surgery, the physician may not bill the patient for the balance of $2,000. The $1,000 is the maximum the physician will receive for it. The same rule applies to Medicaid. There is, in effect, a way around this limitation for Medicare (probably impractical for Medicaid).

A provider may decline to participate in Medicare, establish the prices he or she wishes to charge, bill the patient, and help the patient receive reimbursement to the extent Medicare permits it. In the example above, the physician would bill the patient for the $3,000 surgery. The patient would then seek reimbursement from Medicare,

> Medicare and Medicaid have a large number of compliance requirements.

which should reimburse it at $1,000. And the patient would, in effect, pay the additional $2,000. Of course, in the market this provider would be disadvantaged for Medicare patients relative to other providers, so most providers with services that are viewed by most patients as more or less indistinguishable from the others would find this difficult to pull off. Other providers, whose patients are willing to put up with paying extra and billing Medicare themselves, are able to do this.

Medicare and Medicaid compliance requirements relate not only to proper reimbursement, but also to safety in the workplace, quality of care, and electronic record-keeping. The compliance requirements are ignored, or corners cut, at the peril of the provider. The Centers for Medicare and Medicaid Services and other federal and state agencies may deny payment or demand repayment for services provided, disqualify a provider from participating in the programs, institute a fraud and abuse investigation, impose civil penalties, and undertake criminal investigations in some cases for failure to comply with the Medicare and Medicaid laws. In all but the smallest providers, formal compliance efforts are essential, and a compliance officer with special training may be warranted.

Private Insurance

The other major reimbursement mechanism, covering the vast majority of non-Medicare/Medicaid patients, is private, employer-provided insurance. From a legal standpoint, health insurance is primarily contract law. There are, of course, many issues of risk, economics, and financial incentives, but ultimately it is simple: it is a contract. A provider who signs it *is* bound by it. How does it interact with other contracts the provider already has? Does it provide a "most favored insurer" provision that could reduce the agreed upon rates considerably? Does it allow cancellation with limited notice? Does it provide for arbitration that can be unfair to the provider and favor the insurance company? There are a thousand questions such as these that matter.

Not reading and understanding these provider contracts can be disastrous. If a provider does not review or negotiate such contracts with regularity, it is wise to have expert assistance in working the way through the details.

Fraud and Abuse

These concepts generally apply to Medicare and Medicaid, although they can apply to private health insurance as well. Dozens of federal and state laws are aimed at stopping fraud and abuse, particularly including billing for nonexistent services, billing too much for services rendered, providing unnecessary or slipshod service, and engaging in self-referrals and kickbacks. This discussion later will consider several of the more important laws in fraud and abuse.

FALSE CLAIMS ACT
The granddaddy of them all is the False Claims Act, which was originally not aimed at health institutes when enacted but at faulty munitions in the Civil War.

The act has been amended by Congress several times in recent times to expand its reach. It is even further expanded under the ACA. The federal law is supplemented now by state false claims acts. This discussion will focus on the federal law. There are several provisions of the act, but they essentially come down to knowingly presenting or assisting with a false claim to the federal government for payment or approval. Of course, Medicare and Medicaid, among other federal programs, involve lots of claims presented to the federal government.

The False Claims Act has several powerful and unusual provisions. Most of its effect is civil, not criminal. Criminal charges, however, are possible in the worst cases involving outright fraud. But the power of it comes through its civil damages and its whistleblower provisions. There are civil penalties of approximately $6,000 to $12,000 for each false claim—and treble damages for the government's loss.

The other unusual provision of the law is that it allows private whistleblowers to a *qui tam* action, sometimes informally referred to as a "private attorney general" action. The person, known as a "relator," first discloses all of the relevant information to the government. The government then investigates the matter, and if it decides to take over the case, it proceeds. If it decides not to take the case, the relator may proceed with the case (at his or her own expense). There is a financial incentive to relator/whistleblowers. If the government does take over the case, the relator may receive 15% to 25% of the recovery. If the government does not intervene, the relator may receive 25% to 30% of the recovery. This, of course, can be an attractive mechanism to disgruntled employees or former employees who know of some form of wrongful billing of the government.

The False Claims Act has been used in a wide range of cases in healthcare. From Medicare billing for services that were not actually provided, to billing for "phantom surgery," to off-label promotion by pharmaceutical companies, the False Claims Act has become an everyday part of health organizations. It is one of the reasons that good compliance programs have become an essential part of these organizations.

The US Justice Department provides a good primer on the False Claims Act at http://www.justice.gov/civil/docs_forms/C-FRAUDS_FCA_Primer.pdf.

ANTIKICKBACK STATUTES

Two arrangements in healthcare inherently invite overuse of services, increased charges, and referrals that are less than optimal. One is kickbacks, in which someone receives a fee (bribe) for referring business to a specific health service provider. For example, a physician agrees to send blood work to a laboratory in return for a "handling fee." The second is self-referral in which a healthcare provider refers business to another entity in which the provider has a financial interest. For example, a physician sends the blood work to a laboratory in which he or she is a major owner.

The law has a broad definition of kickback and self-referral, which creates some problems. In the complicated arrangements in healthcare, there are many instances in which some form of self-referral or even kickback may be perfectly legitimate and efficient. The answer to this problem has been to define a large number of "safe harbors," which carve out specific types of arrangements that are exceptions to the prohibition on kickbacks and self-referrals. These safe harbors are generally complex, with exceptions to the exceptions, and with increasing numbers of exceptions.

There is an old cliché that the only cure for law is more law, and the antikickback and self-referral prohibitions, safe harbors, and exceptions seem to illustrate that principle. This discussion will first take a quick look at the kickback prohibitions and then the limitations on self-referral.

The federal Anti-Kickback Act makes it illegal to offer anything of value (cash, in kind, directly or indirectly) to induce some to refer or reward for referring healthcare business. The federal law provides for substantial civil and criminal penalties for violations. It does not directly give private (nongovernmental) parties the authority to bring actions, but by using the False Claims Act, they are in effect able to bring private actions. Examples of the many safe harbors are those related to equipment rental, practitioner referral groups, ambulatory surgical centers, purchase of organizations, and sale of medical practices. For each safe harbor, there are several criteria that must be met to fit within the harbor. There are many shoals for the unwary, and the consequences of not meeting all of the requirements can be serious.

SELF-REFERRAL PROHIBITIONS

Many of the federal laws related to self-referrals are in one of the "Stark laws." The name is not a description of the law but refers to the sponsor of the bills in the House of Representatives, Fortney Hillman "Pete" Stark, Jr. The Stark laws generally apply to self-referrals within federal health programs. Many states also have self-referral prohibitions that cover other medical service programs.

The Stark statutes and related regulations are intended to prohibit the referral of patients to services/providers in which the referring physician has a financial interest or ownership. The referrals include, for example, radiation therapy; magnetic resonance imaging (MRI), computed topography (CT imaging), and ultrasound; laboratory services; home health supplies; and so on. Referral is broadly defined to include various forms of order, request, or plan of care. The law is based on good evidence that self-referral increases the frequency and costs of referrals. Violation of the Stark laws may result in substantial civil penalties.

As with the antikickback laws, the prohibition on self-referrals has a large number of exceptions and safe harbors—some count 35 to 40 of them. As with the other safe harbors, these commonly are multiple part tests, where all parts must be met for the harbor to be safe. And the consequences of missing even one of the requirements for the safe harbor can be severe.

Private Insurance Fraud

Most of the federal fraud and abuse statutes, of which the discussion above is a sampling, apply specifically to Medicare, Medicaid, and other smaller federally funded or assisted programs. State statutes sometimes expand the principles (e.g., kickback prohibitions to private insurance programs). Many kinds of fraud, and some abusive practices, are violations of federal or state consumer protection and fraud and theft laws. Health organizations engaged in ongoing, concerted mail fraud, for example, may also violate the Racketeer Influenced and Corrupt Organizations Act (RICO).

There are also laws increasingly targeted at making it easier to find and prosecute criminal fraud in the private healthcare and insurance areas. For example, the Federal Criminal Health Care Fraud law makes it illegal to defraud any health benefit program. Violation of these laws may result in liability, civil fines, criminal penalties, and loss of licensure or certification.

Emergency Medical Treatment and Active Labor Act (EMTALA)

EMTALA presents the question: is a parking lot a hospital? (More about that in a moment.) EMTALA is a federal law that requires hospitals (those receiving Medicare, Medicaid, or some other federal funds) to provide emergency medical treatment and labor-related services to anyone who presents to the hospital. EMTALA is not a general care requirement—it is a requirement of emergency care. A hospital must conduct a minimum examination and treat or stabilize the person. It can discharge or transfer the patient only if another hospital is better equipped to treat the patient, the patient is refusing treatment, or the patient wishes to leave or is stabilized.

EMTALA's original purpose was really to prevent "dumping"—one hospital transferring nonpaying patients to another hospital (usually a charity hospital). Because the vast majority of hospitals are covered by EMTALA, it has become a focus of uncompensated care for the indigent. Hospitals commonly go well beyond the technical requirements of EMTALA because of local laws or a sense of mission or charitable commitment. In fact, most states by common law or statute require that hospitals provide emergency services for those who are at the hospital.

There have been many issues of interpretation of EMTALA, which is where the parking lot comes in. Is a patient in a hospital's parking lot present "at" the hospital? Essentially the answer is yes. The general rule is also that a patient within 250 yards of the hospital is at the hospital, which, of course, is subject to its own set of interpretation.

The consequences of violating EMTALA (for hospitals or physicians) are civil fines, potential loss of Medicare/Medicaid eligibility, and civil lawsuit from a hospital on which the patient has been "dumped." There may also be civil lawsuits by patients who are not evaluated or treated properly.

Electronic Medical Records (EMRs) and the Health Insurance Portability and Accountability Act (HIPAA)

The federal government has been pushing for the adoption of EMRs, both in an effort to improve reimbursement for and auditing of Medicare/Medicaid services and to improve health services generally. With the adoption of the Health Information Technology for Economic and Clinical Health (HITECH) amendments, the push has become a shove. Medicare/Medicaid-eligible entities are required to move toward a "meaningful use" of EMRs, and the modest incentives to do so are becoming requirements. (See Chapter 3.)

The rub has been that development of EMRs is expensive, the transition to them is difficult, it is very complicated to make one system compatible with others, and the antikickback laws limit the ability of hospitals to pay for the EMR equipment of nonemployee physicians. There is little doubt that almost all healthcare entities will have to move to EMRs. The ACA is increasing the pressure for EMRs to become universal sooner rather than later. Along with the adoption of EMR systems, there are a variety of associated legal obligations, including the obligation to ensure the accuracy of the records, as well as their security and privacy. Here comes HIPAA.

HIPAA began a process of federal requirements to protect electronic health records. HIPAA and the amendments to it in HITECH have authorized mountains of regulations concerning the security and privacy of health information. Chapter 5 on ethics discusses HIPAA and related issues dealing with confidentiality and privacy.

Human Subjects (and Animals Too)

The regulation of the use of human subjects in research begins with international law. The gross abuse of human subjects was considered a crime against humanity, or war crime, at the Nuremburg trials. A Nuremburg code announced basic principles of legal use of subjects, which include obtaining voluntary informed consent, avoiding unnecessary risks, assessing the risks and benefits, and allowing withdrawal from the study.

Federal law regulates most human studies through the leverage of the funding of research and approval of new pharmaceuticals. The Common Rule ("common" because it is used by most federal agencies) and similar rules are promulgated by the FDA for studies that will be used to seek approval of new drugs. The core of these rules is the prior review by institutional review boards (IRB) of the proposed study, plus some monitoring of the study as it is undertaken. Ordinarily, any organization that is subject to the Common Rule also agrees that any studies conducted within the institution, federally funded or not, will be subject to IRB review. The Office of Human Research Protections maintains a very helpful website that helps explain the intricacies of federal law. It is available at http://www.hhs.gov/ohrp/policy/.

Institutions that violate the federal requirements for protecting human subjects risk disciplinary action, including disqualification for federal research funding or an immediate cessation of ongoing research. Although unusual, these sanctions have been imposed, in some instances against some well-known institutions. In addition to the legal mechanisms, there are voluntary accreditation programs, primarily under the Association for the Accreditation of Human Research Protection Programs, to assist institutions in ensuring that they comply with ethical human research protection.

In the case of federally funded research, the institutions in which the researchers are working have undoubtedly made assurances in the granting process that the research

> Researchers who undertake research on human subjects have significant obligations.

will have IRB approval before human subjects are used. Even in the absence of federal funding, it is likely that the institution in which the research is conducted will have requirements that all human studies receive prior review. Furthermore, many foundations and private funders require IRB review.

Some states have laws that deal directly with the use of human subjects, but these play a relatively minor role compared with federal law. However, state laws regarding informed consent, abuse reporting, tort liability and the like all apply to human research activity as well as any other healthcare.

Federal and state laws also regulate the use of animals in research studies. A particularly good summary of these laws is maintained by the Association for Assessment and Accreditation of Laboratory Animal Care, the accreditation program for laboratory animal care, at http://www.aaalac.org/resources/usregs.cfm.

Dangerous Patients

One narrow exception to the general "no duty to rescue" rule described in the Torts section of this chapter may be the dangerous patient. Most states have either a statutory or common law obligation under which certain mental health professionals are required to take reasonable steps to avoid a known danger to identifiable individuals. This is commonly known as the *Tarasoff* duty, based on the name of a California case that established the duty. It is also known as the "duty to warn" case, although that is a bit of a misnomer. The duty is to take reasonable steps, given the circumstances, to protect the identifiable victim. This may include warning the intended victim, but it is not universally required.

Under some other circumstances, health entities may be required to take action to protect the public. Abuse reporting laws as well as sexually transmitted disease and communicable disease reporting obligations have already been discussed. Beyond the legal obligations to report, it is generally accepted that there is authority or permission to report voluntarily a range of serious risks, even though it is not required. For example, a patient who represents a serious, imminent threat of shooting up part of a town (even though there is not a specific, identifiable victim) may be reported to authorities without any real risk of legal liability. All of the protections of confidentiality, including HIPAA, have some form of exception that allows such disclosure of information.

Peer Review

The processes of peer review (broadly to include all manner of professional assessment and analysis) are of considerable importance to the ongoing process of quality improvement and error reduction. (See Chapter 15.) They do, however, have some legal risks. Claims of defamation, breach of contract, misrepresentation, and antitrust problems, for example, have all been made in the course of these processes.

Society thus has a stake, along with the medical profession, in ensuring that these review processes work successfully. For that reason, there are a number of special privileges that protect peer review processes. For example, there are testimonial privileges that limit the ability of courts and parties to lawsuits to compel disclosure of communication in the peer review process. Defamation law generally offers a qualified immunity to limit liability. Antitrust violations are possible but unlikely in the normal course of events. There are, of course, some exceptions to the protection of confidentiality, as evidenced by the requirement of reporting to the National Practitioner Data Bank, discussed earlier.

Most of the defenses and protections of the peer review processes rely on a level of good faith (especially not using the processes of inappropriate or vindictive purposes). They also depend on the assumption that these processes not be used to limit competition by preventing other qualified practitioners from entering or continuing in the healthcare marketplace.

A legal debate continues. Is it better to rely on demanding individual responsibility as a way of reducing errors and improving quality or to focus on systemic changes in this process? The National Practitioner Data Bank and the proposals to expand reporting requirements are examples of the first approach. The second approach is illustrated by error reduction programs patterned after the Federal Aviation Administration's effort to improve air safety by encouraging self-reports of errors and thereby focusing more on systems changes and less on individual punishment. This second approach requires that the law modify some aspects of traditional personal responsibility. (See Chapter 15.)

Starting, Joining, and Leaving a Practice

Many of the general legal principles discussed early in this chapter and those more specifically directed to healthcare in this section come together when a physician begins a new practice, joins an existing practice, or leaves a particular practice or retires. Those are times of particular vulnerability, and a particularly good time to do a review of changes in the law that may be important to the practice. These issues are considered in the chapter on risk management chapter (see Chapter 17).

PRACTICAL CONSIDERATIONS

In summary, all of this may seem a little overwhelming. Even in scratching the surface of legal issues relevant to the healthcare professional, the bundle of law seems reasonably substantial. In part, this reflects the importance of medicine in society. It also reflects the very complex arrangements in which modern healthcare is delivered and the fact that at least 18% of the economy is devoted to healthcare.

The ACA brings a whole new level of law to healthcare. The statute itself is hundreds of pages, the initial regulations are many thousands of pages, and the courts are just beginning to weigh in. The ACA will result in very significant changes in health law over the next decade.

Most of the laws that affect healthcare make sense, at least in broad sweep. Sometimes the law is misguided, badly drafted, or sloppy. But mostly laws are reasonable efforts to avoid problems that have arisen, sensible attempts to deal with competing values and interests, and difficult decisions to fairly and efficiently use scarce resources. Still, at the level of the details of the law, it becomes difficult because of the need to deal in a regulation or statute with a wide range of situations to which the law will apply. (See Chapter 15.)

For years people have been advised that they should have an annual physical checkup. The authors are going to return the favor: healthcare professionals should periodically have legal checkups. Preventive law is as important as preventive medicine. That requires several things.

Here is the most important sentence in this chapter. **Physicians and other healthcare professionals should have an ongoing relationship with a trusted attorney.** That will often be someone engaged by the health professional. In other cases, it may be an attorney in the general counsel's office. It is essential to actually consult the attorney on a regular basis—not just when there is trouble. This is another time it is a good idea for both professionals to have a list of things they want to talk about. And it is important to listen and to act on the advice.

Every effective leader and manager in healthcare must be aware of relevant legal issues and be able to work with lawyers. The fundamental lessons are that there are a number of legal areas in which any leader or manager must have a sensitivity; an openness to understanding the law and working within the prescribed limits is both critical and possible; and it is essential that healthcare providers have an ongoing, trusting relationship with a lawyer who is an expert in health law.

CASE STUDY

One of your partners calls you from the office, upset. He has received a letter demanding compensation from a woman he saw 3 years ago. The patient was allergic to a medication and went into anaphylactic shock in the office (which a local hospital maintains for the partnership as long as the partners admit at least 150 patients per year to that hospital). Although the patient was quickly revived and went home later that afternoon, she blames the physician for "scaring me to death." Your partner wants to know whether he will have to pay money to her and lose his license. He says he has pulled the patient's record and can insert a note that he warned her of the risk of shock.

Questions

- What factors are likely to play an important role in determining whether he would be liable?
- What would you advise him to do?
- In addition to potential malpractice liability, do you see any risks for the partner?
- Do you, as a partner, have any risk of liability?
- What should you do?

SUGGESTED READING

Hall MA, Ellman IM, Orentlicher D. *Health Care Law and Ethics in a Nutshell*. 3rd ed. St. Paul, MN: West Publishing; 2011.

Institute of Medicine. *To Err Is Human: Building a Safer Health System*. Washington, DC: National Academies Press; 1999.

Showalter JS. *The Law of Healthcare Administration*. 6th ed. Chicago, IL: Health Administration Press; 2011.

Teitlebaum JB, Wilensky SE. *Essentials of Health Policy and Law*. 2nd ed. Burlington, MA: Jones & Bartlett Learning; 2012.

7

Quality Improvement in Healthcare

ERIC J. BIEBER AND WILLIAM ANNABLE

KEY POINTS

- Value is becoming the new currency in healthcare and is represented by quality and efficiency.
- There is a move from a fee-for-service to a pay-for-performance (P4P) environment, where healthcare providers and entities are financially rewarded for quality and efficiency attainment.
- It is difficult to define exactly what quality is.
- Value-based purchasing (VBP) is a type of P4P that continues to evolve over time.
- Disincentives such as readmission penalties and eliminating payment for hospital-acquired conditions (HACs) and "never" events (e.g., operating on the wrong body part) are becoming more common.
- It is unclear what model of P4P will create the greatest or the most sustainable change.
- There will be ever increasing transparency of pricing and results as the healthcare environment becomes more consumer-centric.
- Building a culture of quality and safety takes broad engagement from multiple stakeholders.

Quality has become the buzzword for this generation of healthcare providers. It is constantly talked about, and now hospitals and providers will be judged and paid according to their "quality." Value, represented by quality and efficiency, has also become critically important as healthcare systems seek to differentiate themselves and avoid payment penalties while concomitantly reducing their expenses. This chapter explores the concept of quality beginning with the challenge of merely defining the word and looking at the evolution of the concept of quality over the past century and the progress that has been made. It considers the impact of healthcare reform and how legislation in the United States is driving P4P. It discusses the challenge of identifying appropriate metrics to gauge true quality and how these metrics are being incorporated into payment reform and alternate payment methodologies. It concludes by discussing the importance of transparency in the ongoing quality dialogue and how to create a "quality culture" within an organization.

DEFINITION OF QUALITY

Although most people believe that they can recognize quality healthcare, asking them to define it becomes problematic. In fact, a good definition of healthcare quality really did not exist until after the Institute of Medicine (IOM) report on American healthcare, *Crossing the Quality Chasm* in 2001. The disappointing and devastating statistics presented in that report sharpened national interest and began an ongoing effort to improve quality and safety in the United States. The IOM defined quality as "The degree to which health services for individuals and populations increase the likelihood of desired health outcomes and are consistent with current professional knowledge." It was assumed that this care should be based on the best-available clinical evidence and provided in a technically and culturally competent manner with good communication and shared decision-making. Although this definition seemed better than those used before it, it was lacking in several key areas such as recognizing the concepts of safety and cost. This led to the development of the "Six Aims" of the IOM.

- Safe—avoiding preventable injuries, reducing medical errors
- Effective—providing services based on scientific knowledge
- Patient-centered—care that is respectful and responsive to individuals
- Efficient—care that avoids wasting time and other resources
- Timely—improved wait times, better workflow
- Equitable—care delivered regardless of patient characteristics or demographics

When care is provided in a manner that achieves these Six Aims, it is deemed to be "quality care." Many institutions have subsequently developed their own personalized versions of the Six Aims. For example, leaders at the University Hospitals Cleveland further added that it is necessary "to foster an environment in which our patients experience no needless deaths, no needless pain and suffering, no helplessness in those served or serving, no unwanted waiting, and no waste."

As the definition of quality broadens, there have been attempts to simplify it and to optimize health system performance in the process. Notable among these is the Triple Aim, as introduced and defined by the Institute for Healthcare Improvement (IHI). It is IHI's belief that new models must be developed that simultaneously pursues three dimensions: improving the patient experience of care (including quality and satisfaction), improving the health of populations, and reducing the per-capita cost of healthcare.

It has been pointed out that in most healthcare settings today, no one is accountable for all three dimensions of the Triple Aim. To be truly successful, all three aims must be addressed simultaneously. Much of healthcare reform is designed to achieve the Triple Aim; in directing programs to achieve it, we benefit patients individually, contribute to population health, and help provide society with the necessary affordable healthcare. Perhaps the greatest impact of the Triple Aim so far is the realization that from a patient's perspective, excellent medical care is the least a healthcare organization can provide. The patient's experience matters greatly.

Another aspect of quality healthcare is the process of striving for and reaching well-defined standards of care. This includes, but is not limited to, accrediting physicians, ambulatory settings, and hospitals. Improving the quality of patient care is the driving force behind all the standards and regulations that exist. Performance improvement is designed to improve processes to achieve the standards and regulations.

Still another aspect of defining quality care is the often-confusing relationship between patient safety and quality care delivery. Many organizations view quality healthcare as the umbrella under which patient safety resides. The IOM considers patient safety "indistinguishable from the delivery of quality health care." Patient safety was defined by the IOM as "the prevention of harm to patients." This requires a system of care delivery that prevents errors, learns from those errors that do occur, and is built on a culture of safety that involves everyone. Many safety practices have developed such as simulation centers, bar coding, and team training. The causes of harm have been grouped by the National Quality Forum as:

- Latent—removed from the practitioner and involving organizational policies, procedures, and resources
- Active—direct contact with the patient
- Organizational—failures involving management, culture, protocols, communication, and external factors
- Technical—indirect failure of facilities

Patient safety is a key component of high-quality healthcare. It is strongly linked to all definitions of quality whether the definitions explicitly state it or not.

Despite multiple attempts to define quality, there is general agreement that the perfect definition does not yet exist. This perceived lack of definition, however, has not slowed the quality movement. In fact, as the definitions have evolved, the momentum to improve quality in healthcare has only increased.

THE EVOLUTION OF QUALITY

"Every hospital should follow every patient it treats long enough to determine whether the treatment has been successful, and then to inquire 'if
not, why not' with a view to preventing similar failures in the future."

ERNEST CODMAN, *1914*

The focus around quality is not a new one. In the 1910s, Ernest Codman began
to speak about a concept where patients and their outcomes should be tracked to
evaluate the effectiveness of various treatments. He called this the "end result"
system. Unfortunately, some people were not enamored with his insistence of
tracking outcomes, and ultimately he resigned his position at the Massachusetts
General Hospital to open up the Codman Hospital. In 1918, he published the book
"a study in hospital efficiency" where he reported on the outcomes of his hospitals
first 5 years in operation, including errors—certainly an interesting study in early
transparency! He was also pivotal in the
formation of the American College of
Surgeons (ACS) and its development of
the minimum standards for hospitals,
a program that ultimately became the
Joint Commission. In 1926, the ACS
issued the 18-page "Manual of Hospital Standardization"—arguably the first
manual on quality in the United States.

In 1951, the Joint Commission
Accreditation of Hospitals (JCAH) was
formed.

The Joint Commission, evolved over time to the Joint Commission on
Accreditation of Healthcare Organizations (JCAHO) and ultimately to the Joint
Commission. From the onset, the organization was a not-for-profit group that
built its accreditation of hospitals around meeting minimum-quality thresholds.

The famed public health scientist, Avedis Donabedian, published his ground-
breaking treatise "Evaluating the Quality of Medical Care" in 1966. In this and
many subsequent publications over the next three decades, Donabedian discussed pivotal quality concepts such as using structure, process, and outcome
in the evaluation of medical interventions in the assessment of quality. It was
this work and many others that drove national interest in the quality agenda and
saw the creation of the IOM in 1970; the formation of the National Committee
for Quality Assurance (NCQA) in 1979; the Agency for Healthcare Policy and
Research, which ultimately became the Agency for Healthcare Research and
Quality (AHRQ) in 1989; the IHI in 1991; and the National Patient Safety
Foundation (NPSF) in 1996.

Importantly, the NCQA became responsible for accrediting managed care organizations in the early 1990s, and out of this work came the formation of health
effectiveness data and information set (HEDIS) measures, a set of measures that
continue to be used to this day. The initial set of measures focused around six
domains: access and accountability, effectiveness of care, utilization of services,
member satisfaction, cost of care, and plan stability. Although the measures and

definitions have evolved over the past three decades, it is interesting that most are still key measures of quality.

There is no question that the IOM's publication in 1999 of *To Err is Human* and the 2002 publication of *Crossing the Quality Chasm* have catalyzed the quality field. The Joint Commission also created additional focus when they released National Patient Safety Goals, which brought attention to specific areas of concern and helped drive patient safety. Also in July 2002, core measures that had been piloted for several years were first put into place in the national landscape. These initially included measures for treatment of patients with acute myocardial infarction as well as heart failure. Subsequently, a number of clinical conditions have been added, and ultimately these were made part of VBP, which will be discussed later in the chapter.

Another advance was the initiation of quality reporting in ambulatory physician offices. This began in 2006 as a voluntary effort, the Physician Quality Reporting System initially offered reporting doctors a 1.5% payment increase. This was later increased to 2.0%. In 2013, it included 138 measures with the focus around preventive care, care coordination, acute and chronic care management, and procedure-related care. The Affordable Care Act (ACA) decreased the increase to 0.5% in 2013 and 2014, with penalties beginning in 2015 of 1.5% and increasing to 2.0% (penalty) in 2016 (which is based on the 2014 reporting year). It can only be anticipated that there will be increasing rigor around not only reporting but on actual achievement of outcomes and that third-party payers may develop similar programs.

PAY FOR PERFORMANCE (P4P) AND HEALTHCARE REFORM

In an attempt to continue the momentum to improve quality in healthcare in the United States, many changes in the fee-for-service payment methodology have been suggested. Healthcare reform is in many ways a laboratory for examining and testing those possible alternative models. The emerging front runner at this time appears to be some variation of P4P where providers are financially rewarded for achieving or exceeding specific targets. All are a fundamental change from fee for service.

The passage and signing of the Patient Protection and Affordable Care Act, commonly called the ACA, in 2010 significantly changed the focus around quality and quality reporting (for additional information, see Chapters 3 and 6). The legislation was ultimately upheld by the US Supreme Court on June 28, 2012. This legislation calls for a number of sweeping changes in the healthcare landscape, but more importantly it calls out specific areas highly tied to quality. Many of the requirements are occurring over time, and many are likely to further evolve as has been seen over the past several decades.

The legislation calls for certain preventive services to be covered free and without copayments or deductibles. There was an elimination of lifetime limits and denials for preexisting conditions. Accountable care organizations (ACOs) were mandated to be brought forward by 2012 for traditional Medicare recipients. A program for VBP was created: a type of healthcare P4P program. In addition, a program to penalize hospitals for readmissions was introduced. The legislation also calls for the creation of a bundled payment pilot to encourage hospitals, physicians, and other providers to work together in more collaborative ways.

Broadly, P4P, also known as VBP, rewards hospitals, medical groups, physicians, and other providers for achieving certain performance measures for quality, efficiency, and safety. In many scenarios there are also disincentives such as eliminating payment for HACs and other "never" events such as surgery on the wrong patient or wrong body part. Although there is considerable support both from professional provider groups and hospital administrators for incentive programs, there is also considerable concern regarding the validity of some of the data and with the uneven comparisons between physicians and hospitals.

There also continues to be concerns regarding which metrics are prioritized and even how individual metrics are defined. HEDIS measures, now almost a quarter century old, continue to be evaluated and reevaluated. Programs such as VBP have changed quite dramatically from their inception when core measures, which are largely process measures, were changed to a focus on outcome measures. In some cases, practitioners are forced to use intermediate or surrogate measures such as hemoglobin A1C or adherence to a diabetic bundle, knowing that they are most interested in actual outcomes and diminishing diabetic complications such as diabetic retinopathy and blindness, myocardial infarction, and peripheral vascular disease.

The debate over P4P becomes progressively more confusing, but it is no longer theoretical. VBP and readmission penalties were called out in the ACA, and HAC reductions were created through the Deficit Reduction Act of 2005. Thus, these P4P programs have been in existence a number of years, and penalties and rewards are being assessed and creating a new focus around these areas. Physicians themselves are not immune, with the value-based modifier and other incentive programs. Is it working so far? In the last few years, there have been reports saying it works and others insisting that it does not. One reads that it is destroying professionalism and that it needs to be strengthened with more severe penalties. The evidence is far from clear, even though some of the metrics (readmissions, patient satisfaction and others) have improved. One experiment testing P4P has been Medicare's Hospital Quality Incentive Demonstration program. It examined a small bonus program involving 253 hospitals in the Premier network. After 6 years, it found essentially no improvement in outcomes when comparing the control and bonus groups. Although there was a small improvement in some process measures, it did not translate into improved outcomes (lower mortality). Another such intervention was the Physician Group Practice Demonstration, a 5-year evaluation of 10 organizations that were eligible for shared savings if quality metrics were achieved and there were savings from predicted Medicare spending. The effort did suggest some success, with 7 of the 10 organizations ultimately achieving shared savings. However, the results were modest and quite variable among the participants and the savings appeared to be largely in the group of dual eligible patients (Medicare and Medicaid). Suffice it to say, the evidence that the P4P approach works is yet incomplete.

The three key P4P programs (VBP, readmission, and HAC) have completely different approaches to bonuses and penalties. The VBP program is zero-sum to Centers for Medicare and Medicaid Services (CMS) because it redistributes monies from poorer performing hospitals to the better performing ones based on achieving certain metrics. The readmissions program is a pure penalty program in which CMS assesses penalties to those whose readmissions rates (observed to expected) are above the benchmark. The HAC program only assesses penalties to the worst quartile of hospitals in number of HACs. It is much too soon to say which program, if any, will stimulate more improvement.

A brief summary of each will help one understand the principles involved.

Value-Based Purchasing (VBP)

CMS calculates a VBP incentive payment percentage for each hospital based on its total performance score. A hospital's adjustment factor can be positive, negative, or neutral—no change to the payment rate that would apply absent the VBP program. VBP is zero-sum to CMS, but at least $1 billion will change hands. It is a fluid program, and the measures will change each year as will the weighting and the dollars available. Initially, it included only process measures and patient satisfaction scores, but outcomes, efficiency, and safety measures have been added. An impact analysis shows that so far 44% of hospitals have a change in base operating amounts between –0.2% and +0.2%. The largest effects are for high disproportionate share hospitals and small hospitals in urban settings.

Readmissions Reduction Program

This program reduces payments if readmissions exceed an expected level. The calculations are based on a formula that compares payments for actual readmissions to payments based on an estimate of expected readmissions. All calculations are risk adjusted. Initially, the program applied to patients with heart attack, pneumonia, or heart failure. If the calculated ratio exceeds 1.0, every Medicare discharge is penalized. Of all the programs, this is perhaps the most controversial.

Hospital-Acquired Condition (HAC) Reduction Program

Hospital-acquired conditions are undesirable conditions that develop during a stay in a hospital. Patient safety indicators are measures of patient harm. Both of these categories have already been addressed in payment/penalty schemes such as VBP and adjustments to diagnosis-related group (DRG) payment. Neither of those approaches showed much effect, so a third program was added. As mentioned above, the penalty (1% payment reduction) applies to any hospital that, relative to the national average, is in the worst quartile. In a recent year, an impact analysis revealed that large (as determined by number of beds), urban, and teaching hospitals stand out as disproportionately represented in the worst quartile and that half of the teaching hospitals are in the worst quartile.

The Medicare Shared Savings Program, otherwise known as Medicare ACO, also has a significant component of quality attached. In this particular program, which is called for by the ACA, organizations will have any shared savings they are eligible to receive reduced if quality thresholds are not achieved. In the early years of the program, participants simply need to report their quality metrics, but over time these migrate to actual attainment. The 33 quality measures in the program are divided into four areas: patient/caregiver experience, care coordination and patient safety, preventive health, and at-risk populations. It is likely that as ACOs increase in the Medicaid and commercial marketplace similar paradigms of both efficiency and quality attainment will be required to achieve full shared savings.

Most P4P programs have similar goals:

- Redesign systems to improve quality and efficiency
- Reduce errors
- Reduce costs
- Advance information technology (IT)
- Broaden delivery of care beyond the office
- Put direct responsibility on physicians and providers to get it right the first time

And most agree on the attributes of performance measures:

- Proven feasibility
- Financially important
- High priority for maximizing health
- Noted variations in care
- Based on clinical guidelines
- Well-defined specifications
- Documented reliability and validity

Whether the goals can be reached is uncertain, but there is no question that people are in the midst of the greatest P4P experiment ever created. So far the results seem to be mixed but if nothing else, the experiment has propelled the quality age.

TRANSPARENCY

Most hospitals in the United States are still not being held accountable for their patient satisfaction, safety record, clinical effectiveness, and cost-effectiveness. At the same time, it is well accepted that some transparency is becoming mandatory. What is not as well accepted is what degree of transparency is required to truly drive significant quality improvement. Transparency holds the key to better hospital performance. An increasing number of hospitals are putting transparency at the top of their strategic priorities.

Don Berwick, former interim director of CMS and the founder of IHI has stated, "Healthcare is a fragmented system. It has many defects and broken parts, so it's impossible to isolate one element of it and say what's wrong." In an attempt to find the "defects," the key participants—purchasers, health plans, patients, and even many providers—are starting to demand the same thing: universal transparency. Transparency is often the first step in a radical shift in the way people think about institutions, whether they be political, economic, or in this case healthcare. In the best case, transparency can lead to patient empowerment. This then leads to an increased demand for evidence-based medicine because it is effective and creates great outcomes. This will improve the quality of care. If this occurs, the better care will lead to lower overall costs. It has even been stated that transparency will redefine how healthcare organizations compete and in the best of all possible worlds it would move healthcare away from a market driven by plans focused on cost and price to one driven by the consumer and focused on quality.

Most everyone agrees on the basics:

- Define goals and metrics and create common standards
- Design and implement an IT system that will report outcomes
- Create process improvement methods to drive successful results
- Create a means to monitor improvement
- Reward positive outcomes and/or penalize poor results

The ACA, although quite complicated in its overall methodology, attempts to implement the basic concepts noted above; none will function without transparency. So whether the desire is to improve an individual hospital or to improve healthcare for the nation, transparency is a necessary ingredient for success.

Who Drives this Transparency?

There is an implicit trust that goes on among the board, the community, and the hospital. Key to that trust is transparency, and only with sufficient transparency can people be certain that all areas of the institution are as they believe them to be.

Before a hospital can become transparent to the community, it must first become internally transparent. This requires the support of both the employees and the board. It also requires the regular sharing of key strategic initiatives and performance metrics with all interested parties. A hospital can literally decide to become transparent overnight, but the full journey to transparency is not quite so easy. It is frequently a process that can be painful, costly, and frustrating. It demands a cultural change and it requires the development of systems and processes that did not exist before. When the inevitable push-back occurs, it requires courage to stay the course. It is critical to understand what we are asking people to do because it is frequently contrary to human nature. Most people are not easily ready to broadcast their mistakes. And it is very difficult to watch as things appear to get worse before they get better. A leader at Dana Farber Hospital stated, "Our goal is to have as complete reporting of errors as possible. If people don't report mistakes, you can't fix them." This is perhaps the simplest but most truthful rationale for transparency.

The journey to transparency is different in every institution that makes the choice. In some places, the board leads it. The chief executive officer (CEO), legal team, or a combination of both lead others. Over time, all have proven effective. But there is general agreement that the most difficult issue to overcome is physician fear and resistance. Providers, as a group, have no training in communicating errors. Physician fear of lawsuits is often the biggest barrier to moving forward. Most agree that programs for physicians must be developed to include teaching of the rationale, training in communicating errors, and providing support when things go wrong. Making a "just culture" part of the day-to-day environment can make acceptance much easier.

With internal transparency achieved, it is an easy leap to external transparency, also known as public reporting. There are many audiences for health performance information:

- Policymakers. Officials responsible for oversight and monitoring would benefit from transparent, accurate data.
- Consumers. Consumers can use this information in selecting a healthcare plan or a provider.
- Employers/purchasers. Employers need information to use in selecting health plans or self-insured options.
- Health plans. Plans may have access to their own data but not enough information to evaluate the price and quality of all physicians, hospitals, and providers.
- Providers. Hospitals, nursing homes, physicians, and other providers would benefit from transparent price and quality information.

Whatever the many merits of transparency, it is a broad-scale initiative that leads to change.

CREATING A CULTURE OF QUALITY AND SAFETY

Many healthcare institutions have invested heavily to improve quality and patient safety, and yet many fail to reach an environment that is truly safe and also fail to sustain their intermittent success in quality improvement. Many factors may be involved in this failure to achieve and sustain goals; however, the most common is that the culture has not changed sufficiently to nourish sustainability. Although it may be hard to develop such a culture, it is relatively easy to recognize when it has been attained. The steps in developing a quality and safety culture have been well described, but it has also been accepted that each institution has to find its own path. More than likely, this occurs because the system barriers to improvement are different at each institution.

A few of these barriers are:

- Culture of blame. It is not uncommon for institutions to use errors to take punitive action rather than take the more difficult route of looking for systemic improvements that may be needed.
- Lack of teamwork. Healthcare is complex and interdisciplinary, and teamwork and communication are essential in building a culture of quality and safety. Teamwork training is often necessary to achieve the goal.
- Human nature. It is perhaps human nature to want to hide mistakes, and it certainly was part of the culture especially with physicians for many years.
- Incident reports. It is often time-consuming and difficult to report errors, and in the name of efficiency it is often left undone.
- Excessive regulations. Old rules and policies are often not updated, and the complex layering of the old with the new makes it difficult to comply with the latest policies.
- Physician buy-in. Often listed as the main barrier, buy-in can be difficult to achieve without a clear explanation of the strategy and goals.
- Inadequate leadership. In many institutions, the board's involvement is not aligned with that of senior leadership, which itself may not be aligned with the clinical staff.
- Quality strategy. If it even exists, the strategy may not be aligned throughout the organization and may not be communicated well to all levels.
- Accountability. There may be a lack of personal accountability, and there may be lack of a "just culture."
- Trust. Trust or intimidating behavior may not be assessed or addressed.

Given the complexity of the barriers, how then does an organization move toward the desired culture of safety and quality? An implied question is: why must such a culture be developed in every institution?

Most experts agree that establishing a culture of safety and quality is the right thing to do. Such a sentiment has been around for decades and yet, little has been accomplished before the last decade. Spurred by the IOM's *Crossing the Quality Chasm*, organizations, governmental agencies and many individuals felt compelled to act. The ACA set in motion many forces that will create and sustain change, including more robust public reporting and linking payment with quality. Through a mixture of bonuses and penalties as well as strong support for innovation, healthcare reform is supporting the change in culture that has been proven to be essential.

The following are best practices for achieving the desired culture of safety and quality.

- Board. The full board is totally committed to achieving the culture desired. During board meetings, the time spent on quality matters is equal to that spent on financial matters. The board is involved beyond the board room and in setting goals and strategy.
- CEO/leadership. The CEO and senior leadership leads in the development and implementation of the quality strategy. The CEO meets with quality leadership and has a strong hand in improvement.
- Physicians. Physicians are deeply involved in improvement projects and participate directly in achieving the objectives.
- Goals. Goals are clear and aligned at all levels. Front-line staff participates in any reward program.
- Strategy. Quality is near the top of strategic priorities and preferably is first.
- Transparency. The organization is transparent internally and externally and incident reporting is expected and is the norm. A "just culture" is observed.
- IT. The IT department supports the quality efforts and optimizes the electronic medical record (EMR) for all quality needs.
- Accountability. A clear accountability mechanism is in place at all levels, including physicians, front-line staff, and ancillary staff.
- Mission. Quality and safety is incorporated into the teaching and research missions of the institution.
- Regular assessment. Measures of safety cultures are used routinely.
- Improvement methodology. An improvement methodology is taught and used.

Achieving a true culture of quality and safety will require hospitals to make major changes that cannot take place overnight. It will require a committed leadership, a willing staff, involved physicians, and much more. It will also require resources that must be used wisely. It will require a strong vision and a willingness to see things seem to get worse before they get better. But in the end, a culture of safety and quality will take healthcare providers to where their patients have a right to expect them to be.

CONCLUSION

Quality has now entered into the mainstream, and all healthcare providers and leaders will need to have a degree of expertise in the discipline. For years, if one asked how to best define quality, there would have been a wide range of answers. The first section details the continuing heterogeneity of responses, and the government as a payer and third-party payers has in part defined quality. It is clear that there will continue to be an evolution in this dialogue, but quality as a way to judge clinical performance is here to stay.

The publishing of IOM's *To Err is Human* started a conversation, but it is each physician's responsibility to continue the dialogue and to train the next generation of care providers who will embrace the concepts of continuous quality improvement as an integral part of a lifelong journey of attaining excellence in patient care. Providers are in a time where metrics will continue to be refined as they move from surrogate clinical endpoints to actual outcomes. The conversation will hopefully be iterative as evidence-based medical science catches up to their desire to pick the correct metrics and clinical end points. In the end, they each have to embrace the transparent dialogue among themselves and our patients and continue to drive to a culture that expects and reward transparency.

CASE STUDY

You are the administrative leader for quality in a medium-sized acute care hospital. You have been made aware of a recent case where a patient on a medical-surgical unit received the wrong dose of a medication. The error was recognized several minutes after the nurse administered the medication. The patient had to be moved to the intensive care unit for observation but ultimately did well. Now nursing is upset and is blaming the pharmacy for the error. Pharmacy states that because of recent staff reductions and volume increases, they are overwhelmed. The ordering physician is upset and is blaming hospital administration, and your colleagues in leadership are wondering why a $30 million investment in an EMR system has not corrected these type of problems. You are left to sort out the issues and suggest a plan of action.

Questions

- Define what a root cause analysis (RCA) is and why it might be useful in this case.
- How would you manage nursing, pharmacy, physicians, and staff through this process?
- If the goal is to have all errors reported, how would you recommend beginning a blame-free culture?
- Would you involve risk management as part of the process? Why?
- How would you monitor for success of interventions put in place? Whose responsibility is it?
- What thoughts do you have on posting metrics in your hospital units or even online?
- How would you use electronic infrastructure to aid these processes?
- Who would you put on interdisciplinary teams to evaluate potential opportunities?
- How as a leader would you support process redesign and innovation by your staff?

SUGGESTED READING

Institute of Medicine. *Crossing the Quality Chasm: A New Health System for the 21st Century.* Committee on Quality of Health Care in America. Washington, DC: National Academies Press; 2001.

Institute of Medicine. *To Err is Human: Building a Safer Health System.* Committee on Quality of Health Care in America. Washington, DC: National Academies Press; 1999.

Joynt KE, Jha AK. The relationship between cost and quality. *JAMA.* 2012;307:1082–1083.

McKinsey and Co. Healthcare Systems and Services Practice. The post-reform health system: Meeting the challenges ahead. http://www.mckinsey.com/client_service/ healthcare_systems_and_services/latest_thinking/the_post-reform_health_ system. May 2013. Accessed August 4, 2014.

Roland M, Campbell S. Successes and failures of pay for performance in the United Kingdom. *N Engl J Med.* 2014;370:1944–1949.

Schoen C, Guterman S, Shih A, et al. Bending the curve: options for achieving savings and improving value for US health spending. The Commonwealth Fund. http://www.commonwealthfund.org/publications/fund-reports/2007/dec/ bending-the-curve–options-for-achieving-savings-and-improving-value-in-u-s– health-spending. December 2007. Accessed August 4, 2014.

Stukel TA, Fisher ES, Alter DA, Guttmann A, et al. Association of hospital spending intensity with mortality and readmission rates in Ontario hospitals. *JAMA.* 2012;307:1037–1045.

8

Strategic Planning: Creating a Culture of Quality and Safety

ERIC J. BIEBER AND JENNIFER RADIN

KEY POINTS

- Business models based only on fee for service may become antiquated as the transition from volume to value picks up pace.
- The keys to future success include collaboration, coordination, productivity, integration, alignment, innovation, and enhanced revenue generation.
- Population health is becoming increasingly important as a key horizontal integration strategy.
- Continuum of care will be optimized by integrating services across geography and product line.
- The current fragmentation of care by physicians and hospitals will be replaced by coordination and integration across the care continuum.
- Organizations will need to choose what they own versus what they outsource or collaborate on.
- New leadership structures, roles, and matrices will need to be created to facilitate sustainable success.
- Healthcare organizations will be adopting a lifetime value approach to patient engagement and connectivity.
- In the future, market share may be based more on responsibility for lives or populations.

- Successful organizations will continuously innovate through making small but sustainable changes to their models of care delivery.
- Given the significant changes occurring, organizations should build short-term strategic plans that are frequently refreshed and adapt to the changing healthcare landscape.

For hospitals, clinics, and physician practices and the people who run them, it has never been more important to develop and execute a strategy that is well planned. Strategies that effectively served the industry for so long are no longer predictors of success; operational and marketplace demands continue to shift, and new industry partnerships align.

With increasing frequency, health system leaders are coming to believe that business models based on fees for service may become antiquated. Many of these leaders are beginning to reassess their operational and organizational direction, investing in changes they hope will build an operating engine powered by collaboration, coordination, productivity, and integration—and lead to more efficient alignment, innovative growth, and increased revenue generation.

Our own prescription for strategic planning and development is based not only on what is cost-effective and predicts better patient care but on what creates organizational and operational structures that allow us to deliver effectively on an entirely new vision. Systems are moving from the old modes of institutional healthcare delivery, concentrated in siloed facilities and functions, to an emphasis on population health. Healthcare planning, development, and personnel deployment decisions will be made in the advancement of a continuum of care across the lifetimes of patients.

There are a full range of benefits in transitioning to population health as the strategic foundation for healthcare systems. Administrators can minimize duplication of services and redundancy of effort across local institutions, raise operational standards, and clarify decision-making. Operating margins may improve. New, increasingly efficient and more representative leadership models will emerge.

What are the key lessons that can help build out organizational models? First, there is no "one size fits all" solution. It will vary according to vision, depending on unique services, geographies, patient demographics and need, and access to the most appropriate data. System leaders and administrators should identify resources available in the system to provide insight and feedback; gather information from adjudicated claims, laboratory results, and electronic medical records; and clarify the role these data will play—immediately and on an ongoing basis—in creating new structures.

Second, the broad transformative changes facing the healthcare industry cannot be adequately assessed without understanding the dramatic implications for corporate culture. It is impossible to understate the cultural ramifications of what amounts to a fundamental shift in healthcare system strategy and operation. Rethinking the value proposition and its impact on the marketplace, how new systems of care are structured and supported, and developing a new generation and type of leadership expertise will require a new mindset and acceptance of innovation and new ideas on the part of all system stakeholders.

The process is highly complex and will no doubt be complicated. Strategic planning for hospital leaders has rarely been as challenging. Options for hospital and healthcare leaders are complex and diverse. In the continuum of care, no one owns all the pieces. We need to be increasingly introspective. What do we as system administrators and advisors own? What do we buy, and what do we spend? How do we link services together, and with whom should we partner? How do we reach a level of integration that ensures marketplace competitiveness?

Different healthcare organizations find themselves at different points in this evolution and may be more or less adaptable. What could be possible a year from now may not be today. If there is insufficient scale to compete in the marketplace, how will changes be implemented to remain competitive and guide strategy to future effective levels? Going forward, strategic considerations will rest on a range of factors to succeed in the "new normal." Organizations that are especially nimble, adaptive, and able to factor risk-taking into their strategic vision are the ones likeliest to survive.

ASKING THE RIGHT QUESTIONS

As healthcare leaders transition to healthcare models driven increasingly by population health and the wiser use of resources, these are some of the key strategic questions these leaders should be asking of themselves and their teams.

- What patient populations and markets should we serve?
- How do we communicate most effectively with our patients and internally with ourselves?
- Where are we headed as an organization?
- What operating model works best for us from a cost and sustainability vantage point?
- How do we effectively integrate physician leadership into organizational management design?
- What is the proper balance between systemwide standards of consistency and potential conflicts of local patient preference?
- How do we develop a system of shared services and hone outsourcing to meet planning priorities?
- What does the workforce of the future look like, and how do the priorities of generation Y factor into longer-range thinking?
- What metrics and analytics are most important to ensure best outcomes?

Clearly, the weight of the current set of economic and regulatory challenges brings more intensive pressure on hospital systems to reduce costs, streamline processes, improve outcomes ,and work toward a more seamless alignment of physicians. Resetting organizational strategies and demanding more of stakeholder behaviors can help in achieving these objectives.

Most healthcare executives understand that they have already entered a brave new world of care delivery, structure, and program development. The individual hospital is not the center of our universe any more. The market is not confined to a single facility. Value, not volume, is becoming the guiding operating principle. Conventional business units are giving way to new, innovative service lines. The old ways of doing business are disappearing.

VERTICAL/HORIZONTAL DESIGN

In an effort to predict the future, it is worthwhile to review the past. Historically, the hospital was a community anchor, physically and socially, and a symbol of security. Its president or chief executive officer often was better known and more influential and respected than the mayor. These facilities were stand-alone pillars of good health and comfort, treating and healing people with nearly all the tools needed to do so at their direct disposal.

Hospital administration was fairly cut and dry. Market share was based on inpatient service, with individual hospitals providing virtually every aspect of required patient service. Today, the local hospital is more likely to exist as part of a larger health system. They are no longer stand-alone facilities but essential components in a highly collaboratively, interconnected network designed to provide multiple channels of patient care.

It is a critical time for hospital leaders and the institutions themselves.

Should these leaders continue to support the historical vertical hospital-based models, and still be reasonably independent? Or is a horizontal strategy promoting a broader continuum of care and redefining operations a better fit? A majority of health systems are beginning to choose the latter, but is it best in all cases?

For facilities operating vertically, it is still about "place." Leaders may follow a strategy of conventional management. Hospital leaders tend to organize by facility and put less credence in building a network on the basis of geography. They do not think much of accountable care organizations (ACOs). The status quo is just fine.

Horizontal strategies are underpinned by a growing involvement in population health. Continuum of care is at the strategic center of this approach, based on integrating by services, geographies, product lines, and new modes of care delivery. These systems view patient-centered medical homes and ACOs as a constructive method of care delivery, if not the most important element. Even bundled payments may be more relevant as a care model than as a payment model by emphasizing the interaction of multiple care providers over at least a portion of the continuum. Advantages to leaders of horizontal systems are many, but they too face challenges in planning and execution. Examples of both strategies are show in Figure 8.1.

Neither structural approach is absolute. There is considerable momentum in building horizontal networks. But many are reluctant to put all of their eggs in the population health or conventional management baskets. In fact, most of them probably live somewhere in the middle; They may be hybrids banking on specialties and their individual core service offerings while stretching to develop collaborative arrangements with an unfolding cast of service partners.

Adapt or die, goes the old adage. Certainly, everyone needs to adapt, but there are inherent risks in which model—vertical, horizontal or something in the middle—to implement. It is difficult to predict how quickly these models will become the standard and whether there will be continued regional variation with this adoption, as there was with managed care. Adapt too quickly, and a facility or system risks organizational disruption that alienates patients and employees. Affect change too slowly, and it might find itself left behind—or worse, out of business. The trade-offs are shown in Figure 8.2.

DEFINING THE VALUE PROPOSITION

Healthcare stakeholders still tend to think of healthcare as linear. It is not. It operates in a three-dimensional reality, with patients and other stakeholders frequently moving in and out of different areas of the system. Boundaries are more permeable, with nontraditional players seeking an expanded role and a place at the table. Wellness and chronic care are not mutually exclusive when it comes to treating patients. Strategic choices depend on measuring and managing value more appropriately in the current environment.

Volume to Value

The first step is transitioning from a volume-based operational premise to providing (and rewarding) highest value. This transforms the model, taking it from acute episodic care to a continuum of care as the organizing principle. Traditionally, quantity has paid the bills; the future financial health of healthcare systems will almost assuredly depend on how leaders create, market, and manage quality (see Chapter 7). They continue to strive for optimal patient outcomes but now are more cognizant of the need to accomplish them in a wider and more elastic patient care continuum. Institutional demands will always be important, but patient-centric choice—and a system of payments rooted in value shaping the care/quality agenda—is at the center of enhanced quality and better care (Figure 8.3).

Operating Model Components	Holding Company	Strategic Guidance	Strategic Control	Integrated Operating Company
Operating Structure	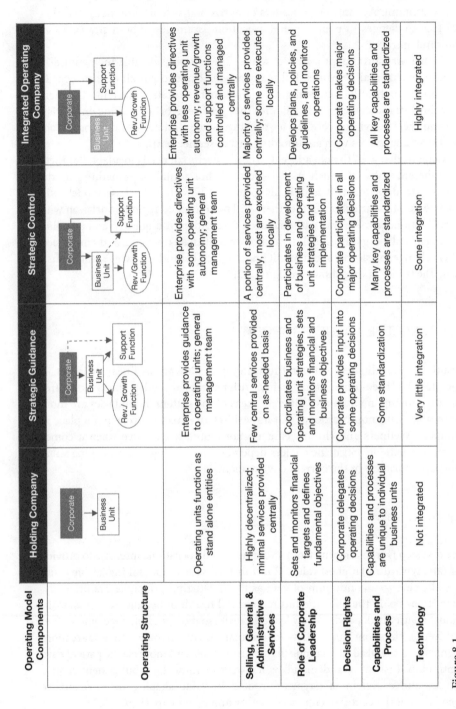 Operating units function as stand alone entities	Enterprise provides guidance to operating units; general management team	Enterprise provides directives with some operating unit autonomy; general management team	Enterprise provides directives with less operating unit autonomy; revenue/growth and support functions controlled and managed centrally
Selling, General, & Administrative Services	Highly decentralized; minimal services provided centrally	Few central services provided on as-needed basis	A portion of services provided centrally, most are executed locally	Majority of services provided centrally; some are executed locally
Role of Corporate Leadership	Sets and monitors financial targets and defines fundamental objectives	Coordinates business and operating unit strategies, sets and monitors financial and business objectives	Participates in development of business and operating unit strategies and their implementation	Develops plans, policies, and guidelines, and monitors operations
Decision Rights	Corporate delegates operating decisions	Corporate provides input into some operating decisions	Corporate participates in all major operating decisions	Corporate makes major operating decisions
Capabilities and Process	Capabilities and processes are unique to individual business units	Some standardization	Many key capabilities and processes are standardized	All key capabilities and processes are standardized
Technology	Not integrated	Very little integration	Some integration	Highly integrated

Figure 8.1

The shift from vertical to horizontal operating structures.

Legend: ● = Current State ● = Future State

Trade-Offs for Desired Future Operating Model

Consideration		Trade-Offs for Desired Future Operating Model
1	Systemness	**Local:** Retain operating unit decision authority to allow for local market responsiveness ⟷ **Central:** Shift decision-making authority towards the center to allow for strategy execution across the system
2	Value Drivers	**Differentiated:** Focus on creating and sustaining differentiated market offerings that drive high margins in each of the unique patient populations, outcomes variable ⟷ **Efficient:** Improve role clarity and reduce redundancy/duplication of efforts, and create repeatable processes and programs to reduce waste and drive consistent outcome measures
3	Shared Services (Nonclinical)	**Stand Alone:** Services and resources in each operating unit (or market) are separate, allowing for different responsibilities based on local needs and business plan ⟷ **Consolidated:** Share resources and processes to achieve economies of scale and consistent levels of service across operating units; decision authority at the system
4	Physician Integration	**Detached:** Create structure that attracts talent and allows for physicians to practice without deliberate attempts at alignment, performance metrics vary based on location, local councils and governance encouraged ⟷ **Integrated:** Create a joint decision making framework and develop incentive models to drive consistent, evidence based practices, behaviors and performance metrics, supported by a single system entity
5	Clinical Services	**Siloed Services:** Clinical services remain separate, focusing on providing their specific services/procedures to patients and are organized by competency; services are not rationalized across the system; staff and physicians identify locally/by facility ⟷ **Service Line:** Clinicians are integrated system wide to provide end to end services and consistent experience and outcomes across the patient lifecycle; services are rationalized and planned for at the system level; staff identify with system
6	Geography	**Hospital:** Operating unit focused, develops care delivery strategy and organization structure based on ministry location; staff identify locally ⟷ **Population/Market:** Focused on broad geographic footprint, develop organization structure and patient population strategy to deliver the full continuum within a market; staff identify by market or system

Figure 8.2

Design considerations as trade-offs.

Figure 8.3
New structures and new capabilities.

ORGANIZING MODELS

Organizing a health system and equipping it with tools and resources to operate efficiently can take a number of different strategic shapes. This can be done in various ways.

- Organize by facility. The individual hospital continues to stand as the center of the patient care universe for health systems.
- Organize beyond hospitals, clustering into geographies, an approach that could be dictated by populations. Geographies determine the operating model with regional or system leaders matrixing with individual hospital leaders.
- Adopt a third, more forward-thinking model that transcends facility and geography—organized around services. Location/region and individual facilities are still critical but become support mechanisms in the development of healthcare structure built upon the care continuum and the range of services provided.

Institutional Organization

Facility-based care—the conventional bricks-and-mortar centrality—can supply sufficient rationalization for maintaining the status quo. Cost and breadth of service, however, can vary from one location to another, from inner city and high-acuity hospitals to suburban and rural hospitals, from ambulatory centers to medical offices.

But the system is not just about bricks and mortar any more. Increasingly, the model does not revolve around the individual hospital or clinic. It is about geographies and developing service lines that not only feed business units but *are* the business units. All large, complex organizations that span wide geographies depend more and more on digital and virtual operating practices. The evolving healthcare system is no different.

The disadvantage, in the movement from structural anchors for care delivery to service models, is that systems today can rarely be built from scratch. One cannot plan a healthcare system, for example, the way designers and planners carried out their vision for Washington, DC, when the nation was new—the Capitol here, other monuments there, and parks located in central areas. Leaders have to create a new care delivery and management paradigm based on existing facilities—and by dramatically altering the way patients and healthcare professionals think about medical treatment.

Geographic Foundations

Strategic growth across geographies depends on reverse engineering the system, and reverse engineering requires a certain amount of retrofitting. The geography of access demands it. The challenge is how to enable a better, more coordinated system. Some of the questions are nuts and bolts: where, physically, should the cardiologist be located? But healthcare leaders do not get to plan and build a brand new physical plant. They are more or less stuck with facility design. And even if they could rebuild from the ground floor up, economic realities might constrain construction of new facilities.

The Service Line Model

Take a typical small health system operating in the United States. It has a number of community-based hospitals and ambulatory centers or clinics, several of them affiliated with a college, university, or other academic center. These are the places where physicians, nurses, administrators, and support staff come together to serve patients. Historically, they have been the cost centers and discrete business units. An example of a service line model is shown in Figure 8.4.

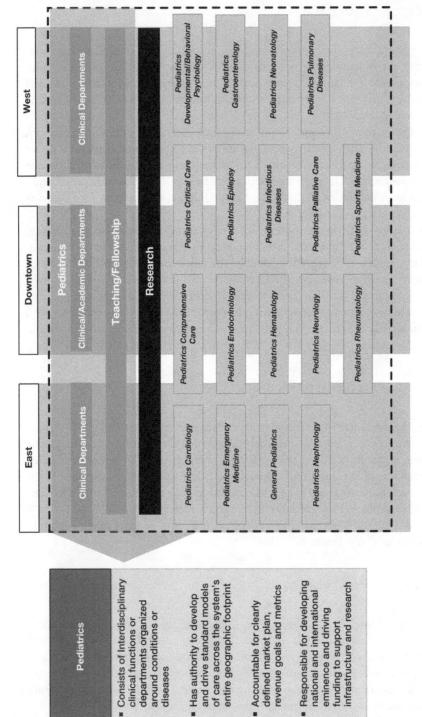

Figure 8.4
Service line institute case example.

Now think of providing care and developing payment networks based not on buildings or geographic connections but on services. That means looking at profit and loss in the context of a specific healthcare service line. This is the most promising strategy of all and one that may steer healthcare in an exciting new direction. For example, cardiovascular treatments—everything from radiology through high-end cardiac and vascular surgery—become a coordinated service, a type of cost center, regardless of the facility where the procedures are performed. That requires a network of physicians aligned across multiple disciplines and, possibly, geographies. It also requires a payment system that is not based on episodic care but instead rewards an entire collection of appropriate care.

These units could be responsible for patient acquisition and retention using the following principles: develop "sticky" strategies; determine the best way to treat patients within the service line; and think broadly about care that goes beyond cardiovascular considerations, tapping into other services within the healthcare system.

All successful systems must be both proactive and responsive. But it requires a nimbleness to harness the ability to react quickly to changing patient, regulatory, and market demands. And that is something the healthcare system largely lacks. Life sciences companies are adept at reacting quickly to these demands. Not only because of the way they are structured but because it is in the DNA of these organizations, because they are driven by a model of maximizing profit. To remain competitive, these enterprises cannot take their foot off the pedal.

OPTIMIZING INTEGRATED SYSTEM PERFORMANCE

Managing populations is an excellent foundation on which to establish a new health system paradigm. One may start by defining health systems as single, integrated organizations, not a loose collection of independent facilities operating under the mantle of a somewhat distant and disconnected health system. These integrated organizations will be endowed with clear decision rights and accountabilities. This strategy fosters sustainability and steadier long-term growth, and it may well show significant cost savings in the short term by aligning physicians, administrators, and staff through enhanced and more profitable care delivery interactions.

As with any effort to transform an industry, it is necessary to remember that there are plenty of moving parts, many of which do not fit neatly with one another. How effectively all the disparate elements of personnel, resources, and assets are integrated will determine prospects for system viability and marketplace success. But integration is only one element of how that success is ultimately measured.

No transformation, regardless of the strategic model imposed, comes easily. No single solution responds to the breadth of conflicts and controversies that arise along each step of the transition. By its very nature, it is a difficult process that will ruffle feathers, sow confusion, and lead to the discarding of some modes of operation that have been decades in the making. It demands more than a few compromises and trade-offs.

In facilitating this large-scale transitioning, those trade-offs—their impact and their place in the operating model—must be thoroughly considered. For example: Should a system organize first by geographic locations and a dispersed network? Or should markets or specific types of patient care serve as the guiding force? Is the best future approach organizing around services delivered? What will yield optimal benefits in setting new economies of scale and providing frameworks for increased service consistency delivered across communities?

All of these considerations should be weighed in the context of organizational mission. What is the service market and what, at the end of the day, does the organization want to achieve? Depending on the foundation, whether old single clinics, smaller suburban models, or sprawling regional networks, the business model must reflect the mission. If the goals and reason for being are not clearly thought out or if service delivery is opportunistic, driven by funding and personnel availability, then how much does the selection of a defined model really matter?

There are a number of choices around integration that health leaders should consider as part of the strategic mix.

Changing the Role of the Hospital Leadership

Expanding horizons—that is the view senior hospital leaders must adopt. Shifting the leadership oversight role from individual institution to the wider system is an important change. A key component is creating an executive structure to facilitate sustainable success. The new strategic model has to assess the impact in the decision-making hierarchy as roles and accountabilities move from singular facilities to more regional or marketplace control. Beyond that, how it affects the roles of people operating within the expanded system will be an important strategic point, as well as something for a leader to recognize could be a source of staffing upset.

System transformation means that acute care hospitals will have to deal with decreased utilization and a possible spike in cost pressures. This new hospital leader may garner efficiencies through growing systemic complexity to best serve patients and the goals of the system through clinical improvements, driving innovation and revenue.

Healthcare organizations will have to adopt a lifetime value approach to patient engagement. Concepts such as "repeat business" and direct referrals, as well as offering new products and innovative services that fall outside a specific service channel to other lines of business within the system, are cornerstones of this new strategy. These might include health, wellness, and complementary and integrative medicine strategies that in prior times were mere afterthoughts. Some of the new concepts in healthcare that are appearing, and which must be part of the operational equation, are built on the idea of improving the customer experience broadly, embracing a customer-service sensibility and making it an integral part of the strategic purpose.

Developing Effective Levels of Clinical Integration

Developing clear clinical pathways, patient flow, or lines of service is strategically important. Providers can maximize clinical patient outcomes by moving away from organizational and service line silos. The application of advanced analytics can enable this level of clinical integration.

Analysts can do their best work in this emerging organization structure by being able—and encouraged—to collaborate across traditional departmental boundaries, such as operations and information technology. Outcome measurement and cost data are more effectively exploited during the full cycle of care. Creating a data-driven management capability that drives efficiency and accountability, both within the system and externally, will facilitate integration.

Aligning the Decision-Making Structure

Without adjusting management techniques to reflect these new realities, structural realignment is just something that looks interesting on paper. It is important to resolve questions of duplication of effort, internal political conflicts, and poorly executed plans. Identifying key issues and how to resolve them is a continual undertaking for system leaders; decision-making and how it is carried out is one of the essential areas of review. Decision-making should be established in a style that supports the operating model chosen. It is necessary to create a "decision framework" that clearly defines the lines of decision for all stakeholders. This is demonstrated in Figure 8.5.

Consolidating Reporting Relationships

Too often, decentralized organizational structures have become fragmented and difficult to control. For example, one institution develops a leading practice built around quality or cost containment. If that model is not shared with other facilities throughout the system, an opportunity could be lost and the consistency sought may be undermined. Health system leaders understand that centralizing some services can improve outcomes and lower costs but not if they do not close the loop with their peers and collaborating facilities.

One decision that must be made is the degree to which centralization is appropriate for each area and the associated deployment strategy, especially when the

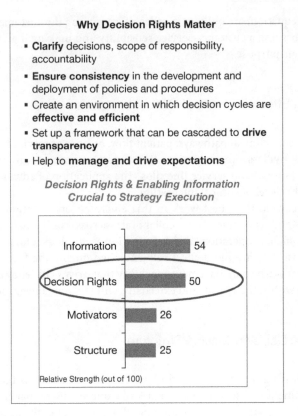

Figure 8.5
Why decision rights matter.

unique attributes of local patient populations may require customized activities. The degree of centralization can be determined through an adaptive cost management exercise, wherein cost-cutting priorities are paired with investments needed in strategic operations, such as local delivery capabilities. Each organization will have to calibrate accordingly, but there appears to be a great opportunity to challenge traditional thinking on what clinical services should be controlled at the local level and which ones may be as good or better when managed regionally or centrally.

Establishing Higher Standards of Service

Centralizing a reporting structure may sustain a more efficient level of standardization. But it is not an absolute. It is not just about structure but quality of service across the continuum. And the implementation of a higher set of standards systemwide does not work if there is not corresponding attention to its impact. This is mainly driven by evidence-based medicine, the funding imperative generated by the need to meet certain standards to earn bonuses in a pay-for-performance environment, and the desire to avoid penalties or the prospect of losing revenue by not hitting set targets. Clarity and transparency is critical when it comes to the connection between different operating units and how it affects employees, patients, and other stakeholders.

At the top of any leadership/planning "to do" list is making sure managers specify the relationships between functional units—how they interlock and how they complement one another. When hospital leadership, whether at the executive or lower management level, is making decisions irrespective of their impact on the rest of the organization, consistent delivery becomes more difficult to attain. By standardizing processes, policies, performance expectations, and demands, health systems can operate at a more integrated strategic level.

Implementing Shared Services

As the healthcare industry has expanded, as systems have evolved, shared services as a basis of operation and the outsourcing of services that were not core to the system internally have grown correspondingly. That is changing. Harmonizing and coordinating services can dramatically reduce expenses and should be a part of any system's organizing strategy.

Service Line Implementation

The community hospital used to be organized around acute care, acute care locations, and specific functional departments. As the industry becomes increasingly focused on outcomes as the measure of quality and success, an innovative way of organizing as a superior vehicle to achieve our objectives becomes apparent. Emerging service lines have their own plan, business model, and strategy. They have distinctive marketing campaigns and tactics, even as they fit into the larger organizational whole. They can manipulate the latest in technological advances to drive predictive analysis and segmentation as it pertains specifically to their service line. This is an exciting development but still in its formative stages.

MARKETPLACE CHANGES

The definition of market share is changing, as healthcare moves toward collaborative care expressed through the growth and maturation of ACOs and other vehicles to promote a care continuum over volume. In the healthcare space, volume has always been the driving force. The acute episodic care environment mandated that more would always be better. The conventional payment approach influenced this practice, as did the growth of ultraspecialization and growing technologies that delivered ever more sophisticated treatment. Unfortunately, in some cases the treatments were overly complicated, expensive, and fragmented, occasionally with little tangible evidence to support cost efficacy.

In the value-based world, more is not necessarily better, and more volume is not necessarily good volume. How does one measure performance in the marketplace? Value-based markets reflect different results and demands, and future market share could revolve around the numbers of lives being managed across the continuum instead of procedural volume.

Imagine market share as a healthcare environment based on populations, on lives, and how and where patients access key decision-makers. With that in mind, consider some of the key questions that should be explored:

- How does one adapt to a marketplace where everything is shifting so rapidly?
- What does one mean by market share and, given all of the changes altering healthcare, what does one mean by market?
- How does one form partnerships—and with whom?
- Working increasingly in a value-driven marketplace, how does this shape movements toward capturing bigger market share?
- How does one measure how people are doing in the marketplace? In a value-based market, there are not only different results and demands, but the level of market share and extent of service delivery may be well rooted in the continuum of care and around the numbers of lives benefited.

In the evolving valued-based world, more is not necessarily the best option. This is a fundamental shift in thinking. Less, in a manner of consideration, becomes more. It is a question of how to manage it, carrying interesting implications about patient acquisition and investment in the context of a lifetime of service. Few hospital systems, however, give this enough thought. Chief marketing officers might preferentially focus on "how do I acquire and retain patients?" If they are headed back to global capitation environments, understanding and placing stock in value as business drivers is imperative.

To facilitate the capture of market share, healthcare leaders should examine their own core competencies, determine what they can do best, how it should be developed and applied across the system, and what areas are better served through external partnerships. For example, an independent company that provides nursing or rehabilitation services affiliating with specific hospital systems makes good fiscal and operational sense.

That said, there are other potential factors that need to be reviewed to balance quality of service and cost-effectiveness. For example, if the fit turns out to be less than ideal, the amount of time and energy spent on managing the relationship could become prohibitive. It is also necessary to consider other issues and challenges: interoperability of devices, transfer of information and data, privacy and security, and hospital requirements to monitor business associates under the Health Insurance Portability and Accountability Act (HIPAA) Omnibus rule.

Moving from the fragmentation of all providers (physicians, hospitals, clinics) to a system of coordination and integration necessarily requires a fundamental change in how the healthcare market functions. Markets, reacting to changing business or geographical drivers, can serve as the organizing principle moving forward. It is fair to say that most health systems are just starting out on this journey to population health and still sorting through how it will affect the marketplace and their own organizations. The critical issues are how to strategize around that thinking and how best to apply those strategic choices so that they have the greatest and most productive impact on healthcare operating models of the future.

This paradigm shift will likely continue to shape the way mergers and acquisitions are weighed and completed. Strategically, as systems continue to engage in merger and acquisition activity—always looking to fit and fine-tune facilities, services, and offerings—hospital leaders should be cognizant of market factors important to development.

CULTURAL CHANGE TO MAXIMIZE PERFORMANCE

None of the sweeping transformative changes facing the healthcare industry can succeed without a corresponding change in corporate culture. Culturally, all of these factors—redefining the value proposition, assessing new marketplace demands, structures and opportunities, developing an organizational framework based on distribution of services—require a new mindset on the part of all of the system's stakeholders.

Today, there continue to be people who work within healthcare systems that are still focused on traditional views. They see the hospital as their corporate and community anchor. In the new paradigm, culture becomes the sum of collaboration with accountability across all departments. Hospital leaders need to align their incentives to affect change and develop their customer service strategies.

Those who are the most forward-looking understand that they are creating new and very interesting cultural anchors. Patient wellness over a lifetime becomes as much a pillar of cultural change as a medical center. Moving inexorably toward a continuum of care model that includes virtual medicine, vertical care, and the medical home, the patient's thinking is not necessarily, "I go to this place to get better," but "I have an overall responsibility to be well." It is a seismic shift in patient attitude.

The path is not easy. How does pediatric care interact with endocrinology? How should mental health services, psychology, and other behavioral treatments be integrated into this new structure of comprehensive healthcare? For patients, how do healthcare leaders drive shared accountability for wellness? How should patients be incentivized or disincentivized to drive these behaviors? Just as important, these leaders need to value their work differently and acclimate to new ways of doing it. They have not created a reward system that acknowledges superior work in making those points of connection. The leaders that achieve success on this new level are not necessarily rewarded for it.

In an acute episodic payment environment, all people are paid for their part of the process. There is often little accountability or incentive available to persuade leadership to apply their expertise outside of their own silo. As incentives grow, what is the impact on staff? Are people more willing to work in this new environment? Healthcare professionals who have been in the same institution—even the same position—for 35 years are much more likely to express resistance to these dynamic systemic changes. The newer generations of physicians and other medical personnel, however, will view it differently. Studies have shown that young people, the cohort known as generation Y, bring a far different sensibility to long-accepted ideas of work, pay and career path than those who have gone before them.

These young people have grown up in a world more dependent on teamwork and less on individualistic concerns and self-interest. They are not keen on sacrificing everything for the job and are seeking a more satisfying work/life balance. They are more content to grow in teams, so the concept of broader collaboration and being open to innovate new ideas within their profession is already more comfortable to them than it has been to previous generations of healthcare employees. Collaboration is an intrinsic part of their work culture. They realize that incentives and care models need to change and that this will improve the system and their place in it.

This is where interdisciplinary teams can thrive. They offer a combination and coordination of different (and, ideally, fully compatible) approaches to managing the "whole person," or the entire episode of care. Healthcare leaders need to determine how best to ensure that their employees are synergistic. The leaders want to create an incentive program that rewards new behaviors. It will always be a work in progress. And they want to train people in an environment intertwined with other disciplinary teams, where people are thinking about this from the beginning. There has been some progress, but if the reward system does not change, if the pay scale does not change, will it succeed?

CASE STUDY

Your organization has decided to create a new service line, and you have been named the administrative leader. The organization considers itself an integrated delivery system, but to date no other service lines have been created and the thinking has been quite traditional regarding span of control. Your particular department has 10 different offices spread over 6 counties, which span 50 miles east-west and 30 miles north-south. There are single specialty practices at each of these sites, and most were acquired over the past decade as independent physicians were bought by the hospital system. There are three different hospitals that the providers work from, including a large hospital at the urban site where the "chair" of the department is employed. To date, her attention has been focused on the providers at that facility, and little attention has been focused on connecting the other providers. Over the past 3 years, market share has been declining and going to your main competitor. In addition, new patient volume is down—as is individual physician productivity (now below the 50th percentile) and surgery. Your organization has recently announced a large ACO agreement that will be covering 30,000 lives over the six-county region.

Questions

- How will you partner with the chair to develop a service line?
- How do you define a service line?
- What data will be most helpful as you build the mission/vision/strategy for the service line?
- How will you integrate the physicians that are currently part of the system but disengaged from the department?
- What type of incentives would you recommend for the physicians and employees of the service to create the correct alignment around quality and productivity?
- What will be your key performance indicators and metrics of success?
- What is the relevance of the coming ACO to your service line and providers?

SUGGESTED READING

Combes J. Physician leadership: the implications for a transformed delivery system. *Hosp Health Netw.* 2014 (Feb);88(2):12.

Kahn LH. A prescription for change: the need for qualified physician leadership in public health. *Health Aff.* 2003;22(4):241-248.

McAlearney AS, Fisher D, Heiser K, Robbins D, Kelleher K. Developing effective physician leaders: changing cultures and transforming organizations. *Hosp Top.* 2005;83(2):11-18.

McDowell T, Radin J. It's your decision. http://www.deloitte.com/assets/Dcom-UnitedStates/Local%20Assets/Documents/us_consulting_Organization DecisionMaking_051111.pdf.

Mostashari F, Sanghavi D, McClellan M. Health reform and physician-led accountable care: the paradox of primary care physician leadership. *JAMA*. 2013;311:1855–1856.

Porter ME, Teisberg EO. How physicians can change the future of health care. *JAMA*. 2007 (Mar 14);297(10):1103–1111.

Wiesenthal AM, Kaplan J, McDowell T, Radin J. The new physician leaders: leadership for a dynamic health care industry. *N Engl J Med*. November 21 2013.

9

Organizational Development

DAVID JAVITCH

KEY POINTS

- Definitions of organizational development (OD) and organizational behavior (OB)
- Reasons why OD and OB are gaining in importance worldwide
- Seven objectives of OD
- Derivations and values of OD
- Eight challenges and opportunities of OD
- Five factors that make it possible to understand people from different cultures through OD
- Role of perception in forming opinions in the workplace
- Four theories to help understand organizations: leadership, motivation, change, and team building

---

OD is a collection of planned changes and interventions that seek to improve organizational effectiveness and employee well-being. The discipline is based on humanistic-democratic values and encompasses an interdisciplinary field of studies, which investigates the individual, the group, and the organization in its interplay with each other.

OD and its related cousin, OB, are currently taught in many business schools and departments of psychology across the world. OB looks at how the organization and its people, policies, resources, and structures behave to affect each other. Most people use the two terms OD and OB interchangeably due to their overlapping similarities and purposes.

OBJECTIVES OF ORGANIZATIONAL DEVELOPMENT

The objectives of OD are:

- To increase the level of interpersonal trust among employees
- To increase the level of satisfaction and commitment from employees
- To confront problems instead of neglecting them
- To manage conflict effectively
- To increase cooperation and collaboration among the employees
- To increase problem solving abilities in organizations
- To put in place processes that will help improve the ongoing operation of the organization on a continuous basis

Because the objectives of OD are based on specific situations, they vary from one organization to another, and programs need to be tailored to meet the requirements of a particular environment. According to OD thinking, OD provides managers with a vehicle for introducing change systematically with the application of a broad selection of management techniques. This in turn leads to greater personal, group, and organizational effectiveness. Broadly speaking, the objectives for all OD programs include:

- Developing awareness of the vision of the organization and in helping employees align with that vision
- Encouraging employees to confront and solve problems instead of avoiding them
- Strengthening interpersonal trust, cooperation, and communication for the successful achievement of organizational goals
- Encouraging employee participation in the planning process to promote "buy-in" and the greater feeling of responsibility for the implementation of the project
- Creating an atmosphere in which employees are encouraged to work and participate enthusiastically
- Replacing *formal lines of hierarchical authority* with personal knowledge and skill
- Creating an environment or trust that makes change more easily acceptable

The objective of OD, then, is to improve the organization's capacity to handle its internal and external functions and relationships. This would include such things as improved interpersonal and group interactions, better communication, enhanced ability to cope with simple and multifaceted organizational problems, more effective decision-making processes, more appropriate leadership styles, improved skill in dealing with destructive conflict, and higher levels of trust and cooperation among organizational members. These objectives stem from a value system based on humanistic values and an optimistic view of the nature of man—that (people) in a supportive environment (are) capable of achieving higher levels of development and accomplishment. Essential to organization development and effectiveness is the scientific method of inquiry, a rigorous search for causes, experimental testing of hypotheses, and review of results.

In 1972, Margulies and Raia (see References) articulated the humanistic values underlying OD as follows:

- Providing opportunities for people to function as human beings rather than as resources in the production process
- Providing opportunities for each organization member, as well as for the organization itself, to develop to his or her full potential
- Seeking to increase the effectiveness of the organization in terms of all of its goals
- Attempting to create an environment in which it is possible to find exciting and challenging work
- Providing opportunities for people in organizations to influence the way in which they relate to work, the organization, and the environment
- Treating each human being as a person with a complex set of needs, all of which are important in work and in life

OB continues to gain in importance and practice as the globe continues to shrink. Organizations with employees from different races, cultures, ethnic backgrounds, religions, values, and other orientations must work together to succeed. This is especially true in the healthcare industry for a great number of reasons, among them medical tourism and the influx of patients emigrating from one country to another. In North America, in particular, where administrators, practitioners, technicians, and patients come together from across the planet to gain access to high quality medical care, healthcare workers must deal with people with multifaceted backgrounds and beliefs. Therefore, employees up and down the hierarchy must respond effectively to these changes.

OB differs somewhat from OD. OB is founded on principles derived from the fields of anthropology, psychology, sociology, and political science. The basic model involves independent and dependent variables. The former are the individual, the group, and the organization. Working with these three entities, every intervention the OB practitioner implements seeks to affect these important dependent variables, resulting in increases in productivity and employee satisfaction and decreases in absenteeism and turnover.

With those in mind, one can see that organizational life offers many challenges and opportunities for OB. Some of them are as follows:

- To improve quality and productivity
- To improve people skills

- To manage workforce diversity
- To respond to globalization
- To empower people
- To stimulate change and innovation
- To cope with temporariness
- To address declining employee loyalty and to improve ethical behavior

"Self-managing work groups" allow the members of a work team to manage, control, and monitor all facets of their work, from recruiting to hiring and from training new employees to deciding when to give them rest breaks. An early analysis of the first self-managing work groups found that employees would:

- Assume personal responsibility and accountability for their work outcomes
- Monitor their own performance and seek feedback on how well they are accomplishing their goals
- Manage their performance and take corrective action when necessary to improve their output and that the of other group members
- Seek guidance, assistance, and resources from the organization when the team does not have what they need to do the job
- Help members of their work group and employees in other groups to improve job performance and raise productivity for the organization as a whole

HOW TO UNDERSTAND DIFFERENT CULTURES IN THE WORKING ENVIRONMENT

Geert Hofstede, a well-known international researcher in the field of cultural differences, proposes six dimensions or lenses from which to observe, understand, assess, and interact with individuals from across the world and even within one's own organization.

- Power distance: the degree to which people in a culture accept that power in institutions and organizations is distributed unequally. This has an impact on and defines the figurative distance individuals keep between themselves and their leaders, their caregivers, and their patients. For example, in a high-power distance healthcare setting, a patient would only reluctantly, if at all, question a caregiver.
- Individualism versus collectivism: the degree to which people act as individuals rather than as members of a group and how much people expect others in the group to take care of them. Caregivers who understand this would be aware of when to provide information to and

ask for decisions about care directly from the patient as opposed to the patient's family.

- Masculinity versus femininity: the degree to which the culture favors traditional masculine roles (achievement, power, and control) versus high feminine cultures where men and women are equal. In high feminine cultures, people see little differentiation between male and female roles. Here, males and females can equally aspire to high status medical positions; also, both males and females can equally share in the decision-making about a patient's selection of procedures and outcomes.
- Uncertainty avoidance: the degree to which people prefer structured to unstructured situations and their ability to deal with uncertainty and ambiguity. Some patients and their families are better able than others to cope with the unknowns of medical treatment.
- Long-term versus short-term orientation: the degree to which people looked forward to the future in making decisions and also valued tradition and persistence versus the latter, people value the present and more readily accept change as commonplace. Caregivers working with people with a short-term orientation can feel comfortable trying a variety of tests and procedures, for example, and adapting decisions and further treatment as a result.

UNDERSTANDING ORGANIZATIONS

Armed with this information about OD, OB, and cultures, Marvin Weisbord presents a six-box model for further understanding organizations and knowing how individuals (especially leaders) and groups can interact in their organizational setting to improve process and outcome.

- Purposes. The organization members are clear about the organization's mission, purpose, and goals. They also support the organization's purpose.
- Structure. How is the organization's work divided? Is there an adequate fit between the purpose and the internal structure?
- Relationships. These exist between individuals, between units or departments that perform different tasks, and between the people and their job requirements.
- Rewards. Individuals should determine for what the organization formally rewards and punishes members.
- Leadership. Who is it and who is watching for blips among the other boxes to maintain balance among them? (See Chapter 4.)

- Helpful mechanisms. Are there adequate coordinating technologies that align people, mission, vision, and goals? How are these discussed and remedied if problematic?

THE ROLE OF PERCEPTION

Perception is generally seen as a process of using one's senses to take in information to gain perspective, appreciation, and understanding of the differing elements in the environment.

Perception plays an important role in everyday organizational life. Caregivers, often in a hurry to see the next patient, make quick judgments about their patient's maladies, sometimes in the first 15 seconds of an encounter. In all situations where perceptions come into play, the perceiver tends to believe that his or her perceptions are reality; however, an enlightened person must decide to what degree that their impression is substantiated with hard facts. Here are some specific situations where the effects of perception can be seen.

- Employment interviews. Interviewers often form some opinion, positive or negative, but hopefully neutral, about the interviewee within the first minute of the beginning of the meeting. Based on what the interviewer perceives and then interprets from the interviewee's responses, the outcome of the meeting can go in many different directions.
- Self-fulfilling prophecies of performance. Both the leader and the employee have views and opinions as well as wishes and aspirations about performance. A job applicant, heading into an interview, might begin thinking, "I am so nervous that I am going to make a mistake and I will not get this job!" As the applicant focuses on his nervousness and the fear that the job opportunity will be lost, he will become even more anxious and end up fulfilling the "prophecy," and he will not get the job!
- Performance evaluations. These semiannual or annual work events unfortunately tend to be wrought with often-unsubstantiated perceptions. Many people have experienced being inaccurately evaluated because of a misunderstanding or miscommunication. Similarly, some fortunate individuals have been positively evaluated and even promoted based upon a positive, yet also inaccurate interpretation of an event.
- Employee effort and employee loyalty. "Beauty is in the eye of the beholder." Without specific and measurable criteria, some leaders in their evaluations overestimate or underestimate the amount of effort and loyalty an employee demonstrates. Conclusions are based on the employee performance the leader believes or perceives he or she is seeing, with an often-incomplete amount of information.

*Mis*perceptions also provide unfortunate shortcuts when evaluating and judging others. Leaders, especially caregivers, might want to ask themselves if they used these shortcuts during the evaluation process:

- Selective perception. Here, the perceiver only recognizes and deals with a portion of the total situation, either because of desire or lack of knowledge.
- Halo effect. The perceiver places a virtual halo over the head of another individual, seeing only the positive and believing that the other party is capable of far more than he or she actually is. Sometimes this is the result of an individual being effective in one situation and therefore the perceiver automatically believes that person to be effective in another situation—whether true or not. At other times, the halo is placed on an individual because the perceiver likes that person and wants to believe that party performs better than she actually does. In healthcare, if a caregiver has a patient who has done well on a certain regimen such as exercising or taking medications, that caregiver can inappropriately assume the same result on another regimen, such as diet.
- Contrast effects. This occurs when the perceiver compares an individual to another individual who ranks higher or lower on similar characteristics.
- Stereotyping. This occurs when the perceiver judges another person solely based on the racial, ethnic, or religious background; work team; or group to which the person belongs.

IMPORTANT THEORIES TO CONSIDER WHEN WORKING WITH ORGANIZATIONS

In addition to the concepts already mentioned in this chapter, the following theories are significant when understanding organizational life: leadership, motivation, change, and team building. The first two have been described in other chapters.

Organizational Change

John Kotter of the Harvard Business School is perhaps the best-known researcher in the area of organizational change. He cautions change agents to realize that change takes a very long time and must be accomplished one step at a time. He states that, "Making critical mistakes in any (of the following) phases can have a devastating impact, slowing momentum and negating hard-won wins." Nonetheless, Kotter sees change taking place in eight phases when leaders:

- Establish a sense of urgency. To achieve change, at least 75% of the leadership team needs to be convinced that the status quo is no longer acceptable. Unless a high percentage of the leaders concur, the team will not be strongly enough committed to carrying the message throughout the organization. People must believe that something is wrong or missing in the current state to be motivated enough to participate willingly in a change process. Because human beings are creatures of habit, they resist efforts that encourage them to do something differently. The key to bringing about a change involves perceiving some level of "threat" to everyday behavior, thus requiring a change. In healthcare, financial concerns (e.g., need for increased reimbursements), better payer mix, facility fears (e.g., lack of availability of beds or operating suites), or medical scares (e.g., outbreak of a nosocomial or drug-resistant infection) can stir the staff to implement changes.
- Form a powerful guiding coalition. Three to five "true believers" need to be organized to begin the effort of spreading the word throughout the organization. The members of this group need to be seen as powerful and credible, so that others will look up to them, listen to them, and be willing to move forward with them.
- Create a vision. This is a future view of the outcome the organization wants to achieve. The vision, however, must be concrete enough for people to understand it and motivating enough so that they will be willing to "get on the bandwagon" and put the plan into action; the ups and downs of the implementation process may interfere.
- Communicate the vision. Do this by using every possible means of communication, such as voice mail, e-mail, social media, posters, newsletters, meetings, and "by walking around," so that all employees repeatedly hear, clearly understand, and greatly appreciate the new direction the organization is taking during this time of change.
- Empower others to act on the vision. Management and nonmanagement employees should be allowed opportunities to offer suggestions, to modify proposals, and to adjust the vision, as long as the overall message is not adversely affected. Assign and reassign key people to affirm and reaffirm the vision continuously. Allocate resources (time, people, money, and materials) to this effort. The goal is to reduce or remove obstacles to the change process.
- Plan and create short-term wins. Recall that an effective change process and implementation take a long time. During that period, employees can lose sight of the many steps necessary to achieve the overall goal and thus can become "demotivated" during the change process. This is why they need to see continual examples of progress along the way.
- Consolidate improvements and sustain the momentum for change. It is certainly very tempting after one or more gains have occurred to

state that the change process has "succeeded." However, doing so before the entire process has been completed (which may take many years, depending on the project) might have the unfortunate impact of muting enthusiasm for reaching the goal.

- Institutionalize the new approaches. "Until the new behaviors are rooted in social norms and shared values, they are subjected to degradations as soon as the pressure for change is reduced or removed." Therefore, leaders must emphasize the changes that have resulted in positive outcomes as soon as possible. Then once the changes have become part of everyday life in the organization—all the while leaders are continuing to reinforce the new norms—it can be said that the change process has been successful.

> Kotter concludes that in reality even successful change efforts are messy and full of surprises.

Team Building

Here is a short parable, based on actual experiences, that captures the challenges of teamwork and team building.

This is a story about four people named EVERYBODY, SOMEBODY, ANYBODY, and NOBODY. There was an important job to be done and EVERYBODY was asked to do it. EVERYBODY was sure SOMEBODY would do it. ANYBODY could have done it, but NOBODY did it. SOMEBODY got angry about that, because it was EVERYBODY'S JOB. EVERYBODY thought that ANYBODY WOULD do it but NOBODY realized that EVERYBODY would not do it. It ended up that EVERYBODY blamed SOMEBODY when NOBODY did what ANYBODY could have done.

In this classic example, roles and responsibilities were not clearly defined. Neither were the leadership tasks. As a result, there was little cooperation, poor focus, and few accomplishments—not altogether uncommon problems in poorly led teams. To avoid similar difficulties and many frustrations, the strong leader might consider the following six factors when building a team or diagnosing a malfunctioning one.

- Environment. Settings and surroundings, circumstances, and conditions often have a great impact on the team. Policies; the systems of rewards and communications; procedure; markets; the economy; the customers; local, regional, state, and federal guidelines; and the structure of the organization itself (horizontal, vertical, tightly or loosely structured, silos, and a formal or informal hierarchy) can influence success or failure in an organization. Is your work environment positive?

- Goals—what the team is to accomplish. To be most effective, goals need to be very specific and measurable so that the team can march in the same direction and can easily determine to what degree the objectives are being met. Each team member needs to understand the goals and be firmly and openly committed to working toward meeting them. Furthermore, each member needs to know who owns the goals. Are the goals being worked on those of the boss, the team leader, or each and every team member? In healthcare, the patient needs to know if the goals and changes he or she is working on are actually the caregiver's goals or those the patient has agreed to and will work toward.

- Roles. Everyone needs to understand what his or her role is and ideally, those of every other team member, too. When each team member takes care of his or her own responsibilities, friction is reduced—"good fences make good neighbors." This does not mean that each team member cannot or will not assist others, for participation by everyone is required. In addition, all members must know and agree to follow the team leader. Finally, it is crucial that all team members participate fully and come prepared for work activities and meetings. When roles are clearly defined, it is easier to hold an individual responsible for the completion of the task at hand.

- Processes. This systematic series of actions leading toward a specific end enables a team to accomplish its work. Interwoven into the processes is the leader's style. It may vary depending on the situation; the leader's personality; the work objectives; and the team members' experiences, knowledge bases, or skills. At times, the leader may be autocratic or democratic, or only willing to use the team as an advisory group. Communications systems play a big role and are key to a successful outcome. It is crucial that all members be kept aware of the progress of the sessions, the between-session meetings, conclusions, and follow-up assignments. In addition, everyone must know exactly how the team and the system work together. How are materials ordered? How are complaints and suggestions filed? How are new candidates hired? How are employees terminated? How are operating room, clinic visits, and other schedules made or changed? Finally, how are conflicts and disagreements handled within the team? The process of conflict resolution needs to be explicitly stated at the beginning of the team's tenure rather than waiting for a conflict to arise and then have to decide what to do about it.

- Trust. The belief the members have in their leaders and in each other. This factor is based on a person's integrity, competence, consistency (reliability, predictability, and good judgment), and his or her openness and willingness to share ideas and information freely between the leader and the team members. Trust is potentially the strongest element in a relationship, for without it, the team will certainly flounder.

- Interpersonal relationships. Interactions between workers who are congenial, cooperative, and collaborative moves the team forward. Those elements have been determined to be important factors in team success. However, it is a myth that for a team to be successful all its members must be very good friends and even socialize together. What is required for teams to function effectively is that the members need to have a positive working relationship, devoid of extreme negativity, which can doom even a successful project. Even within successful work groups, conflict can occur. And that is not altogether a bad thing. Many times when there is conflict and tension, a good leader can facilitate problem-solving solutions, provided that the intensity of the conflict is kept in check (see also see Chapter 4).

PLANNING FOR THE FUTURE

The lifeline of any organization depends upon fallible human beings putting forth their best efforts to constantly change and update their best hypotheses about what to expect in the near-term and the long-term.

CASE STUDY

Dr. Alice Hardee is the chief of cardiology at a 300-bed teaching hospital in Atlanta, where she has worked the past 5 years. She did her residency in Dallas and took a fellowship in Detroit. She came highly recommended to this hospital because of her success in Michigan. She reports directly to the chief medical officer. In the 38-bed cardiology unit, 16 physicians, 2 nurse practitioners, and 1 physician assistant report directly to her. She gets along moderately well with the chief nursing officer.

Working in a major city such as Atlanta has provided Dr. Hardee with experience dealing with employees from many different cultures. In the past few years, for example, she has had several Englishmen, a few Mexicans, an Ecuadorian, one Israeli, and two Egyptians on her immediate staff. Nonetheless, she prefers to hire Americans, whom she feels have better knowledge and training and are usually smarter. She actually dislikes practitioners from eastern Europe and South America because she believes their training has not been as good, and as a result, they are not as qualified or as effective as "our people." She believes that she is very adept at sizing up job candidates and usually makes her hiring decision within the first few minutes of an interview.

In the past 6 months, two physicians who had been on the staff for a long time resigned to join a hospital 8 miles away—a competitor. One year prior, two other important physicians left for that same hospital. Dr. Hardee is not fazed by these departures or the rumblings of discontent in her unit.

Even though nurses report to the chief nurse, Dr. Hardee interacts with many of them on a daily basis. Many of these nurses, mostly women, tend not to be very assertive when carrying out her orders. In truth, several of them are afraid of her because they fear she can get them fired, if she so desires. Nursing turnover in the cardiology unit has been above average for the hospital. Morale seems to be decreasing on a weekly basis. Recently, Dr. Hardee implemented several new policies dealing with on-call schedules; the way physicians select their nursing staff; and the priorities for allocating time between teaching, research, and patient care. Much of this has happened without consultation or involvement of the staff. Her physicians complain that because of the high turnover in the nursing staff, along with an above-average number of nurses who call in sick, patient care and satisfaction are at risk.

To address these issues, Dr. Hardee convened a team to come up with recommendations for improvement in the work environment. Dr. Hightower, a close colleague of Dr. Hardee, is the team leader. After the first 3 months of meetings, the team remains uncertain as to the real purpose of the planning sessions. Some believe that they are supposed to plan for downsizing the unit, others think they are there to cut costs, and yet others firmly believe that they have to improve procedures on the unit but are not exactly sure which ones. Because of the team's lack of progress and the continuing complaints about the unit that were reported to the Human Resources Department, an OD consultant has been called in to help address the situation.

Questions

- How should the consultant best approach the issues?
- How can this person implement changes in this situation?
- What should the consultant's immediate and longer-term strategies be?
- Is Dr. Hardee at fault? If yes, can she be reeducated/rehabilitated or should she be terminated?

REFERENCES

Beckhard R. *Organization Development: Strategies and Models*. Reading, MA: Addison-Wesley; 1969.

Bradford DL, Burke WW, eds. *Reinventing Organization Development*. San Francisco, CA: Pfeiffer; 2005.

Carter LL. *Best Practices in Leadership Development and Organization Change.* San Francisco, CA: Jossey-Bass; 2004.

Kotter J. Leading change, www.power-projects.com. Summary of "Leading change: why transformation efforts fail." *Harv Bus Rev.* 2007(Jan);85:96–103.

Margulies N, Raia A. *Organizational Development: Values, Process, and Technology.* New York: McGraw-Hill; 1972.

Robbins S, Judge TA. *Organizational Behavior.* 12th ed. Upper Saddle River, NJ: Pearson Education Inc; 2007.

Shonk J. *Working in Teams: A Practical Manual for Improving Work Groups.* New York, NY: AMACOM; 1982.

Sullivan R. *Practicing Organizational Development: A Guide for Leading Change.* San Francisco, CA: Jossey-Bass; 2010.

Weisbord M. *Productive Workplace: Organizing and Managing for Dignity, Meaning, and Community.* San Francisco, CA: Jossey-Bass; 1987.

10

Motivation

DAVID JAVITCH

KEY POINTS

- Three definitions of motivation
- Two different types of motivation: internal and external
- Why people want to work with motivated employees
- Theories of motivation:
  - Maslow's hierarchy of needs
  - Alderfer's existence, relatedness, and growth (ERG) theory
  - Herzberg's motivation-hygiene theory
  - Vroom's expectancy theory
  - McClelland theory of three needs
  - Locke's goal-setting theory
  - Pink's theory of the puzzle of motivation
  - Motivating generation X people
  - Motivating generation Y people (millennials)

Did you ever wonder why the cave dwellers drew pictures on the walls of their caves? Did you ever really think about why you do certain things and not do others? For instance, why did you pursue higher education? Why do you go to certain social, athletic, or cultural events rather than others? Why did you go into the field of healthcare? And most importantly, why do you go to work and try to be productive?

The basic answers to these questions are all dependent on a person's *motivation*.

Psychologists and others have defined this important concept by writing that motivation is the willingness to exert high levels of effort toward organizational goals, conditioned by the person's ability to satisfy some individual need. Also, it may be a person's choice to do some task, a desire to expend effort at doing it, and the drive to persist with that effort. Or simply, it can involve getting yourself or others to do something. The field of medicine is rapidly changing due to advances in technology, knowledge, and computers. Other changes include concerns about reimbursement models, downsizing, mergers, ever-increasing costs, and the future of medicine.

The complexities of this "transformation" of the healthcare industry have caused a great number of morale problems. That is why motivating oneself, patients, and other employees is particularly important in healthcare. That is also why there is a strong need to know more about motivation, an important factor in management's desire to improve staff productivity, patient satisfaction, and quality care.

Organizational behaviorists are professionals whose goal is to observe the individual, the group, and the organization. (See Chapter 9.) They then attempt to improve all three, by looking at four key variables associated with organizational life and motivation: increased productivity, increased employee satisfaction, decreased absenteeism, and decreased negative turnover.

Motivation can drive an individual in two key ways: internally or externally. In internal motivation, the person *willingly* performs an activity because it is meaningful, important, challenging, enjoyable, and serves to satisfy some desired need or goal.

External motivation, on the other hand, occurs when an outside source (e.g., a parent, a peer, or a healthcare administrator) tells a person to perform a task. The person motivated by an outside source may perform that requested task, but it is not necessarily completed at the level intended by the other party and it may not necessarily make the individual satisfied with his or her accomplishment.

What of the unmotivated employee? What element is missing that prevents that staff member from achieving the desired level of performance? Is it salary, position, lack of opportunity, knowledge, skills, abilities, resources, good supervision, or something else?

When interviewed about performance, if that staff person is "unsure" why his or her achievement level does not measure up, then the employer's challenge is to decide what, if anything, there is to do about it. Is that person valuable? Trainable? Willing to change, improve, or adapt? Or is termination the best alternative?

Before opting for the latter, it is necessary for the employer to determine if the atmosphere can be improved enough to allow and encourage the person to become more effective. A very important notion to keep in mind is that "everyone is motivated, but for their own reasons." Is it possible to find the reason? The employer's task, if he or she wants to "save the person's job," is to determine what motivates that individual. Remember, even the individual doing nothing is motivated to demonstrate that behavior, even if it is a passive-aggressive behavior.

So why should an employer make the effort to motivate employees? They do so because motivated employees:

- Come to work more regularly
- Are more supportive of colleagues
- Generate a motivating atmosphere for others
- Work more productively
- Are more flexible
- Are more enjoyable to work with

Consider the following important theories to gain further insight into the different way people are motivated.

MASLOW'S HIERARCHY OF NEEDS

Abraham Maslow created a hierarchal pyramid of five needs or motivators. He theorizes that everyone is driven to satisfy his or her needs in a sequential order to reach the top of the pyramid. At the pyramid base are physiological and safety needs (classified as lower order needs), followed by social, esteem, and self-actualization needs (called higher order needs) at the peak of the pyramid.

The lower order needs are most often satisfied by an external source (e.g., someone who offers or provides shelter and/or protection). In contrast, the higher order needs and motivators must be satisfied by the individual. How the person meets, approaches, and satisfies any or all of those needs will determine the level of a person's fulfillment in life.

Let us take a look at these needs now in more detail. The first and most basic need is physiological. It is the foundation for life and is the base of Maslow's pyramid. To survive, an individual must satisfy needs for hunger, thirst, shelter, sex, and other bodily demands. Once this physiological need is met, the individual moves up the pyramid to address the second need: safety. Here the individual is concerned with freedom from physical or emotional harm. In addition, the person is looking for and motivated by a sense of structure or consistency, such as in expecting a regular paycheck, following specific rules, or a certain schedule.

The higher order needs revolve around social issues, such as love and belonging and the need for affiliation, camaraderie, friendliness, and interaction with others. In the workplace, this need can often be satisfied by meeting with others around the break-room coffee area, connecting with social media, and attending company or team activities.

The next need that a person is motivated to satisfy is that of esteem. People want and need to feel good about themselves, gain self-respect, autonomy, achievement, status, recognition, and attention. People come to work every day to, among many things, have their self-esteem reinforced. A hospital can help with this by recognizing and rewarding staff for excellent patient care, or colleagues can congratulate someone on an exceptionally well-done task.

The final and highest level in the hierarchy is the need for self-actualization, which is defined as the drive to become self-fulfilled by achieving one's desired potential. The chief resident, the nurse manager, or the attending physician, who serve as mentors and advisors, often are satisfying this need by "giving back" to others.

One important and interesting aspect of this hierarchy is that no matter what level on the pyramid a person occupies at any point in time, when distressed by a lower order need, that individual drops from the current level. For instance, if someone is at the level of gaining esteem and is confronted by a family emergency, a job loss, or termination, then the current motivator no longer has prime importance, because the person now must address the lower level need.

Maslow did not submit his research findings to the public, and some of his concepts have not been borne out by further research. However, his theory is still widely appreciated, taught, and applied.

ALDERFER'S EXISTENCE, RELATEDNESS, AND GROWTH (ERG) THEORY

Alderfer has examined, questioned, and reworked Maslow's ideas with positive research results. He concludes that there are three, not five, motivational needs and condenses them into his ERG theory, stating that anyone can be working on several of these motivators at the same time. The needs are:

- E or Existence needs: basic existence and physiological requirements, financial and nonfinancial matters, and work concerns
- R or Relatedness needs: relationships (social, belongingness, and affection) plus respect and esteem
- G or Growth: growth in self-fulfillment and pursuit of interests

HERZBERG'S MOTIVATION-HYGIENE THEORY

Herzberg's theory is very popular and its principles are widely applied, serving as a foundation for many other motivational theories. (Note: Here "hygiene" refers not to cleanliness but to the environment.) His concepts, however, diverge markedly from that of others. His research is based on the premise that the opposite of job dissatisfaction is not job satisfaction but rather no satisfaction. Furthermore, he differs from all other motivational theorists by dividing his ideas into two types: motivators and demotivators. Motivators, the first category, are intrinsic factors that encourage an individual to be more productive. Demotivators, the second category, are those factors that are necessary for an individual to be at least minimally motivated; however, having more than an adequate amount of these factors *will not motivate anyone*. In terms of motivators, he lists achievement, recognition, growth, the work itself, responsibility, and advancement. These elements are specifically related to job satisfaction and autonomy. Not having the opportunity to attain satisfaction will decrease an employee's level of motivation.

On the other hand, examples of demotivators (those issues that a person needs an adequate amount of) are supervision, work conditions, salary, status, security, and relationships with others. Typically, most people are quick to say that money is a motivator; that is true, but only in the short term (as in the months following a bonus). Many more months down the line, the extra money no longer serves to motivate that person. To repeat, if certain factors are not adequate, as in a hospital not providing sufficient or appropriate examination instruments, access to the electronic medical records or other resources, an individual will be demotivated. As long as his or her computer has enough memory, for example, a person will be motivated. But if the amount of memory needed increases by a factor of two, it will not have a motivating impact.

The most significant aspect of Herzberg's theory is that he determined that employer's giving recognition to staff was often more important than anything else.

VROOM'S EXPECTANCY THEORY

"Expectancy theory is about the mental processes regarding choice, or choosing. It explains the processes that an individual undergoes to make choices." In the study of organizational behavior, expectancy theory is a motivation theory first proposed by Victor Vroom of the Yale School of Management.

One of the first questions the reader must ask when reading about expectancy theory is: whose expectations are being referred to as a source of motivation? The reader's? The chief medical officer's? The nurse manager's? Others? And when the boss tells an employee what is expected of him or her, what determines if the staff member will buy into it and fulfill that expectation? To what degree? How will it be evaluated and by whom? What will be the repercussions? The following aspects of Vroom's theory will help answer these questions.

Here are a series of fundamental questions that the employee can ask himself or herself.

- Will any effort that I exert result in a solid performance of the task? In other words, can I do it? Do I have the knowledge, skills, abilities, resources, and support to complete the assignment to an acceptable level to achieve my goal or attain success?
- Will my performance result in the expected, anticipated, stated, or implied outcome or reward? In the process, will my performance follow

the guidelines or specifications made by my boss? Can I demonstrate
the required creativity, productivity, or initiative required? Will these
latter two factors be allowed, appreciated, or valued?
- Will the rewards result in achievement of or the attainment of my personal
objectives or those of the organization without regard to my interests,
growth, or goals?

The answers to these important questions as well as others generated by the discussion contribute to describing the level of motivation any individual possesses
because they specifically relate to expectations.

MCCLELLAND'S THEORY OF THREE NEEDS

McClelland's research has determined that for individuals to be motivated, they
need to satisfy three sources of needs: the need for achievement, the need for
power, and the need for affiliation. Like many of the other theorists, he maintains
that different individuals have different need levels that will lead to satisfaction
and productivity.

His first factor, the need for achievement (recall Herzberg) is the drive to get
ahead, do well, and succeed. His research demonstrated that individuals who have
a sufficient amount of this need strive to be better, more effective, faster, and so on,
than other people. They want to receive rapid feedback on their performance so
that they can change or adapt their approach, if necessary. Unlike entrepreneurs,
they are not high-risk takers or even low-risk takers, contrary to popular belief.
Challenge, however, is important to high achievers. Success coming from low-risk
projects is not appealing either to those seeking to accomplish great things,
because easily attained success does not really represent true achievement. Those
with this high need for achievement prefer to gain success with projects that have
moderate odds in their favor. The latter lead to true feelings of achievement and
satisfaction (again, recall Herzberg).

Yet, just because someone has a high need for achievement does not necessarily
mean that he or she will be an effective manager or leader. Two of the drawbacks
of these high achievers are that they may not be concerned with managerial effectiveness or concern for others.

McClelland's second factor is the need for power. People who possess this need
want to influence and control others and make other people behave in ways that
sometimes they would not have behaved. Again, they are more concerned with
achievement than with making people happy or creating a happy working environment. They are clearly competitive, and they are concerned with status and
prestige.

The third need that McClelland researched is the need for affiliation. Ironically,
this seems to be inconsistent with the need for power, as explained in the previous

statement. This affiliation motivator encourages affiliation-oriented people to be friendly and liked and to enjoy close interpersonal relationships. They enjoy working cooperatively with team members as opposed to being sole practitioners. They seek mutual understanding and like to work within a consensus with agreed-upon goals, processes, and procedures. The best way to explain this seemingly contradictory need is that more successfully motivated people combine their need for affiliation with their need for power and balance them effectively.

Think about chiefs of services, nurse managers, and chief nursing officers here. Which one(s) of these three needs is paramount in each role, and what kind of impact will it have on others?

LOCKE'S GOAL-SETTING THEORY

Do you or your bosses ever make comments such as "do a good job," "your work is wonderful," "your work is subpar," or "you need to work harder on dieting or taking your meds"? These comments, either positive or negative, really have little meaning, although caregivers frequently say them to their patients. They are not specific enough. The follow-up response to the above statements is "What does 'good job' mean?" or "How or why is my work wonderful or subpar?" In his goal-setting theory, Locke explains how to counteract the vagueness and ineffectiveness of these and other similar statements and how to turn them around to increase motivation.

One way is to get the individual to participate in the process of setting the goal. Then that person is likely to be more motivated to complete a difficult task or project than if the goal were dictated by a boss or team leader. Individuals are more committed to choices if they have participated in the process of selecting them (recall autonomy).

This concept of "participation" is the central focus of an older, yet very time-tested practice: management by objective. That practice is a result of the boss and the employee jointly discussing and at times developing compromises on goals, processes, timetables, resources, and outcomes. Just think about how your outcomes may be more effective if you made joint decisions with your patients! (The second aspect of Locke's theory is to provide feedback on goal achievement [recall Herzberg and McClelland], especially when the feedback is self-generated. Obviously, feedback leads to greater success than a lack of feedback.)

One cautionary note, however: according to anecdotal reporting from personal experiences with parents, professors, caregivers, and at the workplace, it seems that a great deal of feedback offered tends to be negative. Even the absence of feedback says something. So when the boss does not offer feedback, many individuals assume their performance is lacking, even if they were anticipating positive comments. Certainly, there are people who say, "I know what kind of job I'm doing, so I don't need feedback from others." These individuals tend to be the exceptions rather than the rule.

The third and final facet of this theory is to gain commitment to the goal from each individual and every participant. Without that commitment, preferably expressed publically (e.g., by voice mail, e-mail, social media, in person), then there is no certainty that a person has internalized the goal and will work to achieve it, consistent with the best of his or her abilities. So when the caregiver assumes the patient will follow directions for lifestyle changes in medicine, diet, and or exercise, the patient needs to state that agreement verbally to the caregiver about how this process will work.

One way to increase commitment to a goal, as previously expressed, is to have the team "buy into" the goals because they mutually created them and/or agreed upon them (and had the consent of their coaches, mentors, or caregivers).

Participation leads to motivation (recall Maslow), which leads to commitment, which most often leads to cohesive work performance. Another motivational aspect of this commitment is the belief that the individual is capable (i.e., possesses the knowledge, skills, abilities, resources, preparation, training) of attaining the goal. If an individual in the group lacks that belief, then one of the supervisor's or caregiver's tasks as a motivator is to try to "turn around" that person or the situation.

DANIEL PINK'S THEORY OF THE PUZZLE OF MOTIVATION

Consistent with previously described theories, Pink's research demonstrates that contingent factors such as "If you do X, you will get Y" or the carrot-and-stick approach does not work for complex tasks. In fact, it is just the opposite. In research performed at the Massachusetts Institute of Technology, Carnegie-Mellon, and the University of Chicago, organizational behaviorists concluded that high levels of rewards for cognitively challenging tasks actually decrease the quality of the result.

Further outcomes of this research state that there are really three types of motivators: autonomy, mastery, and purpose. These motivator types support the concept of intrinsic motivation as described earlier. Workers with autonomy can personally control their life direction, time, opportunities, and provide self-direction. These are reminiscent of Herzberg's concept of achievement as a motivator.

Mastery is the next motivator. Here, an individual can perform a job or task quickly, efficiently and effectively, and generally without error. Mastery of a skill, particularly one of intricacy and complexity, provides a strong feeling of accomplishment and often comes with praise and recognition, which are very important motivational factors. (Recall Herzberg.)

The third and final component in Pink's theory is purpose. That entails the yearning to do something larger or better than one's self because one believes that one is doing something that is important and that it matters (recall Maslow once again!).

These factors play an important role in educating healthcare professionals who frequently enter the field seeking a higher purpose in their lives, which is one reason they turn to helping others. In addition, when they master their skills and prove themselves, they can seek more autonomy in their roles. Do you as professionals help or hinder them in that process?

MOTIVATING GENERATION X AND GENERATION Y GROUPS

At this point, it is easy to think that these theories and approaches are important, easy to apply, and can increase your understanding in such a way that you will be able to improve the motivation of your and your employees. You might also think that these ideas about motivation apply universally to all people who work. However, when it comes to the younger generations, often called generations X and Y, other challenges exist.

Motivating Generation X People

"Gen Xers" is the term often applied to approximately 50 million people born between the mid-1960s and 1980, the offspring of the "baby boomers." Now between the ages of 28 and 48, many of these gen Xers grew up as "latch key" kids; they came home to an empty home after school because both of their parents worked or they had single parents. On many occasions, they saw their parents married to the workplace, often devoting long hours to their jobs. The result? Well-meaning parents sacrificed time at home with their families. In the economic downturn of the 1980s, many of these hard workers lost their jobs.

The children of gen Xers were forced to become more resourceful and often had to fend for themselves. Looking at the plight their parents found themselves in, many of the youth growing up in the 80s became disillusioned with the lack of work/life balance and the lack of loyalty shown employees by their employer.

With these facts in mind, leaders need to alter slightly the way they work with and motivate gen Xers. Accordingly, in working with them, a leader would:

- Offer clear statements of goals but allow them—within reason—to decide on how to achieve those goals.
- Provide opportunities for them to make choices. Because this generation has become accustomed to "being on their own," it is

important to provide options—options for task selection, options for challenges, options to formulate new processes, and options to work toward creative, yet appropriate conclusions.

- Offer strong, relationship-oriented mentorship, yet be certain not to micromanage them or suggest rigid guidelines to complete projects.
- Allow them the freedom to use their own resourcefulness, independence, and creativity to achieve success.
- Build on their interest in gaining new skills and knowledge by providing opportunities to grow on the job.
- Rely on their attitude of "work hard, play hard" in accomplishing a goal.
- Manage by walking around—that is, spend time with them and offer clear and frequent feedback on their progress.

Motivating Generation Y People (Millennials)

The approximate 70 million "gen Yers," born in the mid to late 1970s through the late 1990s, came next. They have often been called the "trophy kids" because on sports teams and in school, each child, regardless of capability, was given a chance to perform, and it seemed as if everyone was given some kind of a certificate or award just for having participated. Winning—achievement or competency—did not appear to matter. To ensure that the young people of this era maintained and raised their "self-esteem" and "self-worth," they were praised lavishly by parents, teachers, and coaches in the hope and with the expectation of better and more positive outcomes. This was a far cry from the less "esteem-conscious" days, when young people "received credit" only for having beaten the other team and winning the contest, as was typical in previous generations.

Besides daily school classes, gen Yers were involved in many (some would say an abundance of) extracurricular activities (e.g., sports, music lessons, social events, or art classes) in addition to school. They can be thought of as the "overscheduled" generation.

There is a direct relationship between the experiences growing up and methods to motivate the gen Yers. To attain success with this population, it is important to consider these approaches:

- Provide more than one task to accomplish at a time; they are accustomed to multitasking. They look forward to the challenges of having several tasks to perform at once. However, leaders need to be cautious about "piling on" tasks, they can get overwhelmed.
- Create work teams or partnering situations. They are accustomed to working in tandem with others.
- Provide structure and clear guidelines and at times, specific processes or approaches for achieving goals. Although they appear confident, they still need input from management.

- Encourage and allow them to use the latest technology in the work setting.
- Positively challenge their interests, abilities, and achievements.
- Create a bonding relationship with them so that they feel comfortable asking for input and direction and can feel that they can rely on you—the authority figure—when the need arises.
- Reward them frequently with positive feedback and citations for successful accomplishments and milestones on the road to longer-term achievements.
- Set up specific and regular times to meet with them and supervise them.
- Demonstrate sincere interest in their professional growth and success.
- Understand that they prefer using electronic means to communicate with you as opposed to face-to-face meetings. This generation is far more fluent and comfortable with technology than any other group.

Leaders need to ensure that their employees are productive and eager to do the best job possible. This is especially true during today's challenging economic times. Continue to provide and expect a high-quality product or service. All employees need to work up to their full capacity.

So what can leaders do to "motivate" this generation of employees and patients? First, leaders need to realize that motivation cannot be imposed on anyone!" "You can bring a horse to water, but you can't make it drink," as the old adage goes. What they can do, though, is work to create the atmosphere that allows and encourages the employee to perform at high levels. But that is not all. Good supervisors need to engage their staff. That means getting involved with that person to understand what he or she is interested in doing. Also, it is important to determine which parts of the job description are exciting versus boring. Then, try some of these techniques:

- Set up situations that allow the employee to feel a sense of accomplishment (see Herzberg).
- Praise the employee for specific aspects of a job well done—or even partially well done.
- Involve the employee in creating a more satisfying career path, including promotions, based on concrete outcomes.
- State your expectations clearly for task accomplishment.
- Ensure that the job description involves a variety of tasks.
- Ensure that the employee sees how what he or she is doing affects the whole process or task that others will also be part of.
- Make sure that the employee feels that what he or she is doing is meaningful.
- Provide performance feedback along the way, pointing out both positive and negative aspects.

- Allow for an appropriate amount of autonomy for the employee based on previous and anticipated future accomplishment.
- Increase the depth and breadth of what the employee is currently doing.

CASE STUDY

Ingrid is a new manager in a 65-bed nursing home in the Midwest. She was promoted after being on the job for only 4 years. She is not sure exactly why she was selected over some other candidates, but she was very pleased to have been chosen. Her supervisor is very relaxed about Ingrid's responsibilities. When Ingrid was promoted, her supervisor told her that she has faith in her and is confident that she will do a good job managing 155 employees.

Ingrid has only seen her supervisor twice in the past 8 months. The last time, things did not go well between the two of them. Her supervisor criticized her, and Ingrid felt badly about that because she did not think she deserved the rebuke. Ingrid is having trouble managing the budget. She tries hard to keep to the budgetary guidelines and financial restraints, but things just are not working out. She does not know how she can manage through the rest of the fiscal year.

Some of Ingrid's employees are complaining about lack of job satisfaction and lack of guidance or direction. Ingrid cannot understand their problems because when she was in their position, she enjoyed what she was doing and felt she was doing a good job without the need for a lot of input from her manager.

Mrs. Cartwright, one of the most reliable nurses in the nursing home, has long been known as a very diligent worker, spending extra hours with patients and helping other nurses and medical assistants. However, she only seems to receive criticism from certain physicians and never a compliment for all her hard work. Her morale is rapidly deteriorating, and she is finding it increasingly difficult to go to work every day. She is also pulling back from taking the needed extra shifts inserted into the schedule because of the nursing shortage.

One of the newer physicians, recruited away from an important hospital nearby, works 16 to 18 hours daily. Although young and well respected, he is also beginning to burn out. His chief is too busy to give him the advice he seeks and only reluctantly agrees to sit down with him to discuss difficult cases and scheduling. The new physician is wary of discussing his problems with others but somehow believes they know what is going on.

Ingrid has so many demands on her that she does not know what to do first. Being new at her job is difficult, and she feels that she may not succeed. She has no one to confide in, so she keeps her misgivings to herself. She believes that if she asks for help from her supervisor, she might appear incompetent and may be demoted. Although she knows she is inexperienced in management and therefore has made some poor decisions, she truly wants to succeed. However, Ingrid fears that she will fail.

Questions

- How would you rate Ingrid's level of motivation? Job satisfaction? What factors support your responses?
- What do Ingrid's employees want from her? Are they likely to get it?
- What does Ingrid need to succeed in her new position?
- If you see a morale problem anywhere in this nursing home, what might be the causes and how would you address it?

SUGGESTED READING

Amabile T, Kramer S. *The Dynamics of Inner Work Life.* Cambridge, MA: Harvard Business Review Press; 2011.

Butler T. *Mapping Our Insights—Patterns in the Sand.* Cambridge, MA: Harvard Business Review Press; 2008.

Friedman WA. *Give Me That Old-Time Motivation.* Cambridge, MA: Harvard Business Review Press; 2006.

Herzberg F. *One More Time—How Do You Motivate Employees?* Cambridge, MA: Harvard Business Review Press; 2008.

Javitch D. 5 employee motivation myths debunked. entrepreneur.com. April, 2010.

Javitch D. How to motivate generations X and Y. entrepreneur.com. April, 2010.

Nohria N, Groysberg B, Lee LE. *Employee Motivation—A Powerful New Model.* Cambridge, MA: Harvard Business Review Press; 2008.

Pink D. *Drive: The Surprising Truth About What Motivates Us.* New York, NY: Riverdale Books; 2011.

Robbins S, Judge T. *Organizational Behavior,* Prentice-Hall. 12th ed. Upper Saddle River, NJ; 2007.

11

Negotiations

DAVID JAVITCH

KEY POINTS

- How common it is for people to negotiate daily yet often deny they are doing so? Definitions of negotiations are very important.
- Perception plays a major role in how people form ideas and images of the other party in the negotiations.
- Three different types of negotiations include simple, representational, and symbolic and how people react to each.
- There are differences between distributive and integrative bargaining and how people's views of each determine their negotiation styles and desired outcome.
- Lewicki's five steps in the negotiation process include:
  - Prepare and plan
  - Define ground rules
  - Clarify and justify
  - Bargain and problem solve
  - Close and implement

Fisher and Ury's famous principled negotiations are:
  - Separate the people from the problem
  - Focus on interests, not positions
  - Invent options for mutual gain
  - Use objective criteria
  - Decide issues based on their merit

- Marcus, Dorn, and McNulty's four stage theory of negotiations
  - Self interests
  - Enlarged interests
  - Enlightened interests
  - Aligned interests

People negotiate constantly, whether they realize it or not. Yet so many say that they do not like negotiating or that they do not know how to do it well. Nevertheless, they negotiate in and out of traffic lanes, to be first in line in the supermarket, at ticket booths, in the drugstore, or elsewhere.

Physicians try to convince patients to take medications, to go for further testing, or to arrive on time for follow-up appointments. Physicians and nurses sometimes negotiate the best treatment approaches or options for patients. Administrators work with their boards of directors, donors, subordinates, patients and their families, and the media to advance their agenda. Patients try, often with great difficulty, to work with schedulers, insurance companies, and government organizations to improve their schedules, their monetary situations, or their outcomes. Pharmaceutical representatives try to meet with physicians and healthcare administrators to encourage them to sell or use their products. Whether people realize it or not, these examples all involve varying amounts of negotiation.

So why do people say that they do not know how to negotiate? Perhaps they really mean that they are unaware that they are negotiating. Alternatively, they might not like the idea of attaching a label to their interactions because it might make them feel they are manipulating a person or an outcome. And that may make them feel self-conscious.

Others might fear negotiating because they are afraid of losing something they have, want, or need. Some people are afraid of some unreasonable or unrealistic major negative outcome from "losing" a negotiation; some of those fears may be embarrassment, loss of pride, respect, status, position, love, or money.

So what is negotiation? There are many different definitions. The simplest one is "the process of exchange." Others include "interacting with someone to get what you want," "the process to determine the exchange of tangibles and intangibles," or, "a process in which two or more parties exchange goods or services in an attempt to agree upon the exchange rate for them." One can even negotiate with one's self over an action, feeling, decision, or desire. However, to be accurately defined as a "negotiation," the process must involve an interaction with at least one person, and then either another person, or a machine, or an inanimate object.

Parties in a negotiation discuss their issues based on how they perceive the different component parts of the interaction. For example, how does one party view, evaluate, or perceive the other? Is the second party bigger, smaller, larger, richer, poorer, more sophisticated, higher, equal, or lower in the organizational hierarchy? Does that other party have more political weight, value, resources, importance, or support? Is the other party of the same race, gender, ethnic background, religion, or appearance?

The role of perception is absolutely crucial in all phases of a negotiation. Social scientists tell us that one person forms his or her perceptions within the first moments of encountering that other person.

Dr. Jerome Groopman, in fact, says that most physicians make their initial diagnosis within 15 seconds of encountering a patient. Likewise, a person's initial views, formed quite quickly, will determine how he or she chooses to interact during a negotiation. For example, as a result of the initial encounter with another party, a person's attitudes, behaviors, strategies, and approaches might run the gamut from being passive to being assertive. Based on his or her perceptions, the range of behaviors might lead a person to become aggressive or condescending, cowering or patronizing, or just overbearing. And, of course, the other party in the negotiation might react with behaviors and attitudes that are positive or negative, productive or unproductive, similar or different.

This is when complex interpersonal dynamics enter into the negotiation process.

The important tactic here is to form as many perceptions as possible, using the five senses and other means to accumulate data, not only initially but also during the entire course of the interactions. The caveat is to delay making firm evaluations until the person's initial perceptions become validated and substantiated by hard data, definitions, or even "gut" feelings. Even then, his or her views will continue to be modified and updated as appropriate due to rethinking conclusions and gathering additional information.

TYPES OF NEGOTIATION: SIMPLE, REPRESENTATIONAL, AND SYMBOLIC

As its name implies, simple negotiations are the most basic form. They involve one person, and only one person, negotiating with another person. Each side may have communicated with or have relied on others for counsel or input; however, at the negotiation table, only one person from each side is present for the interaction.

In representational negotiations, the second form, one or both sides may be representing another group, division, or organization. For example, this occurs when there is a bargaining unit such as a union that hires or uses a negotiator or team of negotiators to do the actual negotiation. Perception plays a key role here when one side is either empowered by or disempowered by the size, value, prestige, reputation, "strength," or importance of the entity being represented by the other side.

Symbolic negotiations, the last form, rely even more heavily on perceptions. Take this cross-cultural negotiation as an illustration of symbolic negotiations. One party is affected adversely by how the other side is perceived. The parties do not really know each other very well, and different biases intercede in the interaction. For example, suppose that Martinez and Company represent the first party.

Box 11.1   THE FOUR STAGES OF NEGOTIATING

Preparation
Information exchange
Bargaining
Implementation

On the opposite side, an American team, Smith and Jones, is handling the negotiation for the second party in the dispute. Assume that Smith and Jones believe that the Martinez team is composed of only poorly educated foreign nationals and therefore cannot be very effective. Smith and Jones might feel quite superior in the interaction that will soon take place. But supposing the case has to do with immigration and the background of the judge is Hispanic. Now the situation turns around. Smith and Jones may suddenly feel intimidated and therefore less powerful.

Similarly, if one negotiator is of a race, gender, or ethnic background that the other side does not like or is prejudiced against, then that second party may feel so distracted by the first negotiator that he or she behaves in a manner that is less effective. The opposite could also be true in the imaginary situation. Stages of negotiation and style is provided in Box 11.1 and Table 11.1.

DISTRIBUTIVE VERSUS INTEGRATIVE NEGOTIATIONS

Before beginning, it is necessary to draw a distinction between bargaining and negotiating, even though most people use the words interchangeably. Bargaining involves one winner and therefore one loser, even though in a typical conversation, people may say that one party "strikes a bargain with another." If one side clearly wins and the other loses, the correct term for this process is bargaining. If both sides gain something, then the correct term is negotiating.

In distributive bargaining, there is a fixed or a limited amount of funds, assets, or means that can be divided among the parties, with one side winning and the

TABLE 11.1   NEGOTIATION STYLE

High Expectations		Low Expectations
Collaborator: Problem solver	Compromiser	Accommodator
Competitor		Conflict avoider

other losing. A scenario like this is very common during budget discussions between departments in healthcare organizations. For example, in the new budget, the chief financial officer (CFO) has only $10 million to distribute among five departments, all of which are requesting additional employees and other resources. Irrespective of the desires of the CFO, who may want to distribute enough money to satisfy everyone's requests, he or she is, of course, restricted to that $10 million figure. So unless every department gets $2 million each, some departments will get more and some will get less.

This then can lead to subsequent rounds of bargaining in which the competing department heads will jockey for position to get as much money as they can, generally without regard to what the others receive. In brief, this results in an "I win–you lose" situation where the disappointed parties might end up harboring long-term antagonisms and jealousies. This invariably leads to another round of bargaining, either at that time or later, where the parties who believed that they did not get their "fair share" the first time will attempt to "beat up" the winning parties, whom they thought received a larger proportion of the resources.

It becomes perfectly obvious then that these types of cyclical negative interactions can continue for a long time and detract from the real business at hand. This encounter clearly describes the negative aspect of distributive bargaining.

A far more positive approach to interactions around resource allocation is the integrative approach to negotiations. In contrast to the distributive approach, the integrative approach is based on an "I gain–you gain" outcome. In the integrative approach, a variable amount of resources can be shared among interested parties. In this less competitive, less antagonistic approach, both sides work together to ensure a positive outcome with at least each side getting some, if not all, of what it was requesting.

The beauty of this approach is that the participants in these interactions go into them looking for that gain-gain outcome. The results are far more positive, and the participants come away with either no antagonisms or desires for revenge or far less intense reactions than if they had participated in a distributive bargaining approach.

FIVE STEPS IN THE NEGOTIATION PROCESS

Lewicki lists five steps that are important in the negotiation process:

- Prepare and plan.
- Define ground rules.
- Clarify and justify.
- Bargain and problem solve (note that he does not differentiate between bargaining and negotiating).
- Close and implement.

Prepare and Plan

One of the most important aspects to take into consideration in preparation for negotiation is to advise the negotiator that the entire process begins way before the actual negotiations take place in a person-to-person meeting. That, of course, means that the individual negotiator must stop and think out—in his or her mind or on paper or computer—exactly how he or she intends the negotiating process to unfold. Many negotiators, especially in less formal settings, are apt to launch into a negotiation without fully considering the process, what they plan to do, possible desirable or undesirable outcomes, and potential ramifications of their actions.

This frequently occurs when one party is lulled into believing that the process will be fairly brief and simple or that he or she, being well experienced and smart, can easily and rapidly deal with this situation without seriously considering the overall issues at stake. Or this can occur if the bargainer becomes pressured to negotiate in an impromptu situation, even if unprepared. This is clearly a grave mistake.

During the premeeting preparation, the negotiator must consider the nature of the conflict. Many questions need to be answered. For example, exactly what is going on in this situation? How did the conflict come about? How serious is it? Do the players have a history with each other? Is there a history of this or similar conflicts that you can learn from? Finally, is there more to the conflict than what appears on the surface? Is there a deeper complexity within the conflict, or are there additional ramifications that need to be considered?

Another crucial consideration at this point are the goals. To what degree do the parties involved want to work toward attaining these goals and actually resolving the conflict? Whose goals are being presented: the parties involved, their representatives, their bosses? Are the goals specific and measurable? If the goals are too global or if they are ambiguous, it may be difficult to reach a satisfactory resolution. Are the goals realistic and attainable within a reasonable time frame?

The last aspect of this initial step is the creation of an objective "best alternative to a negotiated agreement," or BATNA. BATNA is a widely used term that refers to the point at which the negotiator might simply say, "Enough is enough. I am not getting what I want out of this negotiation." Another possibility is, "This negotiation is going as far as it possibly could go, and I want to leave." Or this could be the final or lowest point the bargainer wishes to make or agree to, and says, "This is my bottom line (last offer or last position)." At this point, he or she is willing to walk away from the negotiation. At this point, the negotiator might be thinking, "I am not going to reach an agreement, so what are my alternatives? Can I find another supplier, for example? Can I do the deal without this particular partner? Many negotiations take place without the BATNA being considered until an impasse occurs.

We maintain, however, that many alternatives should be examined before the negotiations begin. Smith, a good negotiator in the preparation before the meeting might say, "My goal is to get Jones to buy my business for $10,000. But hmmm, what if he can't afford it? What if he only has $5,000? Little does Jones know, but I am desperate for $3,000. I have to make a bank payment tomorrow. I am so desperate that I would actually pay him to take the business off my hands. But I can't tell him that." So what if an impasse is reached, and Jones is getting ready to walk away. Smith may say something like, "Okay, you cannot pay me the $10,000 that I am asking. What is the most you can pay?" If Smith knows what his or her best alternatives are—in this case, a range between $3,000 and $10,000, then perhaps an agreement can still be reached or Smith can go somewhere and dump the property and get that minimum $3,000 that he or she needs.

Having that BATNA, the best alternative to a negotiated agreement, might provide an additional leverage point.

Define Ground Rules

The bargaining party must have or must be aware of specific criteria upon which the negotiation will be based. Most importantly, he or she must know exactly who the opposing party will be. Is this going to be a simple, complex, or representational negotiation? Next, he or she needs to know precisely where the negotiation will take place. If one party wants to have the upper hand or "home field advantage," then the negotiation will take place at the party's office, conference room, organizational headquarters, or other familiar place of choice.

The specific time that the interaction will take place must be known so that no party arrives too early or too late. In certain circumstances, it may be necessary to have a restrictive time frame placed on the interactions. There may be a deadline for the existence or extension of a contract or a decision that must be made before a certain scheduled date. Having a real or imagined deadline can sometimes work in favor of one party. For example, if the first party wants to pressure the second party into reaching a decision or making concessions, that party can say that, " I need to leave on a scheduled plane flight" or "Another party will be willing to enter negotiations with me if you do not make a decision or agree to my requirements by a certain date."

Next, there needs to be specific rules for this engagement. Exactly how will the negotiation begin, proceed, and end needs to be specified. Additionally, if the agreement becomes stymied, what do the parties do? Do they take a break, call in additional resources, or break off the negotiations?

One factor that is absolutely crucial to the entire negotiation process is the unambiguous clarification of the issues. One party may frankly state that he or she had a different interpretation of the stated concern at hand. Or one party may believe the negotiation would be about a different matter.

The last aspect of defining the ground rules involves an initial proposal. This is generally viewed as a goodwill gesture in terms of one or both sides being willing to give in or modify the initial offer. Unless one party thinks that his or her position is quite weak, and that he or she must accept whatever is offered, it is rare that the initial offer is ever accepted. After all, this is only the beginning of the negotiating process!

Clarify and Justify

Even though the issue at hand was clarified in the previous step, at this point it needs to be reviewed again. In addition, each side needs to explain exactly what it wants. Each side needs to make the issue abundantly clear to the other party. Furthermore, in an attempt to win over the other party, this party must effectively justify exactly why the position is reasonable and should be agreed to. It is here that the negotiator might want to go into greater depth and identify specific desires, needs, goals, and interests.

Bargain and Problem Solve

Now the action begins with the party who proposed the initial agreement. Again, some minor concessions might be made in an effort to appear willing to negotiate good terms and even modify one's initial position. In practice, some positions are actually realistic, important, just, and fair. Nonetheless, concessions are offered. Once one side makes a concession, the other party often feels obligated to respond in kind.

This reciprocity, however, does not always occur. However, it is very helpful, especially at this point, to emphasize a desire for an integrative or gain-gain approach and outcome. The key is to try to create an open, trusting climate that will encourage a give and take, congenial, and objective quality to the interaction.

It is important to address and respond to the issues being raised and not become enmeshed in the personality or even the possible theatrics of the opposing party. Remaining objective and focused—on the overall goal and desired outcome—is extremely important at this point. Thus, one's argument and approach need to be focused on the target, guarding against mirroring possible theatrics or negative approaches of the other party. A negotiator wants to avoid becoming defensive, thereby risking losing sight of the goal.

Close and Implement

Even though the bargaining process appears to be over, with both sides verbally stating their agreement on the issues, it is of major importance and value for each side to repeat clearly and specifically what each side agreed to, giving all interpretations of the final wording of the agreement. It is here where one side may say, "That's not how I interpret what we agreed to." And therefore, in reality, the negotiations are not complete.

PRINCIPLED NEGOTIATIONS

Fisher and Ury, two former Harvard Law School professors, have become internationally renowned for their Harvard Negotiation Project. The negotiation studies provide a simple, yet in-depth and effective approach to resolving even the most complex negotiations. They describe five aspects for the negotiator to consider when working with the disputing parties.

- Separate the people from the problem.
- Focus on interests, not positions.
- Invent options for mutual gain.
- Use objective criteria.
- Decide issues based on their merit.

Separate the People from the Problem

Here a negotiator must be able to separate his or her relationship and perceptions of the other party from the substance of what is being negotiated. This is not always an easy task, because one of the goals of each party is to convince the other side of the value of the proposal. As stated earlier, this can involve emotional pleas, theatrics, and heavy persuasion. Nonetheless, the negotiator needs to pay attention only to the value and purpose of the other person's argument. Different perceptions invariably arise. The negotiator is encouraged to try to identify and discuss differing interpretations of issues so all participants will be on the proverbial "same page" at the conclusion of the discussions. Obviously, this needs to be done early in the negotiation process and as frequently as needed for clarification.

At times, people on one side or the other may become overly emotional or tearful. It is important to recognize it when it occurs and allow for it. The outpouring of emotions happen. It is normal and human for these emotions to be present. If that kind of breakdown does occur, it is often a good idea to take a short break to permit the affected individuals on each side to regain composure and objectivity.

It is helpful to build positive and open communications so that each side clearly understands what is happening and can contribute to the negotiations process. Where positive relationships can be built, the exchange of ideas, alternate solutions, and acceptance of the proposals on the table can be more easily accomplished.

Focus on Interests, not Positions

Typically, what occurs in the initial discussions is that each party enters the process by taking a firm, seemingly unalterable stand that describes what they want. This "stand" is called a *position*. Inferring that one's position is "set in stone," however, has a definite negative consequence for the entire process and might even end the negotiations. For if one side is adamant about what it wants, even if it gains a good portion of that position in the end, that party will not have succeeded in "winning" the negotiation. If that sounds odd, it is. Because in "principled" negotiations, the strong-armed approach ("I must get it all, and/or the people I represent expect me to 'get it all,'") does not permit the other side to achieve success. Furthermore, "winning" is a distributive and unsuccessful way to negotiate for the reasons stated earlier in this chapter. Additionally, if one party is adamant about its position, there is little room for negotiating changes, thus diminishing the possibility of arriving at a *mutually agreed* upon resolution of the problem—in other words, a successful negotiation.

A far more effective approach involves stating one's *interests* and seeking to find commonality with the other party's issues. This can simply be accomplished by asking a series of "Why?" questions that aim to get at the very basis of what each party wants in the negotiations. Why does one side want a specific version of the issue?

Why are the real purposes or motives of one party different from those of the other party? Why does a person think he or she may lose or gain something in the negotiations? Why is this so important? Why did the person not leave room for negotiations on a specific item of interest in the negotiation? Why is this issue or other aspects of issues motivating the person behind this discourse between parties?

Stating and explaining interests, as opposed to taking a rigid position, also allows for movement and flexibility in the discussions. Whereas bargaining based on a firm position and holding to that position does not permit modification or compromise, and one also needs to consider that total inflexibility may even doom the process. When interests and motives, along with possible alternatives are stated and shared with the other party, communications becomes clearer and resolution becomes far more possible.

Invent Options for Mutual Gain

Assume that the first two steps have been followed effectively and the negotiation is now focused on common interests. This next step seems to flow naturally. Here, both parties work toward achieving a win-win situation and understanding the other side's perspectives and interests. They actively assist their counterpart in movement toward mutual resolution of the problem. Accordingly, both sides enthusiastically participate and broaden their options. By identifying the interests they share, former opponents would become collaborators in sifting through their differing interests to increase understanding and achieving mutually satisfying outcomes.

Use Objective Criteria

In many daily situations, individuals make certain requests of others and state their detailed interests for what they want. To add a firm foundation and ratio-nale behind that interest, the negotiator needs to rely on specific and measurable objective information. For example, when a director goes to the CFO requesting a detailed percentage increase in his salary, the CFO can rightly say, "What do you base that request on other than your assumed positive performance?" If the director can cite an objective standard that, for example, the going industry rate is at "x" or show that 10 of the 15 other in-house administrators at his level, with comparable experience and levels of productivity, are earning a certain salary, then that director has specific, nonemotional data to bolster his case. Without these data, the negotiator loses power.

Decide Issues Based on Their Merit

As a result of proceeding through the previous four steps, negotiators can more easily reach a reasonable, effective, longer lasting, mutually satisfying, and agree-able resolution to their differences. Especially by using objective criteria, both sides can see, appreciate, and negotiate helpful, nonemotional, or nonprejudiced data to guide their interactions and conclusions.

A WALK IN THE WOODS

Marcus and Dorn, two Harvard School of Public Health Professors and nationally known leadership consultants, devised what they call "A Walk in the Woods." This strategy gains its name from an experience that the Russians and the Americans had during the complex Strategic Arms Limitation Talks (SALT) II talks in Geneva. Taking an informal break, the two main negotiators actually took a walk in the woods, where they began to get to know each other better, discussing, among other things, family, and then they moved on to their views on the intrica-cies of the negotiations. "This (approach) employs a series of steps to motivate and guide interest-based negotiations," which in the end leads toward collaborative solutions.

The four steps leading toward a solution are to identify:

- Self-interests
- Enlarged interests
- Enlightened interests
- Aligned interests

Self-Interests

- Identify individual motivations (a unidimensional, one-sided perspective).
- State why your party has come to the table.
- Describe who is involved and who are the other stakeholders.
- Each side listens attentively, participating in an active discussion to understand the other's motives (recall Lewicki) and interests (recall Fisher and Ury).
- As a consequence, each side hears and becomes more aware of the broader scope of issues than they previously thought of or appreciated.
- The discussion no longer is a unidimensional one but in fact becomes multidimensional.

Enlarged Interests

- Each side states his or her agreements and differences, hopefully seeing more commonality than disagreement.
- Similar interests are clearly stated, leading to more possible options and solutions.
- Issues are reframed.
- Misunderstandings are identified (recall Lewicki) and resolved.

Enlightened Interests

- When blocked in discussions, participants are encouraged to generate "inside the box" and "outside the box" ideas to address the problem.
- Discuss feasibility and applicability of each reframed, mutually acceptable, and beneficial option.
- More data and possibilities are advanced to build agreement.

Aligned Interests

- Identify what each stakeholder is willing to give up for what he or she can receive as a result of win-win thinking.
- Reframe interests so that they are aligned with the other party's interests.
- Clearly define achievement and success.

CASE STUDY

Health Care Pays Inc. (HCPI) is a 10-year-old healthcare corporation that includes a 200-bed hospital, a 95-bed nursing home, and a 180-employee home healthcare agency. The latter was just acquired this past year. To all members of the healthcare community, HCPI looks like a growing organization and a wonderful facility for patient care and for employees to work. HCPI shareholders are pleased with the return on their investment.

Two of the original four founders still work at HCPI: Andre LeBeau, the chief executive officer (CEO) and president of the corporation, who earns $425,000 per year, and Lee Martin, the chief operating officer (COO) of the corporation, who earns $300,000 per year. Martin is extremely displeased with his salary. He sees money as a reflection of work worth, status, and dedication. He has strived very hard these past 10 years and considers himself an invaluable resource to HCPI. He wants to increase his compensation and is angry that the other founder, LeBeau, earns $125,000 more. Martin realizes that LeBeau's position is more important but does not think that it is worth $125,000 more. Martin wants at least $55,000 more this year, bringing him up to $355,000.

LeBeau feels confident in his knowledge bases, especially after earning both an MBA and a healthcare management degree at Harvard. He feels self-assured and confident that with his abilities and skills, he can deal with possible fluctuations in the economy and reimbursements, the higher cost of materials and personnel, and other uncertainties. His vision for the corporation foresees continued and sustainable growth.

The Board of Directors is pleased with the corporation's performance to date. It maintains a sharp eye on fiscal issues, especially given the current economic climate that has decreased the number and size of federal grants. Nevertheless, the board remains cautious about the uncertain future of healthcare finances caused by ongoing government changes. It is seeking to expand the corporation by building a possible five-floor addition to the hospital and by creating Centers of Excellence in cancer treatment and women's health.

Martin, who never misses an opportunity to remind people of his founder status, manages and oversees 10 departments in the hospital, as well as the COOs of the other portions of the corporation. He has resolved many complex situations in the past and is fairly popular among his colleagues.

Yet, LeBeau, his boss, would say that Martin's performance has been mixed over the years. Sometimes Martin has been very successful because he has a broad knowledge of what's going on and has the abilities to manage changes, conflict, and growth. At other times, he has only been moderately effective. Then, too, Martin can be sharp-tongued and overly critical at times. Overall, however, he is valued.

Martin has a cousin on the Board of Directors and is very friendly with at least four other members. He actively participates in the community, sits on two other boards, and is seen as a civic leader. His family has lived in the community for three generations. He recently went to the CFO for her opinion and data about what she thought he should be earning. Although not totally backing Martin's request, she was optimistic and encouraging.

The nurses in the corporation's facilities do not belong to a union, but LeBeau knows that they are disgruntled, with salary and related work concerns. He fears that they may try to organize a union if their issues are not addressed.

Questions

- How should LeBeau and Martin begin their negotiations?
- What are their positions and interests?
- What tactics should each one use regarding all the issues HCPI faces?
- What pressures might LeBeau feel at this point to either give in to Martin's demands or simply quash Martin's request for now?
- What process should LeBeau and Martin follow in trying to reach some sort of settlement, if both of them agree to try to work something out?

SUGGESTED READING

Fisher R, Ury W, Patton B. *Getting to Yes: How To Negotiate Agreement Without Giving In*. 2nd ed. New York, NY: Penguin Books; 1991.

Lewicki R, Saunders DM, Barry B. *Essentials of Negotiation*. 5th ed. New York, NY: McGraw-Hill; 2010.

Marcus LJ, Dorn B, McNulty EJ. *Renegotiating Health Care, Resolving Conflict to Build Collaboration*. 2nd ed. San Francisco, CA: Jossey-Bass; 2011.

Robbins S, Judge TA. *Organizational Behavior*. 12th ed. Upper Saddle River, NJ: Pearson Education; 2007.

12

Communication Skills

SHRUTI MALIK AND JOSEPH S. SANFILIPPO

KEY POINTS

- Strong communication is the basis of the physician-patient relationship and should be established at the first visit.
- Physicians should strive to be mindful of a patient's concerns and fully engage the patient during the course of the patient encounter.
- Always outline the goals for an office visit so that realistic expectations can be determined.
- Communication can be a tool to build trust in the relationship between patient and healthcare provider.
- Extra time and focus is often necessary for obtaining informed consent, delivering bad news, or discussing medical errors.

BASIC KEY COMPETENCIES FOR PATIENT COMMUNICATION

The primary competencies needed for strong patient communication are well outlined by Wendy Leebov and Carla Rotering (see Suggested Reading). These include mindfulness, strong openings and closings, engaging patients, effective explanations, empathy, collaboration, and knowing how to approach difficult conversations. These will be discussed further as the chapter progresses and discusses key components each physician should be aware of during a patient interaction.

Optimizing the Office Visit

A new patient visit is the ideal time to establish good rapport with your patient. This visit will set the stage for a long-term relationship and should be treated as such. There is tremendous value in taking the time to introduce yourself, make eye contact, and shake hands with the patient. The American Academy on Physician and Patient described the framework of a medical visit to include three functions: to gather information, build a relationship, and educate the patient. All of these require a good communication base.

> The first key competency involves the **mindfulness** of the physician.

To communicate effectively, healthcare providers need to give patients their undivided attention. With increased patient volume and the advent of electronic charting, it may be tempting to transcribe a patient's history as they speak with you. But it is important to remember that your time with the patient is limited, and focusing completely while he or she voices those concerns optimizes the patient encounter. Your patient has likely waited for some time to see you as well, and he or she deserves the physician's complete focus. According to one study, doing so early in the visit improves patient satisfaction and adds only *six seconds* to the visit time.

A sincere effort to communicate with the patient does take time. Patients are more likely to feel that their physician understands and empathizes with their situation when they are able to provide that time. Evidence shows that the amount of time spent with a patient during routine visits in a primary care setting can also be an independent factor in predicting malpractice claims.

However, in the evolving healthcare setting, time is a precious commodity as physicians are trying to accommodate more patients in the finite hours of the day. Most physicians would like to spend more time with their patients but are limited by the number of patients they must see in order to maintain a practice. Therefore, it is important to optimize the time spent in a patient's room.

> As with any facet of communication, both the **opening and closing of the conversation** must leave a positive impression.

It is best to begin with a warm greeting and genuine concern for the patient's problem as discussed earlier. It is also wise to outline the purpose of the visit and prioritize the concerns of a patient. Focusing on the key complaints will allow for a successful visit while emphasizing that the latter concerns can be discussed at a subsequent time. This also helps immensely in the timing of the visit and setting realistic expectations for a single encounter. Higher satisfaction scores have resulted when the duration of the visit is closer to the anticipated visit time. Always remind a patient that you, the physician, are more than happy to discuss the latter concerns more fully at a later time but would like to focus on any initial complaints first and foremost.

Engaging patients and their families is the first step to empowering the patient in the physician's care. As paternalistic medicine is becoming more obsolete, patients endeavor to take a more active role in their

> To ensure both good patient care and communication, patients must be engaged in the visit.

health. This increased involvement has been shown to improve patient outcomes as well. Encouraging patients to speak up during the visit allows them to voice their concerns and questions freely as well as enabling them to believe they also have control over the visit.

One study noted that most physicians interrupt and redirect patients after *23 seconds on average.* Doing so may not only make it more difficult to obtain a through history but also prohibit patients from voicing their primary concerns at the onset of the encounter. Patients are often aware of the time constraints physicians face and do not want to be viewed as a burden. If their healthcare provider appears rushed, it may be more difficult for them to express their questions and concerns. Focus group studies have demonstrated that even highly educated and affluent patients have difficulty asking questions and inquiring about treatment options for fear of being viewed as a "difficult" patient.

Simple ways to involve patients include the use of language that engages the patient such as "we" and "together" when discussing the plan of care. This can be expanded by verbalizing the physician's rationale for testing and treatment. When electing a plan of care, the practitioner discusses his or her reasoning and what the test or treatment entails in simple terms without depending on medical terminology. This not only gives patients a thorough understanding of the plan but allows them to understand and ask educated questions if they arise.

Patient understanding and *effective explanations* can also be improved using the "ask-tell-ask" model. After allowing for questions, it is good remember to discuss his or her reasoning simply. Be sure to pause for questions if patients appear confused so as to better explain a point before moving on to the next part of the conversation. Providers should finish by asking open-ended questions and allowing patients to review the explanation in their own words.

When closing a visit, physicians/providers should be sure to summarize the visit, including the topics that have been discussed and the plan going forward. It is important to then evaluate patients' understanding of that discussion, the next steps, and allow for any questions at that time.

> Use "we" or "together" when discussion the plan of management.
>
> Explain "why."
>
> Use the "ask-tell-ask" model.
>
> Summarize topics for the patient.

Communication as a Way to Build Trust

The quality of a relationship between patients and healthcare professionals can be a significant segment of the overall treatment. If patients have confidence in their healthcare provider, this facilitates their compliance with the treatment plan.

Trust is perhaps the most important component in the healthcare provider-patient relationship. The fact that one is a good a communicator reflects respect for the patient. Taking into consideration the opinions, point of view, concerns, and feelings of the patient is a wise approach. The good communicator listens to the patient and makes every effort to understand the patient's point of view even if the healthcare professional may not agree with it. This is especially important when religious or ethical beliefs may have an impact on the care of a patient.

Empathy on behalf of the physician can strengthen the patient relationship; therefore, it is important to communicate this throughout the entire encounter. Building rapport with patients at the beginning of a visit has been shown to improve patient satisfaction. Merely recognizing and validating these feelings will help build a strong foundation of trust.

Another less obvious key principle is the **collaboration** of the healthcare team. Here, the focus is on the ability of the physician to communicate with the patient care team, solidify a plan, and relay it to the patient. Physicians should be responsible for coordinating patient care and openly communicating with the nurses, office staff, subspecialists, and other providers. Remember, it will inevitably be more difficult for a patient to contact multiple members of the care team. By advocating for the patient and acting as the team leader, primary physicians can ensure that all providers are working together and act as the chief contact for patient communication.

Suggestions for improving a physician practice are provided in Box 12.1

SPECIAL SITUATIONS

Informed Consent

One of the key pillars of informed consent in medicine is strong communication. When a healthcare provider begins to discuss medical treatment or surgical intervention, it is important to acknowledge that, even in well-established relationships, patient stress and anxiety can lead to suboptimal discussions. A physician must remember that patients may still be coping with a diagnosis or a recommendation to proceed with invasive testing or surgery. Allowing them to vocalize their concerns prior to beginning the consent process may alleviate that barrier and allow for a better discussion. (See Chapter 6.)

It is beneficial to start with inquiring what patients already know about the intended treatment or procedure to establish a baseline for the conversation. From

---

Box 12.1   IMPROVING THE EFFICIENCY OF YOUR PRACTICE

- Do-it-yourself video
- Good medicolegal documentation
- Document viewing of video or CD-ROM
- Lend out videotapes or CD-ROMs
- Color-coded prescriptions pads
- Educational materials
- Detailed informed consents
- Call key patients at home
- Market to referring physicians

---

this point, healthcare providers can build on that knowledge base and better elaborate on the risks, benefits, and alternatives of the treatment. It is beneficial to occasionally stop for a few moments during these discussions to allow for questions or comments. If patients appear to be confused or distant from the conversation, it is best to pause and ask if they have any questions at that point. If patients have family members or friends with them, physicians should be sure to engage them when speaking or asking for questions because they may be thinking in a clearer capacity than patients.

Even the most simple procedure to a physician can be a big step for the person undergoing it. At the end of the discussion, the physician should ask the patient to summarize the procedure and the reasons for it in his or her. It is important that the patient sign the consent form only after all questions have been answered to his or her satisfaction. Ensuring a thorough understanding of the treatment sets the stage for more insightful questions, discussion, and a truly informed consent process.

Difficult Conversations

Delivering bad news may be one of the hardest things for any healthcare provider to do. This can range from delivering bad news to disclosing medical errors. Most often, difficult conversations revolve around the former. Having an established relationship is a strong asset in this setting. If a patient already trusts a physician, he or she is more likely to feel that the physician is acting in their best interest and will do everything necessary to remedy the mistake.

Bad news can encompass any number of things, including unexpected test results, a poor prognosis, or failed treatment. In these scenarios, taking additional time to allow for emotions and questions is very helpful. Start the discussion in an open and honest manner. Remember to assess what the patient already knows as a starting point. Transparency is an excellent tool for the healthcare professional to have in his or her armamentarium. A good healthcare provider lets the patient see through him or her and provides a comfort level for expressing thoughts and feelings. An empathetic humanistic approach on the part of the healthcare professional is always appropriate.

A number of training tools have been developed so that healthcare professionals approach a problem in an empathetic manner. This training, which centers on emotional intelligence, communication elements, social styles, and empathy, can be conveyed by practical workshops (Garcia; see Suggested Reading). Patient satisfaction scores are designed to reflect the empathetic approach of the healthcare professional.

Research finds that basic physical touch, such as a handshake or a comforting hand on the shoulder, cannot only provide comfort and foster trust but also cause patients to feel more satisfied with the visit. Remember to pause as needed during these conversations. As discussed earlier, reassessing the conversation from the patient perspective is necessary as grief or stress can cloud the clarity of the conversation. Otherwise, patients may not feel that the real issues were addressed.

It helps not to engage in "blocking," which is a more overt communication problem where the healthcare professional ignores the specific question, especially if it is difficult to answer. Being clear and honest with the patient can avoid this issue. These conversations may be difficult for a healthcare provider as well.

It is understood that some physicians may have difficulty talking about bad news. Common pitfalls regarding communication include physician domination of the conversion and premature reassurance. Each individual is different. Although some patients need occasional reassurance, this should only be provided when it is a realistic expectation. False encouragement can further damage the relationship between healthcare provider and patient. Other patients may prefer facts over reassurance and even view the latter as condescending. It is important to remain cognizant of the patient's needs and adjust as needed.

One of the most difficult discussions for a physician may be discussing medical errors. Whenever an error occurs in the medical team, the physician should take responsibility for the mistake and express apologies for the incident. (See Chapters 6 and 17.) Always be sure to discuss what will be done to correct the situation and discuss any changes that will be implemented to prevent future incidents, if applicable. Many hospitals or medical practices have legal counsel available for consultation if there is potential for litigation. It is advisable to meet with the legal representatives provided but to always remain honest with the patient. Maintaining that trust is the key to continuing a strong relationship in the future.

CASE STUDY

Ms. Manners comes to see you for a pelvic mass that requires surgical intervention. During the course of evaluation, you have made a distinct effort to have eye
contact and allow for questions. You have been diligent in reminding her that
you are more than happy to discuss concerns she has at a later time but initially
wanted to concentrate on the pelvic mass. You always have encouraged her to
voice concerns she has during office visits and you never appear "rushed." On two
occasions you made it a point to state "we" and used the word "together" in your
explanations of preoperative findings. Whenever you conveyed a point of concern,
you always would pause and allow her to react and ask any questions. During a
recent laparoscopic procedure, hysterectomy, a major vessel was accidentally lac-
erated, necessitating vascular surgical consultation; there is a high probability of
vascular compromise in one lower extremity. You now have the task of explaining
to her and her family the intraoperative events.

Questions

- Is Ms. Manners and her family less likely to proceed with litigation
  based on your effort to establish good rapport?
- Should you approach the discussion alone with the patient and her
  family or should you initially have risk management personnel present?
- What is the best way to convey what happened intraoperatively?
- What do you suggest as a follow-up to this conversation?

SUGGESTED READING

Barrier PA, Li JT-C, Jensen NM. Two words to improve physician-patient communica-
    tion: what else? *Mayo Clin Proc.* 2003;78:211–214.
Bauman J, Kapo J. Vital communication skills at the end of life. *Curr Probl Cancer.*
    2011;35:310–316.
Frosch DL, et al. Authoritarian physicians and patients' fear of being labeled
    'difficult' among key obstacles to shared decision making. *Health Aff.*
    2012;31(5):1030–1037.
Garcia D, Bautista O, Verereo L, Coll O, Vassena R, Vernaeve V. Training in empathic
    skills improves the patient-physician relationship during the first consultation in a
    fertility clinic. *Fertil Steril.* 2013;99(5):1413–1418.
Leebov W, Rotering C. *The Language of Caring Guide for Physicians: Communication
    Essentials for Patient-Centered Care.* St. Louis, MO: Leebov Golde Group; 2012.

Levinson W, Roter DL, Mullooly JP, Dull VT, Frankel RM. Physician-patient communication the relationship with malpractice claims among primary care physicians and surgeons. *JAMA*. 1997;277(7):553–559.

Markides M. The importance of good communication between patient and health professionals. *J Pediatr Hematol Oncol*. 2011;33:S123–S125.

Marvel MK, Epstein RM, Flowers K, Beckman HB. Soliciting the patient's agenda: have we improved? *JAMA*. 1999;281(3):283–287.

Stewart MA. Effective physician-patient communication and health outcomes: a review. *CMAJ*. 1995;152(9):1423–1433.

13

Competitive Marketing

LINDA MACCRACKEN AND RICHARD B. SIEGRIST, JR.

KEY POINTS

- Engaging consumers directly to retain patients and attract prospects has become a key anchor in healthcare organizations because of the need to grow volume amid shifting physician employment and limited access via insurance coverage plans. Increasing business among loyal patients is a faster and less expensive way to boost business.
- Expectations that consumers will stay loyal to providers without responding to online searching and shopping is an invitation to the competition to steal patients with more accessible, personalized service.
- Competitive marketing is effective when service delivery marketing is organized to understand and respond to patient needs and desires in a way that differentiates the health system's strengths compared to the competition.
- Stronger marketing results come from focus on personalized customer insight and outreach using multiple channels among traditional media, personalized outreach, and digital access.

As healthcare organizations seek a competitive advantage in their local markets, they need a greater focus on competitive knowledge and competitive marketing to grow targeted business and increase in-network use and consumer loyalty. Marketing is essential to engaging consumers who increasingly switch providers; select multiple providers for care; and given the increase in out-of-pocket healthcare costs, have greater financial incentives to shop. As healthcare organizations explore new methods of attracting and retaining patients and change their service models to reflect consumer needs and wants, they must identify new ways through a variety of channels, using both traditional and new media, to market their services, medical practices, and provider network.

Healthcare organizations can achieve a competitive advantage through effective competitive marketing.

A healthcare organization with the ability to meet the needs of the market (in terms of services, features, benefits, and pricing) can significantly benefit from a competitive marketing program. The focus of competitive marketing is to engage customers, driving them to select their services over competitors, based on reasons that the customer values most.

Healthcare delivery by hospitals and their associated providers is a mature business with increasing competition. Typically, this occurs as margins decline amid only small pockets of growth, driving a need to revitalize the services and brand(s). If healthcare organizations were new to the market, they would be able to focus marketing efforts on mere education and how to use the services for customer benefits. But that is no longer a viable marketing strategy in most situations.

Providers are shifting their service offerings, adding virtual care to expanded outpatient networks and already declining inpatient services. Innovative care and payment incentives are driving down demand to spur an intensely competitive race among providers for patients. These factors will cause marketing to focus more on channel innovation via expanding physician partnerships, narrow networks with limited provides and new types of service development to entreat customer participation. This focus will require appropriate alignment with the organization's strategy and capabilities to bring patients to services that have capacity and are customer decision sensitive.

NEW CHALLENGES DRIVE A FOCUS ON COMPETITIVE MARKETING

A focus on competitive marketing has become crucial for healthcare organizations over the past decade as they seek to attract and retain profitable fee-for-service business and effectively cross-sell or redirect risk-reimbursed patients. There are several reasons for this new emphasis.

Increased Competition from Non–Acute Care Providers

Many non–acute care providers now have the ability to provide services that can replace acute care or even traditional physician appointments. These competitors

include urgent care centers, retail providers (such as those found in drug-
stores), and self-service online care via
the Internet.

> Increased competition, tiered networks,
> lack of patient engagement, and diffi-
> cult physician relationships are some of
> the new challenges facing competitive
> marketing efforts.

Narrow Networks

Employer-based direct contracts are creating narrow networks with financial incentives to have lower copayments by using selected local providers. Recently, there has been a surge of narrow networks where providers contract directly with employers for specific services using a fixed payment rate for an episode of care (known as a bundled payment) or package deals on specific types of treatment. These narrow networks shift the marketing focus to in-contract prospects, rather than locally based residents. The Cleveland Clinic has arranged with Lowe's and WalMart for specific cardiology patient care, which means that employees would leave their local market to obtain care. Although these arrangements may not seem like large patient redirections, the out-of-market narrow networks remove typically profitable, commercially insured business from the local healthcare organization's market.

Tiered Networks

In insurance plans where hospitals and physicians are tucked into two or three networks, consumers then pay higher costs to use the higher cost providers who fall into a higher cost tier. This shifts marketing from a geographic focus to one that focuses on the patient's sensitivity to price. For certain services, patients may be comfortable with a provider in a lower cost tier, whereas for other services they may be able to be persuaded via marketing that the higher cost is justified by higher perceived value.

Need to Engage Primary Care Patients

Competitive marketing is critical for primary care providers. It serves as a means to find, reach, and engage patients to sustain the health system.

Physician Relations

Healthcare organizations must engage both primary and specialty care physicians, encouraging them to promote in-health system referrals. Marketing to consumers through physician practices is also an effective means to retain patient care in the health system network. Although keeping patients in the network is helpful by marketing to patients already using the system, competitive marketing must address keeping patient using the health system and preventing their service use from leaking outside the system—known as leakage. With increased risk-based payment contracts, effective physician and patient relations are even more crucial for the healthcare organization.

Overcoming Shortfalls in Care

As hospital management teams work to enhance performance and improve cost/quality ratings, new marketing strategies are necessary to emphasize a hospital's benefits and centers of excellence—to both patients and to their own provider network. This approach will help minimize leakage.

Satellite Locations

Some providers are placing satellite locations in far-reaching markets in pursuit of better population health. In several healthcare markets that enjoy a favorable payer mix, new acute care providers have launched freestanding emergency departments, specialty outpatient centers, and accessible physician practices.

New Partnerships

National health system affiliations with local providers have changed these providers from secondary competitors into portals for expert medical services. Healthcare organizations trying to win over consumers have to deeply reengage existing customers and acquire new ones to sustain business, even before considering reduced inpatient rates due to changes in medical practices and prevention effectiveness.

Marketing programs designed to meet these challenges head-on must strike a balance between satisfying consumers' individual wants and their clinically necessary needs to promote true engagement, compliance, and ultimately satisfaction and loyalty.

A SHIFT IN FOCUS FOR COMPETITIVE MARKETING

In the past, much of healthcare marketing has been based on (1) "selling" services not needed by consumers or (2) expensive promotions to the masses with a nonspecific message. Both of these approaches become an exercise in vanity and futility at excessive costs. Studies have shown that messaging about inaccessible or unwanted services does not work. Health systems need marketing programs that show they can fulfill consumers' desires and needs and deliver access by providing the right mix of coverage, price, schedule, and simplicity. Successful marketing must focus on what consumers want and need to buy.

During this shift, the market has also begun to acknowledge that different types of consumers make different decisions. Unique consumer groups show significant differences in healthcare use patterns. This divide has only increased through the introduction of the Internet to consumers. For example, baby boomers and senior citizens who did not grow up with the Internet and digital technology make decisions differently than younger people. Although older Americans do use the same technology, they might be considered digital "immigrants," whereas their younger counterparts, who grew

> Marketing competitively means engaging consumers in terms of what they want, need and value based on their consumer type. Those types include the greatest/silent generation, baby boomers, generation X, and millennials (generation Y).

up with it, are considered digital "natives." As a result, digital marketing reaches different generations in different ways. (See Chapter 10.)

As previously described, marketing competitively means engaging consumers in terms of what they want, need, and value. This engagement differs significantly by consumer group. Today, there are at least four unique types of consumer, using healthcare services in very different ways.

Greatest/Silent Generation

These older healthcare consumers (born before 1942) characteristically rely on their personal physicians to provide medical care direction, and they are prepared to seek information from and defer to their physician. Patient visits, in addition to being more frequent, are also typically longer, due to both clinical acuity and patient preferences around medical care. Most groups in this generation have rigid definitions of good service, and this definition of service—"the customer is always right"—also applies to the nonphysician components of the delivery system. This generation identifies only physicians and nurses as health professionals. Most of the people in this generation (nearly 75%) prefer health reminders via mail, with fewer than 20% preferring phone calls.

Baby Boomers

The largest population group (born 1943–1960), this generation values individual engagement in healthcare. When thinking about their health, these individuals tend to seek counsel from and bring information to the physician and then research physician recommendations. Baby boomers identify only physicians, physician assistants, and nurses as health professionals. This generation introduced the concept of "body age" versus real age (e.g., "I'm not winding down, I'm rewinding"). Another characteristic of this group is an interest in quality, as evidenced by use of third-party comparisons or ratings as a means of self-directing to specialists and providers. Many baby boomers are involved in decision-making for their aging parents while simultaneously informing the health needs of their own children. This multiple-generation healthcare decision-making can cause communication challenges for physician and hospital staff; patients may be expressing the values and concerns of a greatest/silent generation or millennial, whereas the primary healthcare decision-maker is expressing baby boomer values. Health reminders are most preferred by direct mail (40%), followed closely by telephone calls and then by e-mail. (See Chapter 10.)

Generation X

When it comes to healthcare, generation Xers (born 1961–1981) are characterized by an interest in being educated and involved. Relatively healthy as compared with older generations, they are notably curious and actively seek information. They assume physicians and staff are knowledgeable, and they have a strong interest in amenities. Consumers in this generation are more likely to switch physicians and/or hospitals based on their most recent experience, rather than their overall past experience. This group has more in common with the millennials than with the baby boomers. When generation Xers think about medical professionals, their definition is broad and includes nurse practitioners, physician assistants, insurance companies, and pharmacies. Health reminder preferences start with direct mail at more than 40%, followed by e-mail and then telephone messaging. (See Chapter 10.)

Millennials (Generation Y)

Millennials (born since 1982) access the healthcare system through primary care providers, urgent care centers, and obstetricians-gynecologists (OB/GYNs), with a higher likelihood for women to use OB/GYNs as primary care physicians. This reflects their relatively low utilization of inpatient and outpatient services. When they do use inpatient services, they tend to come through the maternity or emergency department. Many groups in this generation use and appreciate technology and a positive, personal relationship with their physician. They value information, and they seek it from multiple sources. People in this generation are more likely to switch physicians and/or hospitals if they lose confidence in the care provided, based on their most recent experience. Two in five (40%) prefer text messages for health reminders, followed by telephone messaging and direct mail.

COMMON MISCONCEPTIONS ABOUT HEALTHCARE MARKETING

To better understand the growing importance of competitive marketing on a healthcare organization's success, it is necessary to debunk some common myths and review the necessary components of healthcare system marketing.

> Common misperceptions include that marketing alone will overcome mediocre service quality, that marketing is not worth the investment or that marketing is easy when you have a good product or service.

These misconceptions include:

1. When healthcare providers have insufficient quality factors to attract and retain patients, they can increase patient flow through marketing.

Viewing marketing as simply a selling tool assumes that the marketing process starts first with the needs of the providers at the expense of the needs of the patients or consumers. However, this is backward. This misconception assumes that providers who market have no other way to find, reach, and engage patients, when in fact healthcare delivery programs change at such a rapid rate that patients *need* education to know how and where to access services. Thus, the correct marketing cycle starts with a focus on the needs and desires of the customers (including patients and their families), payers, and providers.

Effective marketing does not mean promoting products and services to consumers who may not want or need them. Effective marketing starts with the needs and desires of consumers, communicates services priced at feasible levels in accessible locations, and then conveys a message of relevant information to the targeted customer in the medium that they are most likely to access.

2. Marketing is wasteful—it is just an expensive means to engage patients who would have come anyway. Patients will continue to visit the same physician or provider regardless of their desires and needs.

However, studies show that consumers are less loyal to healthcare providers than in the past. Given the degree of population relocation, physician retirements, employer-sponsored insurance shifts, and higher-deductible health plans, consumers have many reasons to consider shifting primary care providers or changing hospitals. Consumers today shop around for healthcare services—often shifting providers even *after* a diagnosis to seek elective treatment based on a variety of factors such as seeking a second option that they may find more acceptable or less costly to them.

Adding to this challenge is the increasing transparency of cost and quality, both major factors in provider selection. Payers and employers are making cost calculations and quality ratings available to their enrollees as a means to limit or reduce the rate of spending. The patient who has to get a procedure has several options and can now see those options more clearly. With a potential out-of-pocket cost difference of $1,800 for a colonoscopy, for example, a patient may ask: "Is this worth $1,800? What else can I do with this money?"

Time-starved consumers want fast, easily accessible services. Providers who do not offer this capability, such as with urgent care or walk-in appointments, will miss out on their business. High-deductible insurance coverage has also forced consumers to consider out-of-pocket costs in their decisions about using health services. For example, an evening illness or injury could either cost (1) a $100 copay, a 1-hour wait, and 30 minutes of drive time each way or (2) a $50 credit card charge, along with no wait, travel, or parking with an online provider such as Doctor On Demand. Unless the patient perceives a much greater value from the first option, they are likely to choose the second. At the very least, they weigh different options.

Because of the increased transparency and competition—factors that go into each and every healthcare decision—healthcare organizations must engage consumers by providing information related to the overarching value that the service provides. Even more crucial to correcting this misconception is the need to address the fact that advertising and promotion are the last steps in the process, *after* the services have been defined. Once services are defined, based on consumer need, price point, and location, then promotions can begin. No amount of marketing can change the fact that a healthcare organization does not offer sufficient value to its prospective consumers.

3. Marketing cost too much.

Although a health system's marketing communications budget may seem extensive due to the mix of staff versus purchased services, these budgets usually require a higher proportion of non–full-time equivalent expense than a typical clinical department.

Marketing budgets are influenced by market challenges and/or campaign targets. A healthcare organization attempting to gain market share in a heavily competitive market is likely measuring a number of factors, including media presence, public relations presence, and competitor tactics—all necessary components for effective counter-positioning. The marketing team needs to address this question, "How can we create a presence comparable to or better than our competitors that leads to effective messaging and target audience engagement?"

Another key driver of the marketing budget is the determination of the covered market. For a healthcare organization striving to double its target customer acquisition to fit a growing network or a national niche presence, the incremental cost of reaching those markets must be incorporated into a budget. The comparative measure of top performers, market share leaders, or new movers in key service lines would also be drivers of budget resourcing.

Industry standards for marketing budgets serve as an excellent baseline. The American Hospital Association's Society for Healthcare Strategy and Market Development 2013 study shows that overall marketing and communications budgets average 0.4%, with a range of 0.2% to 0.7%. Factors such as target market, objectives, brand and product life cycles, and target outcomes influence effective resource allocation decisions.

   4. Marketing will be successful if a product is high quality.

A good product does not necessarily translate to financial success. There are three marketing approaches that health systems often take: the *product-driven approach,* the *sales approach,* and the *market-driven approach.* Typically, concerns over sales or product focus have missed prioritizing the needs of the consumer. Lessons learned from the industry help provide the context about why healthcare organizations should take a primarily market-driven approach.

The product-driven approach prioritizes internal production or operations, assuming that the service quality will be sufficient for service selection and retention. Although this approach provides the best quality (hiring excellent clinicians and building centers of excellence are essential for a health system to thrive), it does not address much of what the market looks for in choosing a provider.

The sales-driven approach prioritizes pushing existing services or products on consumers, regardless of whether there is a clinical need or desire (e.g., encouraging consumers to schedule tests). This approach usually involves offering special pricing for a limited period of time. Additionally, pricing-centered healthcare tactics are usually not effective, given the common expectation of consumers that the cost will be covered. The market-driven approach prioritizes the needs of consumers and buyers and then serves to match such needs to service design, financial access, location, and messaging. The healthcare organization's sensitivity to both consumer (primary) and market sizing (secondary) data to identify demand may show different results than what a company may expect.

Apple, one of the most valuable companies in the world, learned a valuable lesson with its Newton personal computing system. Although the Newton may have been a great computer, its launch was a miserable failure because it did not prioritize the needs of the technology consumer. Postlaunch, consumers determined that it was too expensive and too complicated to use. Apple's true turnaround took place after Steve Jobs took over as chief executive officer—he changed direction toward a market-driven approach. Rather than developing and marketing a good *product,* Jobs focused on solving and addressing a market *problem* (the lack of an easy-to-use digital music player). The first-generation iPod was only the beginning for Apple; the company took the same approach to develop its next-generation iPods—and eventually iPhones and iPads.

Moving beyond these common misperceptions, we can explore how best to develop an effective competitive marketing approach.

CORE COMPONENTS OF COMPETITIVE MARKETING

Strategic marketing within a healthcare organization is not just the responsibility of the marketing team. It is a joint effort that also includes the service delivery team, the pricing/payment team, and the physician or ambulatory network. The structure of the marketing team varies by healthcare organization, but there are several core components that set a strong foundation for ensuring that the health system has a consumer-driven approach to its marketing.

Applying a Market-Driven Approach

Core components of competitive marketing are (1) a market-driven approach, (2) a structured marketing plan, (3) executive commitment, (4) an integrated communications plan, and (5) meaningful evaluation metrics.

Armed with consumer priorities and insights, this responsive marketing approach calls for the examination and shaping of the marketing plan components to respond to customer needs. The traditional marketing components of product, place, price, and promotion shift a bit in application to the healthcare organization. The shifts take place given the target customers' insulation from being a fully engaged buyer due to sharing the role with their employer (for employer-sponsored insurance), the exchange (for public and private exchanges), or the government (Medicare and Medicaid). The marketing plan focuses on the target customer population and their needs. From there the marketing components around a customer-centered engagement approach link valued and needed services that relate to the patients' needs, desires, and interests.

Many marketing teams prioritize specific services for customer prospect outreach and engagement. These services are prioritized based on quality outcomes, profitable performance, available capacity, and delivering an optimal patient experience. The key is to market to target customers for target services as well as establish the brand for the service portfolio. Virginia Commonwealth University Medical Center established a brand around their innovative research with "every day a new discovery" as their tagline. This campaign, in two years, moved the community perception of them to being the leading quality provider in the Richmond, Virginia, market.

The attention to locations and distribution channels is essential to ensure patient access. The physician network is a distribution channel for the hospital's acute care services. The primary care physician office locations are essential to serving local populations. Distribution channels also consider the degree of physician loyalty. For primary care physicians whose work is divided among multiple health systems, the marketing and physician relations teams focus on marketing through the practices directly to the health system, with the goal that patients ask for inpatient services. For the splitting specialists, the marketing and physician relations teams focus on marketing the health system to the specialists. In this regard, most marketing activities include both a direct-to-consumer and a direct-to-physician set of tactics.

Competitive marketing also calls for tactics that deal with attention to consumer access through insurance coverage, with attention to direct payment of deductibles and copayments. If demand is a function of what services are covered or of payment sensitivity, the marketing outreach tactics need to integrate consumer willingness to pay for services. The Affordable Care Act has expanded coverage for primary care and preventive care. With additional coverage comes a greater consumer willingness to use services.

Customer acquisition and retention are essential elements in competitive marketing. Many marketing teams are tracking new patient acquisition via tactics directed at new residents in the service area or attracting new patient appointments for employed physician groups.

Developing a Structured Marketing Plan

Like a business or capital investment plan, a structured marketing plan is a key step toward the effective implementation of a competitive marketing strategy. A formal marketing plan is absolutely crucial to identify market demand and assess competitive offerings. It also promotes goal alignment of the service delivery, finance, and payer contracting teams with the marketing team. Competitively effective marketing is based on aligned services, location, pricing, and promotion, matching the entire offering to the patient's needs and wants. The marketing plan should include several components (Table 13.1).

Obtaining Commitment from the Executive Team

A healthcare organization cannot sell a value that it does not have. To create an effective marketing program, the executive team of a healthcare organization needs to value and prioritize the customer. With a system-wide commitment to customer needs that starts at the top, marketing can play a crucial role in identifying and providing the internal and external customer voice.

TABLE 13.1   MARKETING PLAN COMPONENTS

Executive Summary	Current Situation	Market Opportunity	Market Strategy and Forecast	Marketing Innovation	Return on Investment
Market and business challenges	Historic data/drivers	Competitor profiles and service differentiation	Created service, price, location and promotion strategy	Digital channel outreach	Measures of success:
Target goals: volume and revenue, customer type, value proposition, campaign outreach, leads to conversions and budgeted resources	Current profile of service customer, payer and service mix	Strengths, weaknesses, opportunities, threats (SWOT)	Value proposition of new offerings	Sales outreach to target specialists	Leads
	Targeted customer base	Assessment of current service with responsive tactical assessment and challenges	Communication and sales channels to acquire customers	Target physician referrals	Conversion rates
	Business volume/target customer, payer and service mix profile	Target customer needs assessment	Customer retention and service tactics	Customer experience strategies	New patients
	Strengths/weaknesses/opportunities/threats	Growth options to build business, including stealing from target competitors		Satisfaction strategy requirements	Channel value
	Channel access: payers, employers, primary care physicians, specialists, call centers				High value segments
					Profitable growth
					Market share
					Incremental revenue-to-marketing expense ratio

Promoting Customer Access

Customer access is clearly influenced by payment options and coverage. Extensive consumer research from multiple firms demonstrates increasing cost sensitivity that drives selection and switching. This growing difficulty in paying for care coincided with increasing consumer insurance copays and deductibles, and it led to an 80% increase in those who delayed or canceled physician visits for the next 3 months. Accordingly, an effective marketing strategy requires working with the health system's finance team to ensure that financial barriers to care are limited and addressed.

Nontraditional healthcare service organizations such as Walgreens and CVS have demonstrated success by expanding their health product and pharmacy operations to include walk-in clinics. These "health experts" promote accessible healthy products and services and offer retail care that substitutes a $45 visit for either a $120 physician office visit or a $1,200 emergency department visit. By demonstrating the benefits of accessible, self-serve medical care, these organizations have successfully taken the most common and least costly business away from higher-margin acute care services.

Even more compelling and competitively concerning is the success of online retail clinics such as American Well, MD-On-Demand, and One-Doctor. Through One-Doctor, for example, patients can receive physician consultations via the Web as easily as booking a hotel room online. These online clinics have been able to demonstrate the benefits of digitally accessible, on-demand medical services for patients willing to type in a credit card number. As consumers feel increasingly comfortable making their own healthcare decisions, the competition for their attention is becoming more intense, particularly when it comes to episodic, non–life-threatening care. Healthcare organizations must use effective competitive marketing strategies and tactics to engage consumers and help them recognize the value and importance of using their services.

There are many ways for more traditional healthcare organizations to position their offerings. Hospital emergency departments have the ability to provide assurance that they can treat severe health problems. Physicians' offices can position themselves as providers of integrated primary care, even during a walk-in or short-notice appointment. Retail providers with nurse practitioners or physician's assistants located in grocery or drug stores may position themselves as providers of accessible, limited-use services that are still covered by insurance. Online providers may position themselves as providers of medical care with no need for travel. As consumers pay an increasing share of their own healthcare costs, the concept of taking a half-day off work to see a favorite physician may begin to seem less and less feasible. Many of these consumers are more willing to simply search for an accessible office that offers convenient hours with a good clinician. When it comes to non–life-threatening care, convenience trumps tradition in today's market. The reasons for healthcare organizations to position their services as faster, better, and less expensive are becoming more and more compelling.

Implementing an Integrated Marketing Communications Capability

Given business requirements to profitably grow while attracting and retaining customers, the marketing capabilities must engage prospects while also cross-selling to existing patients and affiliates. Provider marketing teams are creatively engaging their prospect and patient audiences with a blend of holistic marketing activities, including events, sales channels, and digital and traditional marketing. Marketing's charge to grow the business in additional markets calls, amidst an increasing digitally engaged consumer base, calls for cost-effective marketing options. This includes marketing cost savings and provider marketing changes such as (1) personalized direct messaging to a target audience, (2) selective contact shifts from call center to self serve, and (3) compelling events that bridge education and entertainment as in-person offerings with cross-sell scheduling. Marketing budgets must be sufficient to engage prospects and patients with the brand, service line initiatives, and market expansion. Typically, the marketing budget stands out, with a much higher proportion of expenses devoted to non–full-time equivalent expenses than other hospital or health system departments. However, the investment in marketing is pegged as an investment in customer sustainability. An effective approach to marketing resource investment is to generate the evidence of additional appointments or contacts—by integrating calls to action in each impression to appointment centers. Another effective marketing focus is to capture the name and address of respondents to measure the "engagement" experience of the marketing activities. Typically, the marketing activities attributed to a high proportion of service line target patients are those offering stronger budget supports in a cost-pressured industry. Marketing programs are using a mix of marketing tactics that include traditional and new media tactics that demonstrate health system expertise and access. Effective marketing communications activities address the following outcomes:

- Creating brand awareness and selection interest. Consumers must know about the differentiated value that an organization or service offers to drive trial and selection.
- Offering compelling calls to action for service use. It is necessary to creatively convey value of each service, knowing that most consumers have multiple choices for alternative services. The rise of online physicians now means that patients can skip "going to the doctor," because they can use their phones or computers to obtain care. Offering an effective and compelling service with a unique and important value proposition is a test of marketing effectiveness, best measured by customer response.
- Creating a value-driven impression. Positioning customer-valued benefits through a variety of channels, from traditional communication to digital engagement media, is necessary for preference and selection.

- Being customer-centered to create an exceptional experience. A marketing capability must reflect the customer's sought value for the service. Although this will include channels and differentiation, the use of testimonials and storytelling is a compelling requirement to reflect a patient-centered experience.
- Creating calls to action. Marketing campaigns and messages are valuable when driving consumers to take action, make an appointment, or attend an event that is a key trigger for consumer decision-making.

Using Metrics to Size, Prioritize, Target, and Measure Return on Investment

The use of marketing metrics to generate prospects, target campaigns, and measure success are essential in developing an effective program. Quantitative criteria should be applied to marketing projects throughout the organization.

Marketing measurements must be sufficiently specific to encourage action. Without this clarity, marketing resources are wasted and too many or too few prospects are engaged. The use of marketing analytics to target and engage customers who are behaviorally, attitudinally, and clinically likely to seek a service is a cost-efficient way to engage customers. These metrics may include lead generation by content, channel and initiative, and social engagement demonstrated through social media and patient satisfaction.

CASE STUDY: COMPETITIVE MARKETING AT BOLTON HEALTH CARE

Mark Hilton is the Chief Marketing Officer at Bolton Health Care, responsible for setting the strategic marketing direction for the entire health system. Bolton Health Care is an integrated healthcare system, which includes the 350-bed Bolton Hospital; the 40-bed Bolton Rehab facility; and an affiliated medical practice, Bolton Medical Associates. The local three-county market also includes a competing community hospital that has a smaller employed physician specialty group. On the periphery of the market, nearly a 40-minute drive away, is a teaching hospital with a strong pediatric capability and a highly rated cardiology program. This teaching hospital boasts top hospital ratings for performance over the past 5 years.

Recent consumer and market share data show increasing patient outmigration to the teaching hospital and significant splitting among surgeons between Bolton and the local community hospital. The local community hospital has just established a pediatric specialty affiliation with locally based specialists. Bolton's goal is to focus on three strategic services—primary care physician practices, orthopedics, and bariatric services.

The two competitor hospitals have significant direct mail but vague television advertising as part of their marketing programs. However, Bolton Hospital has had stronger ratings in their three target service lines. In each service line, the physician leaders share the same goals for quality outcomes, financial outcomes, and volume gains. Hilton and his team are glad to have these service line leaders committed to fine-tuning their offerings to better meet consumer needs and deliver a superior patient experience.

In reviewing his situation, Hilton knows he cannot effectively promote Bolton as a leading brand without changes in hospital operations oriented toward improved value and outcomes. He considers how quickly he needs to introduce market-driven service line excellence programs in light of the health system's challenges of overall low patient satisfaction and mediocre quality ratings.

In addition, Hilton recognizes his plan would require a complete overhaul of how Bolton has traditionally done marketing. He would need to take his plan to the health system's executive team to secure both their approval and engagement.

Hilton has developed a list of questions to answer so that he and his team can develop an effective marketing plan for Bolton Healthcare.

Questions

- What approach should we take to ensure the service line team members are aligned in patient-centered care design and delivery to achieve high satisfaction ratings and strong quality performance?
- How should our marketing team be deployed to focus on the three strategic service lines of primary care, orthopedics and bariatrics?
- What information is needed about the competition and our comparative strengths and weaknesses in order for us to effectively compete?
- How should we address splitter physicians?
- What type of marketing approach should we follow and what specifically should we put in the marketing communications program?

SUGGESTED READING

Christensen CM, Cook S, Hall T. Marketing malpractice: the cause and the cure. *Harv Bus Rev.* 2005;83(12):74–83, HBR #R0512D.

Kotler P, Keller K. *A Framework for Marketing Management.* 6th ed. Upper Saddle River, NJ: Prentice Hall; 2014.

14

The Patient Experience

RICHARD B. SIEGRIST, JR.

KEY POINTS

- Improving the patient experience of care has become an important focus of healthcare organizations in the past decade because of the need to increase patient loyalty and to respond to government and private payer initiatives that reward higher patient satisfaction scores.
- There are a number of myths regarding patient satisfaction, such as the following: (1) very few patients fill out satisfaction surveys, (2) patients are generally unhappy with their care, and (3) patient satisfaction is primarily a popularity contest.
- Organizations can improve the patient experience by focusing on people (nurses, physicians, and staff), communication, and explanation and the culture of the organization.
- The patient's family can play an important role in how a patient perceives the experience at a healthcare facility, either directly through family comments to the patient or indirectly through the patient's view of how family members are treated.

Improving the patient experience of care has become an important focus of healthcare organizations in the last decade. There are several reasons for this new emphasis. First, nonhealthcare service organizations such as Ritz-Carlton, Amazon, Disney, and L.L. Bean have demonstrated the benefits of

There is a connection between patient satisfaction and quality of care. Patient satisfaction is not a popularity contest.

exceptional customer service in building customer loyalty and enhancing business success. As hospitals and other healthcare organizations have faced increasing financial pressures, attracting and retaining a loyal patient base has become a priority.

Second, recent studies have shown a connection between higher patient satisfaction with care and lower mortality rates, fewer patient malpractice suits, better patient compliance with recommended care, improved patient response to actual treatment, and stronger financial performance. Skeptics have criticized patient satisfaction measurement as little more than a popularity contest that can be easily manipulated and that bears no relationship to the true quality of care being delivered. These recent studies call that perspective into serious question.

Third, as part of its value-based purchasing initiative, the federal government (1) has required the comparative reporting of patient satisfaction for inpatient hospital care since 2008 and (2) began penalizing hospitals in 2013 financially for poor patient satisfaction results. In addition, private payers have been integrating patient satisfaction scores into their determination of network inclusion and provider reimbursement.

To better understand the growing importance of the patient experience to a healthcare organization's strategy, this discussion will review the history of patient satisfaction measurement, debunk some of the common myths regarding patient satisfaction, examine the process for enhancing the patient experience, and introduce the importance of effective family communication as part of the patient experience.

HISTORY OF PATIENT SATISFACTION MEASUREMENT IN HEALTHCARE

The formal measurement of patient satisfaction in healthcare organizations began in 1985 when Notre Dame professors Irwin Press, a medical anthropologist, and Rod Ganey, a sociologist and statistician, started Press Ganey. They brought the science of sound survey design and administration to healthcare.

Over the next decade and a half, more and more hospitals saw the internal value that could be gained from tracking their patient satisfaction and comparing it with other similar organizations. The number of companies providing services correspondingly grew to include such firms as National Research Corporation (NRC), Gallup, HealthStream, Professional Research Consultants (PRC), and Avatar.

Over that same period, the surveys administered expanded from just inpatient to emergency department, outpatient, ambulatory surgery, medical practice, and other areas. The sophistication of data collection, analysis, and reporting continued to increase.

The federal government first became actively involved in patient satisfaction measurement in 2002. That year, the Centers for Medicare and Medicaid Services (CMS) and the Agency for Healthcare Research and Quality (AHRQ) collaborated to research, develop, and test the Hospital Consumer Assessment of Healthcare Providers and Systems (HCAHPS) survey. HCAHPS is a standardized 27-question survey that is administered randomly to adult hospital inpatients after discharge either by approved vendors or by the hospital itself.

The HCAHPS survey was implemented by CMS in October of 2006, and the first public reporting of results occurred in March of 2008, with voluntary reporting by hospitals. Hospitals received a financial incentive for participating in HCAHPS starting in 2007 (i.e., pay for reporting). Not surprisingly, eligible hospital participation improved to essentially universal use soon thereafter.

> The federal government and health plans have introduced incentives for hospitals to improve the patient experience, and patient satisfaction scores have improved.

These financial incentives were further strengthened through the Affordable Care Act of 2010, under which hospital Medicare reimbursement was influenced by comparative performance and improvement on HCAHPS (i.e., pay for performance). Since HCAHPS results were first made publicly available, hospital scores overall have consistently increased with each new release of HCAHPS data.

Table 14.1 illustrates the kind of patient satisfaction information being made publicly available by CMS. It uses the three largest hospitals in Boston as an example for the period from October 2011 through September 2012.

COMMON MYTHS REGARDING PATIENT SATISFACTION MEASUREMENT

The first myth is that very few patients fill out satisfaction surveys. In many industries, the average response rate to customer satisfaction surveys is between 10% and 15%. However, in healthcare, the response rates are substantially higher, likely because of the importance of the healthcare experience compared to other non-healthcare products or services.

Looking at 2012 HCAHPS national results for hospital inpatient care, the average hospital response rate was 32%. Three fourths of the hospitals had response rates greater than 27%, and one fourth exceeded a 37% response rate. Healthcare survey response rates depend on the area surveyed. Emergency department, outpatient, and physician office response rates are typically lower than inpatient,

> A high percentage of inpatients complete patient satisfaction surveys (more than 30%) and patients are generally happy with the care they receive (70% give the hospital a top score).

TABLE 14.1   PATIENT SATISFACTION

Patient Satisfaction Metric	Massachusetts General	Brigham and Women's	Beth Israel Deaconess	National Average
Patients who rate the hospital 9 or 10 on a scale of 0 (lowest) to 10 (highest)	81%	81%	75%	70%
Patients who would definitely recommend the hospital to friends and family	90%	87%	80%	71%
Patients who report that their nurses "always communicated well"	81%	81%	80%	78%
Patients who report that their physicians "always communicated well"	81%	84%	81%	81%
Patients who report that the area around their room was "always" quiet at night	52%	55%	51%	60%

whereas ambulatory surgery response rates are comparable to inpatient rates. (See Chapter 7.)

A second myth is that patients who fill out surveys are generally unhappy with their care. Although this may be the case in nonhealthcare industries, it is decidedly not true in healthcare. Based on recent HCAHPS national results, 70% of patients rated their hospital 9 or 10 overall on a scale of 0 to 10, and 92% of patients rated their hospital a 7 or higher.

This positive experience in turn leads to a high level of recommendation of their hospital by patients. As many as 71% of patients nationally would definitely recommend the hospital to friends and family, and 95% would probably or definitely recommend the hospital to friends and family. Patients are generally pleased with the communication from nurses and physicians. In recent HCAHPS results, 78% of patients said their nurses always communicated well and 81% indicated their physicians always communicated well.

A third myth is that only very unhappy or very happy patients make comments on their surveys. One of the most useful aspects of a patient satisfaction survey may be the comments that patients make on the survey. Although numerical ratings are important, the comments can provide deeper insights for the hospital into what is leading to high or low ratings overall or in a particular area. If only very unhappy or very happy patients were to take the time to add comments, then the comments would be anecdotal and potentially misleading. However, this is not the case.

> About 50% of patients completing a satisfaction survey provide written comments. Those comments are an underutilized resource for improving the patient experience.

Almost 50% of patients take the time to add comments on inpatient surveys, for an average of almost three comments per survey. A recent analysis indicated that patients who gave lower ratings tended to add written comments somewhat more frequently, 59% of surveys, as compared with 47% for patients who gave medium ratings and 45% who gave higher ratings. Given the preponderance of medium and high ratings mentioned earlier, a vast majority of the comments come from patients who are generally happy with their care.

These comments are a rich, often underutilized resource for healthcare institutions to better understand how they can improve patient satisfaction. Sentiment analysis is a new scientific approach to comment interpretation that is starting to be applied in healthcare to gain deeper insights into what patients are saying. It categorizes verbatim comments into meaningful categories and measures how strongly the patient feels using natural language processing to complement the numerical ratings. In essence, it translates unstructured text into structured data for more sophisticated analysis of comment themes and sentiment.

Another myth is that patient satisfaction is primarily a popularity contest because patients cannot evaluate the quality of care that is being delivered. Although patients clearly do not understand the technical details of care, their perceptions of quality from what they see, hear, and feel can be remarkably accurate. Patients seem to be able to distinguish reasonably well between friendliness and competence.

As mentioned earlier, studies have shown that organizations with higher patient satisfaction tend to have higher staff satisfaction, lower mortality rates, fewer patient lawsuits, better patient compliance with recommended care,

> Healthcare organizations can and have dramatically improved their patient satisfaction scores. The Cleveland Clinic is a prime example.

better patient response to actual treatment, and stronger financial performance. At the end of the day, the patients' perception of their care matters from both service and quality perspectives.

A fifth myth is that an organization cannot improve patient satisfaction scores significantly, except over a longer period of time. It is clearly not easy to dramatically improve patient satisfaction scores over a relatively short period of time. It requires a true commitment throughout the organization, constant attention to results, and usually a big change in the organization's culture. Yet, organizations have demonstrated that it can be done.

The Cleveland Clinic is a prime example. As a major academic medical center, it has a long-standing reputation for clinical excellence, consistently being ranked in the top of such surveys such as one in US News and World Report. But until recently, it had not distinguished itself in patient satisfaction. When HCAHPS results were first publicly released in 2008, only 63% of patients from the Cleveland Clinic gave it a top box score of 9 or 10 as an overall rating, putting the hospital around the 55th percentile. By 2013, those results had risen to 82% of patients or the 92nd percentile. Similarly, scores for nurses who "always communicated well" improved from 63% to 81%, and those for physician communication rose from 72% to 82%.

The final myth is that if an organization builds a nice new building, patient satisfaction scores will go up. It is easy to use the lack of recent capital investment in newer facilities or overutilized capacity as reasons for low satisfaction scores. Although it may help in certain circumstances, spending more money will not naturally bring about improved patient satisfaction. Surprisingly, it can lower satisfaction scores in the short term as staff gets used to working in the new facilities or as bottlenecks are moved from one location to another.

If the solution is not more bricks and mortar, what is it? It is relatively simple in concept, albeit difficult to implement:

- It is about the people—nurses, physicians, and staff.
- It is about communication and explanation.
- It is about the culture.

People, communication, and culture, not new buildings or technology, are the keys to improving the patient experience.

As illustrated by the experience of Cleveland Clinic and a number of other healthcare organizations, patient satisfaction can be dramatically improved if one looks beyond the myths to the reality of what can and should to be done to enhance the patient experience.

ENHANCING THE PATIENT EXPERIENCE

As you would expect, there is no one formulaic way to enhance the patient experience. However, there are several core principles that set an organization on the right path to improvement.

First, it is essential to have commitment from the chief executive officer and other senior management to the importance of the patient experience that is demonstrated consistently through their words and actions. This commitment is often formally expressed in the organization's strategy or mission statements, incorporated into executive bonuses tied to satisfaction scores and reflected in the agendas for board and senior leadership meetings. However, unless clinical and nonclinical staff throughout the organization widely recognize this commitment from senior leadership to an excellent patient experience, it is not likely to be an effective motivator.

Second, management and staff throughout the organization need to be held accountable for improving patient satisfaction. This accountability needs to go beyond simply the setting of goals for improvement to influencing how employees are selected, compensated and recognized within the organization. It needs to not just affect leadership or department managers but the staff who interact with patients on a daily basis.

Third, patient satisfaction should be measured on a regular basis, with the results shared throughout the organization on a transparent basis. This measurement needs to be at a detailed enough level to encourage concrete action. Without this type of transparency, it is difficult for an organization to maintain the awareness necessary to highlight issues and monitor improvement in addressing them.

Finally, the organization's culture needs to be focused around the patient experience, not just with patient experience being another problem to be dealt with. Although often difficult, cultural change within an organization to that patient-centered approach, can result in significant improvements in patient satisfaction as well as concurrent improvement in physician, nurse and other staff satisfaction. One of the biggest drivers of patient satisfaction is whether the patient feels that the people they interact with are effective in communicating with them and in explaining what is happening. Communication is a cornerstone of an effective culture.

IMPORTANCE OF FAMILY COMMUNICATION

The patient's family can play an important role in how a patient perceives his or her experience at a healthcare facility, either directly through family comments to the patient or indirectly through the patient's view of how his

> Effective communication with a patient's family members not only lessens family member anxiety, but also can improve the patient experience.

or her family members are treated. Family members can also play a critical role in helping patients understand their condition, encouraging patient compliance with discharge and other instructions and in preventing unnecessary readmissions. In an era of potentially declining admissions, family members are an invaluable source of future business for healthcare facility. Building family member loyalty may be a key success factor for the institution.

Hospitals and outpatient facilities are using a variety of approaches to enhance family member satisfaction. These efforts may start with a patient and family council or committee, with family members as participants to advise the institution on what they can improve. The efforts may involve various social media or other technology solutions that facilitate better communication with and among family members.

Numerous hospitals have implemented surgery patient tracking boards to keep family members and friends informed of where their loved one is in the surgery process. Other institutions have implemented text messaging services that send messages from the patient's care team to family members with routine status updates. These approaches represent a technological advance from the more traditional pagers that have historically been used to contact family members. All of these solutions are designed to lessen a family member's stress and anxiety through meaningful and frequent communication.

> Patient/family councils, electronic message boards, and text messaging to family members are several ways to enhance family communication and strengthen patient and family loyalty.

Whether higher family member satisfaction translates into higher patient satisfaction remains an open question because there has been little research on that connection. Patient responses to HCAHPS questions related to nurse and physician communication as well as overall rating and likelihood to recommend may be influenced by way the patient sees family members being treated.

Expanded satisfaction surveys can specifically measure patient perception of staff attitude toward the patient's visitors, with the ability for patients to add written comments. In a review of those comments, approximately 6% of patient comments relate in some way to respect and courtesy of staff shown to visitors (i.e., family member and friends). So it is clearly something they find important enough to comment on. The comments tend to be some of the most positive comments as measured by the strength of the sentiment expressed, further supporting the importance of the family members' experience from the patient's perspective. (See Chapter 7.)

Anecdotal comments from family members receiving periodic text message updates from the nursing staff indicate the importance of family member communication done well. One patient's daughter commented "It is a great way to keep all family members notified of the patient's condition without all of us taking up the nurse's time." Another patient's daughter conveyed "I live out of town so being able to receive text messages letting me know how my mom was doing made it easier to be away." The wife of a patient said "It calmed my nerves."

Given the documented importance of staff communication with patients, it should not be a surprise that staff communication with family members would be highly valued as well. Just as there have been numerous innovations in the last decade to improve the patient experience as previously mentioned, a similar trend in innovation in family member communication is likely. The end result should be a better experience for the patients and providers as well as the family members themselves.

CASE STUDY

Dr. Tracey Chandler has just become the chief experience officer for Bolton Health Care, where she is responsible for all clinical and nonclinical initiatives to improve the patient experience of care. Bolton Health Care is an integrated healthcare system, which includes 350-bed Bolton Hospital; 40-bed Bolton Rehab; and an affiliated medical practice, Bolton Medical Associates. Many health systems have recently created positions similar to Dr. Chandler's to emphasize the growing importance of patient satisfaction and service to future financial success and quality of care.

The most recent patient satisfaction survey results for the hospital are mediocre at best, with the biggest challenges being in physician and nurse communication. In both those areas, Bolton Hospital is in the bottom quartile in the state and nationally and has been in that position for quite a while.

Recognizing that the hospital's reimbursement from Medicare and private payers will be cut if those results do not improve soon, Dr. Chandler compiles a list of actions that she thinks will help. That list includes:

- Starting hourly patient rounding by nurses to ensure that patients think that the nursing staff is proactively monitoring their needs
- Introducing monthly patient rounding by all hospital senior clinical and nonclinical management to both emphasize the commitment of leadership to improve the patient experience and to help management better understand the needs of the frontline staff
- Incorporating patient satisfaction goals into the annual reviews of all levels of management, with an expected meaningful impact on promotions and bonus levels
- Initiating a new program for all staff that recognizes and appropriately rewards examples of excellent service of both individuals and teams throughout the hospital
- Launching a text messaging service where nurses can communicate the patient's routine status with the patient's family members and friends to lessen their anxiety and indirectly influence patient satisfaction
- Working with physicians on following best practices for patient communication, which includes asking the patient to tell his or her story first and listening, sitting at eye level with him or her, and thanking the patient for his or her business
- Making the results of a performance dashboard regarding patient satisfaction scores by hospital area available both internally and externally via Bolton Health Care's website

Dr. Chandler knows it will take more than just introducing some new approaches such as those on her list. She will have to change the culture of the hospital and health system to one of true patient-centered care. She wonders which of the initiatives will have the most impact. Should she get them all started now or try to phase them in over time? Are there other actions she should be considering and where might things go wrong? She also understands that she will have to take some decisive action soon if she is going to turn things around at Bolton in time to avoid decreasing reimbursement and the eventual drop in patient volume and loyalty.

SUGGESTED READING

Merlino JI, Raman A. Health care's service fanatics. *Harv Bus Rev.* 2013 May;91(5):108–116, 150.

Press I. *Patient Satisfaction: Understanding and Managing the Experience of Care.* 2nd ed. Chicago, IL: Health Administration Press; 2005.

Siegrist RB. Family communication—the next frontier for improving patient satisfaction? Association for Patient Experience, June 29, 2013. www.patient-experience. org.

Siegrist RB. Patient satisfaction: history, myths, and misperceptions. *Virtual Mentor.* 2013;15(11):982–987.

15

The Modern Hospital-Physician Relationship

ERIC J. BIEBER AND ELIZABETH HAMMACK

KEY POINTS

- Changes in the healthcare market and through healthcare reform have changed demand for physicians and healthcare.
- Changes in demand and increasingly integrated health systems are affecting how physicians organize themselves.
- Physician integration with hospitals can take place through medical staffs, administrative roles, peer quality activities, and network relationships, even when physicians are not employed by hospitals or related organizations.
- Employment of physicians by hospitals must be carefully structured to ensure clinical independence and fair market value compensation.
- Hospital employment of physicians allows activities that are otherwise restricted, such as directing physician referrals and access to favorable managed care rates.
- If independent physicians are clinically or financially integrated with hospitals, they may be able to leverage hospital bargaining power to access favorable managed care rates.
- Network relationships between hospitals and physicians may be established through accountable care organizations (ACOs).
- ACOs allow participating providers to share in savings from improved utilization of healthcare services generated for managed care and government payers to align incentives.

- ACOs have allowed providers to participate in managing patient care over the continuum and to look at their care delivery from a patient or consumer perspective.
- ACOs are distinct from managed care because there is access to and use of immediate clinical data to address gaps in care and stratify populations for case management.
- Providing value for both hospitals and physicians becomes more important as patients gain access to data, become more engaged in their own care, and have to pay for a greater share of the cost.
- Integrated systems involving both hospitals and physicians for functional alignment and coordination are necessary to optimize the patient experience, however it is arranged.
- The future state of healthcare delivery will include other providers beyond physicians as nurse practitioners and physician assistants take on a greater roles in patient care.

This chapter explores the evolving nature of the physician workforce and how providers and hospitals are working together in new and unique ways such as ACOs. The physician and provider workforce is continuing to change in part as a response to the evolution of healthcare delivery and the new focus around primary care and prevention. The dynamics of these changes are reviewed because they have broad ramifications for how care is delivered. There continue to be numerous different models of employment available to physicians, and external pressures have caused a number of physicians and physician groups to become employed by hospitals. Significant market consolidation has occurred with hospitals and physician groups attempting to connect these entities into integrated delivery systems. There are still thousands of independent practicing physicians in solo and small group practices, and these physicians are increasingly engaged with hospitals as well. The need for both hospitals and physicians to be connected is inherently challenging given the disparate nature of how they each are structured and how differently they operate. Thus, optimizing their relationship and functions becomes critically important for both parties to be successful in contemporary healthcare delivery.

CURRENT STATUS OF THE PHYSICIAN AND PROVIDER WORKFORCE

A number of factors are placing pressure on hospitals and physicians and having an impact on both supply and demand. These factors, as well as how the physician supply is created, and the nature of the shift in the potential need for physicians, are important to understand. Demand for physician services is not fixed. It may be modulated by the changes occurring within the health insurance marketplace as well as the costs associated with obtaining insurance and the impact of health insurance exchanges resulting from the passage of the Patient Protection and Affordable Care Act (ACA, or healthcare reform).

Data from the Kaiser Foundation show a 180% increase in worker's contributions to health insurance premiums from 1999 to 2012, whereas health insurance premiums have increased 172% during the same period, showing the increasing burden that employees are having to bear for consumption of medical services (Figure 15.1). This increased burden for healthcare costs for workers has taken place in the context of a 38% inflation rate and 47% increase in workers earnings over the same time period. In addition, high deductible or consumer-directed health plans, where the consumer is at risk for significantly higher amounts of his or her own healthcare spending than in the past, are becoming increasingly utilized. Employers use high-deductible health plans to mitigate the costs of their self-insured health plans and to create aligned incentives to limit healthcare expenditures with their covered employees and their dependents. Even in non–high-deductible health plans, employers are creating an increased financial burden on their workers from coinsurance and higher deductibles that are also increasingly used as part of employers' health plan design.

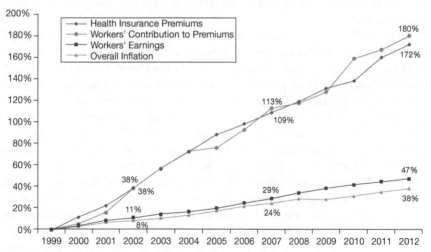

Figure 15.1
Cumulative increases in health insurance premiums, workers' contributions to premiums, inflation, and workers' earnings 1999–2012.
From Kaiser/HRET Survey of Employer-Sponsored Health Benefits, 1999–2002.
Bureau of Labor Statistics, Consumer Price Index, US City Average of Annual Inflation (April to April), 1999–2012; Bureau of Labor Statistics, Seasonally Adjusted Data from the Current Employment Statistics Survey, 1999–2012 (April to April).

The ACA calls for payment by employer health plans of certain preventive care services at 100% with no cost share, where previously these services might not have been covered by a health plan at all. Within the ACA, there are also provisions to allow employers to incentivize their employees to engage in wellness activities. At present, employers may place up to 30% of premium at risk based on activities directed toward wellness or addressing behaviors that might place members at higher risk for health issues. Concomitant with these changes, the advent of narrow networks where less choice may be offered and providers may be within a single health system or grouping of providers is also occurring. These networks may be used to improve coordination of care and connectivity, which may align to greater data sharing and less redundancy and inefficiency in the delivery of care. Narrow networks, with the guarantee of increased utilization, also may provide more favorable rates for medical claims for employers. Health plans and payers are encouraging the increasing prevalence of patient-centered medical homes (PCMHs) based on their belief that a primary care physician (PCP) or provider should be the key to manage patients' medical care and their utilization of other resources to minimize waste and maximize care. The medical home concept is an evolution from a physician gatekeeper model used in earlier managed care models, which required specific referrals to allow coverage of specialty services under restrictive insurance plans. In the PCMH model, PCPs take a more proactive role based on their own clinical judgment and national quality standards rather than the plan design or coverage of a specific patient.

These multiple opposing issues are currently having an impact on physician work force dynamics. The ACA has caused many millions of additional patients to become insured through Medicaid expansion and health insurance exchanges and would suggest that additional providers will be required to care for these "new patients." There have been varying opinions offered regarding potential physician shortfalls because of the aging population—all Americans become enrolled in Medicare at age 65 and post–World War II baby boomers are now coming of age for Medicare coverage—as well as the addition of many new patients who will now have insurance for the first time. Some have suggested this shortfall is well greater than 50,000 physicians who will be practicing medicine over the next one to two decades. Others suggest that many of the activities today's physicians are engaged in can be retasked to physician assistants and nurse practitioners functioning at the "top of their license." They also believe that with the improved use of electronic health records and patient engagement in their own care, such numbers may be overestimates. Unfortunately, the extended timeline to train physicians (currently a minimum of 7 years) does not allow nimble modulation of the provider workforce. Additional challenges include the fact that one in six physicians are currently age 65 or older and that physicians are not geographically well distributed, with limited numbers of providers in rural locations.

As a response to the aforementioned issues of inadequate physician supply, American medical schools and osteopathic colleges have increased enrollment over the past decade. In 2002 there were 125 medical schools. Since that time, 16 additional medical schools have been accredited and 3 more are pursuing accreditation. Also, additional expansion of osteopathic colleges, which have increased first-year enrollment 96% between 2002 and 2012, and allopathic school, which have increased enrollment 18%, has occurred. This has resulted in the first-year medical school class' increasing from 16,488 to 19,517 students; in 2013, for the first time, first-year medical student enrollment surpassed 20,000. A different issue is the problem of lack of increase in funding for graduate medical education since 1996 despite the increases in entering medical and osteopath physician numbers. Most resident physicians in the United States are supported in part through direct and indirect payments that come from Centers for Medicare and Medicaid Services (CMS). Given the need for PCPs, there appears to be an increased need to train such providers. Unfortunately, the mismatch between numbers of specialty physicians and PCPs continues, created by much-higher compensation available for specialists. At present, a limited percentage of all residents are being trained to function as primary care providers. With the increasing focus around wellness and PCMHs, the role of the PCP becomes ever more important.

PHYSICIAN EMPLOYMENT

Over the past decade, there has been consolidation across healthcare providers and a resurgence of provider acquisition by hospitals and health systems as they attempt to become truly integrated. Recent data from the American Medical Association (AMA) showed only 19% of physicians in solo practice, a drop of 6% from the prior evaluation. Although 45.5% of physicians remain employed in single specialty groups, some 29% were either directly or partially employed by a hospital. In addition, there is significant geographic variation depending on the individual marketplace and the amount of consolidation within that marketplace.

Physicians have historically worked for themselves as independent professionals with the protections of licensure and regulations to support their medical judgment. The professional judgement of physicians has been protected through the legal restrictions on who can employ physicians. The prohibition on the corporate practice of medicine, laws that restrict who can employ physicians and share in their fees, was developed to ensure that professional judgment is not compromised by an employer with differing interests (see Chapter 6). The AMA broadened its perspective on these restrictions (2013), but its Code of Medical Ethics provides the following caution to physicians regarding this issue, even in the context of overseeing nurses:

If maintaining an employment relationship with a midlevel practitioner contributes significantly to the physician's livelihood, a physician's personal and financial interests can be put at odds with patient care interests. Similarly, the administrative and financial influence that employer status confers creates an inherent conflict for a physician who is simultaneously an employee and a clinical supervisor of his or her employer (AMA, 2014).

The employment restrictions of the corporate practice of medicine doctrine provide structure to protect the physician-patient relationship. (There are analogous restrictions against corporations providing other professional services, notably practicing law.) State laws, medical boards, attorneys general, and courts provide the applicable restrictions in this context, often through state licensure requirements, reinforcing the individual accountability for professional practice and behavior. In some states, these laws, rulings, and administrative rules mean that hospitals, as well as large corporate employers, are restricted from directly employing physicians.

For physicians who are not owners of or partners in their own practices, they may be part of professional corporations or partnerships that are owned and operated by licensed professionals, meeting the restrictions of the corporate practice of medicine doctrine, but which are held in trust for the benefit of an associated organization, such as a hospital or medical school. Practices may be structured as federally tax exempt entities or for-profit entities. If a practice is a nonprofit group, it is subject to the limitations of any tax-exempt organization, in that its primary purpose must be an approved tax-exempt purpose under the regulations of the Internal Revenue Service. The revenue of a tax-exempt organization must be reinvested in the charitable purposes of the organization and cannot be used to benefit an individual, a limitation that creates restrictions on compensation (Internal Revenue Service, 1993). Although there are opportunities to create appropriate incentives within both nonprofit and for-profit corporations, most frequently, the incentive plans in nonprofit organizations supplement fixed salaries, whereas the physician compensation in for-profit group practices may be based on complete distribution of revenue to physicians in the practice. Notwithstanding these salary models, without an agreement, employment is generally at will, subject to termination by either party upon notice. There are some important public policy protections for at-will employees, including, for instance, hospital employees who report patient care issues (*Wright v. Shriners Hospital for Crippled Children;* see Suggested Reading [see Chapter 6]).

If a physician is employed as part of an integrated system, it allows the physician to access the system's managed care contracts and to direct referrals, and it provides greater ease in the transfer of data. Given this greater latitude under antitrust, fraud and abuse, and privacy laws, physician employment arrangements are subject to greater scrutiny and must be legitimate. Nonetheless, within an employment relationship, physicians should have control of clinically relevant decisions in their practice, including, generally, the diagnosis and treatment of their patients. (Serbaroli; see Suggested Reading). Practically, employment of physicians also requires support for practice management, staff scheduling, medical record management (including electronic medical records), coding, billing, and collections.

OPTIMIZING PHYSICIAN AND HOSPITAL INTEGRATION

Independent physicians are integrated, even in private practice, with hospitals through their participation on hospital medical staffs, administrative roles as medical directors, and peer quality activities with hospitals, through which they clinically review the performance of other physicians for quality improvement activities. However, the fundamental interaction of physicians and hospitals is around the treatment of patients who are treated by both the hospital and their physician. Patients expect that their medical information, although held in confidence for all other purposes, is freely shared among all of their healthcare providers for their medical treatment. The qualitative benefit of sharing information throughout the continuum of care has had policy makers and quality institutions creating incentives for providers to share information. This is evident, for instance, in connecting hospital reimbursement with preventing readmissions and qualitatively measuring whether physicians review and reconcile their patients' medications after discharge from a hospitalization.

> For physicians who wish to remain independent, practices have an increasing need to create data exchange and coordinate with hospitals.

Participation in health information exchanges, easily accessible discharge summaries, and coordination by discharge planners are likewise becoming important hospital alignment strategies. As discussed elsewhere, hospitals' data systems have become more robust, and clinical information is becoming increasingly electronic and accessible (see Chapter 3). Access to these systems allows physicians to have more immediate real-time clinical information to assist in providing proactive patient care; they do not have to rely on patients to initiate appointments or managed care payers to process claims, Over time, different electronic medical records and other clinical data systems have become more accessible and interoperable to facilitate this connectivity.

Besides following patients during and after hospitalizations, immediate access to data facilitates better patient care and ensures complete quality reporting. In addition, independent physicians who integrate clinically or financially with hospital systems may be able to access their negotiated managed care rates, which, as a result of hospitals' greater leverage with payers, often provide better reimbursement. Management services, including billing and collections, practice management consulting, and shared savings arrangements, may be appropriately structured between hospitals and independent physicians without clinical and financial integration. Accessing another practice or hospital's negotiated managed care rates is generally prohibited by antitrust laws, however, without clinical and financial integration.

Clinical integration, by federal agency requirements, typically involves an "active and ongoing program to evaluate and modify practice patterns by the group's physician participants and creating a high degree of interdependence and cooperation among the physicians to control costs and ensure quality [of healthcare services]" (Federal Trade Commission and Department of Justice, 1996). Although integration among independent physicians can include a variety of clinical integration mechanisms, most clinically integrated networks that have been evaluated and approved by antitrust regulators are able to demonstrate the following:

- Goals relating to quality and appropriate utilization of services
- Evaluation of both individual participants and network aggregate performance
- Ability to modify individual clinical practices where necessary
- Implementation and enforcement of protocols to govern utilization of services
- Use of accessible information systems to gather individual and aggregate data

Financial integration often includes the clinical integration infrastructure to appropriately implement and enforce goals. Financial integration requires physicians to share risk so that they are substantially rewarded (or penalized) financially for the achievement (or lack of achievement) of efficiencies. Financial risk-sharing may be structured in a variety of ways, but appropriate risk-sharing arrangements have several common features. Historically, arrangements with substantial financial risk have included:

- Capitation arrangements
- Percent of premium arrangements
- Bundled payments for episodes of care
- Fee-for-service arrangements with substantial payment withholds

ACCOUNTABLE CARE ORGANIZATIONS (ACOs)

Arguably, ACOs were in part created through legislation passed in 2000 calling for the creation of a physician group practice demonstration (PGPD) by CMS that would evaluate a pay-for-performance Medicare program and incorporate evaluation of quality metrics. The PGPD was finally begun in April 2005 and spanned 5 years, coming to completion in March 2010. Ten physician groups, including the University of Michigan, Geisinger, Marshfield, and Dartmouth-Hitchcock, were chosen to be part of the demonstration. This was the first true pay-for-performance demonstration by CMS. The PGPD program participants continued to be paid Medicare fee schedules for medical services, but the groups were eligible to earn shared savings if they were able to save more than a 2% savings threshold from predicted Medicare spending. In addition, the PGPD program required the participants to achieve quality metrics. At the end of the 5 years, there were significant gains in performance measures related to quality. However, only some of the participants were able to achieve the financial savings thresholds for the targeted years. This project ultimately became an important precursor to the future CMS and Center for Medicare and Medicaid Innovation (or the Innovation Center; CMMI) ACO initiatives (see Chapters 3, 6, and 7).

ACOs have increased in significance since the passage of the ACA. ACOs are defined as a group of providers who take on responsibility for a specific group of patients with the goal of increasing the quality of care, improving patient experience, and reducing the cost of care. Generally, patients are attributed to an ACO through their relationship to a PCP who is part of the ACO. This is in distinction to managed care organizations of prior times, which were variations of insurance products and generally required the use of narrow networks. Although there were early ACOs that had been formed prior to the ACA, section 3022 within the ACA, which called for the establishment of Medicare ACOs or the Medicare Shared Savings Program (MSSP), has caused such a rapid increase. The CMMI began early efforts by establishing a pioneer ACO program, which 32 organizations initially joined in early 2012. Subsequently, the CMS began the MSSP program, with the first ACOs beginning in April 2012. Since that time, the number of ACOs has exploded. Estimates suggest that as of late 2013, there were more than 600 MSSP ACOs organized, including some 260 physician group-led ACOs, 238 hospital-led ACOs, and more than 50 insurer-led ACOs. Interestingly, physician groups initially were a minority of MSSP ACOs, but over the past several years, they represent the majority of MSSP ACOs (Figure 15.2).

The significant growth since 2011 can be seen in this figure. It is also worth noting that there is significant regional disparity in the growth of MSSP ACOs, with the highest penetrance in the Northeast, southern California, Arizona, Minnesota, and Florida. It may be that these areas have the greatest collective experience with risk and managed care lives and thus were able to more quickly assimilate into an ACO environment.

In the current structure of MSSP, ACOs are able to choose acceptance of either upside or upside-downside risk. Also, depending on the size of the ACO and number of attributed members, the minimum savings rate, to be eligible for shared savings, varies from 2.0% for the largest ACOs to 3.9% for ACOs, with approximately 5,000 attributed lives. This structure was designed to decrease the possibility of random variation as the cause of reduced costs in the attributed populations.

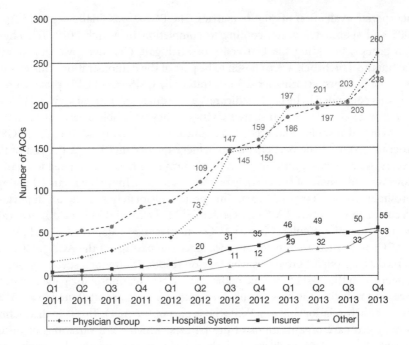

Figure 15.2
Total accountable care organizations (ACOs).

Once the minimum savings rate is attained, MSSP ACOs may share in first dollar savings, half of which are retained by the federal government. To determine shared savings, the projected spending is derived from historical performance and, based on the attributed lives and market trend, the target spending is calculated. If the actual spend is less than the target and above the threshold based on the size of the ACO, savings are shared.

Possibly more important than the ACO financial structure may be the creation of organizational architecture that supports new paradigms of care coordination, case management, and patient engagement. There is no one-size-fits-all solution. Organizations need to uniquely adapt and identify structures that will best facilitate their evolution from volume to value and achieve the highest level of function. Data analytics and personnel should be organized around such structures. Organizations have found that having nurses as case managers or care coordinators/navigators is useful in changing from an acute episodic care focused organization to one focused on value and the care continuum. Medical assistants and even lay individuals who have been trained as patient navigators to facilitate care coordination add significant value to the physicians as well as the ACO in these new structures. Social workers, dieticians, and pharmacists also provide additional ancillary support outside of the physician office setting.

Another aspect that has become increasingly important is who and how to manage care over a complex continuum. Regardless of the population evaluated, a small percentage of patients use significant resources. For Medicare patients, the top 25% account for about 80% of spending, whereas the top 5% account for almost 40% of spending. Similarly, in a Medicaid population, approximately 2% of patients account for 25% of spending and 5.6% account for 50% of spending. Similar statistics exist for both commercial and pediatric populations as well.

Fortunately, most people spend the vast majority of their lives in a state of good health and wellness. However, intermittently they will require acute care, which is where the medical system has historically focused. In a value-based continuum environment, systems must be able to facilitate transitioning patients from states of wellness to acute care to subacute care, such as skilled nursing facilities or even home care, rehabilitation, and so on. Very few organizations have or own all of these parts or subparts. Thus, disparate organizations will need to work with one another to optimize a patient's care over this broad continuum. In addition, ACOs are ideally positioned to be able to optimize chronic conditions such as diabetes, asthma, congestive heart failure, chronic obstructive pulmonary disease, and other chronic conditions that require patients to interact with medical professionals over long periods of time.

Many have asked if ACOs are merely a reincarnation of managed care. Those that are most actively engaged in managing ACOs would argue that the answer is "no." Today, providers have much richer data than ever before, and these clinical data will drive improvements in identifying healthcare gaps as well as stratifying those at highest risk who might best benefit from case management and care coordination. There is no question that data will be the key driver in the quest to improve quality. As quality metrics have continued to evolve, it has become increasingly easy to use these metrics to not only judge quality but to enhance population health. The MSSP outlines 33 quality measures that need to be met to attain the highest possible shared savings percentage. CMS has divided these measures into domains that include patient experience, care coordination, prevention, and management of at-risk populations. Through better data, hospitals are now able to in almost real time identify patients who have visited an emergency facility, and as part of an ACO, ensure that they obtain follow up with a PCP in an appropriate time period. Early identification of patients who have been hospitalized allows appropriate coordination between hospital case management teams and ambulatory care coordination teams to ensure that, regardless of what level of care a patient transitions to, there is continued medical oversight of the patient. In addition, by constantly updating data, it is possible to identify patients who have moved into high-risk categories or who may later become high-risk and thus may be positively affected by more intensive connectivity to care management teams.

There are a number of ways that ACOs can reduce expenditures while concomitantly improving quality. The use of appropriate providers such as medical assistants, nurses, and others who function at "top of license" can help redistribute work from physicians. Adding these additional team members to what is now an interdisciplinary team helps improve overall care coordination and reduces waste and redundancies. ACOs also look to improve internal processes by following evidence-based recommendations. Through optimized data and understanding needs within populations, ACOs are able to enhance prevention and screening efforts as well as identifying individuals who might benefit most from intervention. Most importantly, by placing patients and their families at the center of the care process, patient engagement allows patients to become true participants in their own care, allowing meaningful alignment of incentives.

ARE INTEGRATED SYSTEMS THE ANSWER?

Although ACOs have become quite prominent in more recent times, there are a number of ways that hospitals and physicians may work together. The following are some important definitions of several useful methods:

- Physician-hospital organization (PHO)—an organization where physicians and hospital(s) partner, generally as it relates to insurance contracting
- Independent practice association (IPA)—a group of physicians (and possibly other providers) who contract as a single entity to provide healthcare to insurance groups, managed care organizations, or other third-party payers on a predetermined fee schedule or capitated payment
- Integrated delivery system or network (IDS or IDN)—a connected group of healthcare providers (i.e., hospitals, physicians), which could also include additional entities such as home care, skilled nursing facility or others, who focus around optimizing the continuum of care
- Clinically integrated network (CIN)—a collaboration among physicians (employed or independent) with hospitals or healthcare systems focused around quality improvement and enhanced care delivery efficiency at improved cost

All of these are vehicles to drive toward greater integration of physicians, hospitals, or both. A key question today is what does "integration" truly mean and what is the correct size for an organization to achieve appropriate scale? A further question is: what are the pieces and parts that should be owned to become a system?

The answers to these questions are complex, with a multitude of potential answers and solutions depending on the marketplace. In recent years, there has been increased merger-and-acquisition (M + A) activity, with a number of free-standing hospitals choosing to become part of larger systems or choosing to come together to create systems. This effort in and of itself does not create an integrated

system. Even if a number of the parts such as hospitals, physician group practices, and extended-care facilities (ECFs) are present, there may be challenges in
creating the underlying function of true integration. It used to be suggested that
to get synergy of scale, systems would need to be at total revenue of $500 mil-
lion or more. This now seems small, and many integrated systems are in the $2
to $3 billion range and growing through market consolidation and M + A activ-
ity. Unfortunately, without aligning the disparate portions of organizations, it
is difficult to function as an IDS. As an example, the underlying function of a
rehabilitation hospital is not the same as an acute care hospital and thus must
be managed accordingly. Even if a hospital system has similar component parts,
such as community hospitals, if the parent system does not impose consistency or
economies of scale across the community hospitals, they may continue to act independently, even within common ownership. Because of the inherently fragmented
nature of healthcare today, the transitions to and from these disparate facilities
has not always been smooth. There are also challenges in merging organizations
whose legacy business and electronic medical records systems are incompatible
or poorly connect to the acquiring entity, limiting interconnectivity and flow of
patient data. It will be very challenging to function as in an integrated manner and
to optimize quality and financial performance without ultimately achieving this
type of connectivity.

Just as consolidation by itself does not create integration, having all of the
"pieces and parts" does not allow for integration, either. The size of an organization is relevant only to the extent that it provides natural synergies that are useful.
Numerous failed mergers of health systems serve as a testament to the fact that
increased size does not always provide benefit if cultures clash and the increased
scale does not bring additional value. All of the healthcare industry is becoming
more aligned simply by the increasing transparency of the data and the ability to
view patient care processes over the entire continuum, not just the subparts. There
is also increasing financial alignment with the application of penalties such as the
government's effort to reduce readmissions by adjusting reimbursement based on
hospital readmissions within a 30-day period. It also appears that most healthcare
systems will not own every care delivery piece and thus will have to work with
other institutions to fill holes in the care continuum. This is forcing ECFs, hospitals, and physicians to reevaluate their relationships and how they work together
to optimize patient care across the continuum, not just for their own small portion. Eventually, organizations that are inherently quite different may become virtually integrated and then focus on their core strengths. If care is optimized, it is
irrelevant to the patient whether a given part is owned or not. The realignment of
payment for value and the transition to patient-centered care means that functional integration and the alignment and coordination that this affords is more
important than ownership in the new marketplace—this may be the integrated
system of the future.

The bottom line is there are significant changes to the hospital-physician relationship that are going on today and look to continue into the foreseeable future.

The healthcare landscape is shifting from the acute episodic and hospital-focused environment of the past to a patient-centric, value-focused market of today and tomorrow. ACOs, which did not exist a decade ago, appear to be one vehicle for this transition but will likely also continue to develop over time as experience increases and refinements become possible. Physician practices also continue to evolve, with increasing numbers of physicians choosing to become employed by and/or join larger systems. There will likely be enhanced efforts to train increasing numbers of PCPs and providers such as nurse practitioners and physician assistants as there is a shift to a greater focus on wellness and prevention as well as an increased emphasis on providers who are highly connected to individual patients and families.

CASE STUDY

Your current organization, a large $1.5-billion integrated delivery system, has decided to pursue an MSSP under the current CMS program, and you have been asked to lead this effort. Your health system has numerous employed physicians (both primary care and specialists), a number of hospitals spread over primary and secondary service areas, and relationships with many independent physician practices that work out of system hospitals. The MSSP program only allows primary care providers to be part of one ACO.

Questions

- How and who will you begin to work with to establish the basis for a MSSP?
- What type of governance model will you recommend?
- Who would you work with to begin to discuss how shared savings might be distributed among the various parties if available (i.e., PCPs, specialists)?
- How would you evaluate big data vendors relative to information about financial and quality trends?
- Would you involve independent physicians in this process? If so, how?

SUGGESTED READING

Baicker K, Levy H. Coordination versus competition in health care reform. *N Engl J Med.* 2013;369:789–791.

Chen C, Ackerly DC. Beyond ACOs and bundled payments: Medicare's shift toward accountability in fee-for-service. *JAMA.* 2014;311:673–674.

DeCamp M, Sugarman J, Berkowitz S. Shared savings in accountable care organizations: how to determine fair distributions. *JAMA*. 2014;311:1011–1012.

Fisher ES, McClellan MB, Bertko J, et al. Fostering accountable care: moving forward in Medicare. *Health Aff.* 2009;28(2):w219–w231.

Gawande A. The cost conundrum. *The New Yorker*, June 1, 2009.

Gawande A. The hot spotters. *The New Yorker*, January 17, 2011.

Mostashari F, Sanghavi D, McClellan M. Health reform and physician-led accountable care: the paradox of primary care physician leadership. *JAMA*. 2014;311:1855–1856.

Serbaroli FJ. *The Corporate Practice of Medicine Prohibition in the Modern Era of Health Care*. Arlington, : Bureau of National Affairs; 1999.

Starr P. *Social Transformation of American Medicine*. New York, NY: Basic Books; 1982.

Statements of Antitrust Enforcement Policy in Healthcare, Federal Trade Commission and Department of Justice, 1996, available at http://www.justice.gov/sites/default/files/atr/legacy/2007/08/14/0000.pdf.

Tollen L. Physician organizations in relation to quality and efficiency of care: a synthesis of recent literature. The Commonwealth Fund. April 2008. http://www.commonwealthfund.org/publications/fund-reports/2008/apr/physician-organization-in-relation-to-quality-and-efficiency-of-care-a-synthesis-of-recent-literatu. Accessed August 4, 2014.

Wright v. Shriners Hospital for Crippled Children, Supreme Court of Massachusetts, 469, 589 N.E.2d 1241 (1992).

16

Entrepreneurship in Healthcare

RICHARD B. SIEGRIST, JR.

KEY POINTS

- As healthcare organizations strive to deliver on the triple aim of better health and better care at lower cost, they need to identify new ways to understand healthcare information and introduce new methods of healthcare delivery. Many of the innovations necessary will come from entrepreneurial organizations.
- Key components of a successful new healthcare venture include a good idea that meets a market need, a strong value proposition, an effective management team, a sound business model, and a solid understanding of the competition.
- "Friends and family," angel investors, venture capital, and crowd-funding are potential sources of capital for start-up companies or a hospital system; valuation and the investor pitch are important aspects of securing financing.
- A start-up company or new hospital system needs to consider what is the appropriate legal structure, how to distribute equity among founders, what to do regarding vesting and noncompete agreements, and how to protect intellectual property. Perhaps most important, the company needs to execute well and achieve its milestones to be successful.

As healthcare organizations strive to deliver on the triple aim of better health and better care at lower cost, they need to identify new ways to understand healthcare information and introduce new methods of healthcare delivery. Many of the innovations necessary will come from entrepreneurial organizations. This chapter will explore what is involved in starting a new healthcare venture in terms of the idea, team, business model, structure, financing, execution and exit.

THE IDEA

Having a good idea that meets a market need sets the foundation for a successful venture. A common misperception is that one needs a unique or brilliant idea to start a business. A vast majority of new business ideas are not unique or even great. Apple did not create the idea of a graphical user interface. It commercialized it. Google did not develop the first search engine. It made search results more relevant. Multiple people were in the process of creating an electric light bulb when Thomas Edison did it successfully. The same applies to healthcare ventures.

> One needs a good idea that meets a market need, not a great or unique one, to have a successful venture.

How can a person come up with a good idea? A first useful step is to identify a problem that one can relate to through personal experience. It is also advantageous if he or she has some level of knowledge or expertise regarding the problem. Having identified the problem, it is necessary to consider the following questions:

- How big a problem is it?
- Why do you think the problem is occurring?
- What is the best current solution to the problem?
- How would customers benefit from a better solution?

So if having a good idea is often enough, what distinguishes a successful idea from an unsuccessful idea in launching a new business or a new service line? An important factor is having a compelling value proposition. A value proposition identifies the problem that the product or service addresses and explains why customers will value a particular solution. It should be clear, concise, and verifiable initially through conversations with potential customers and later through actual customer sales.

> A compelling value proposition can mean the difference between a successful and an unsuccessful idea. "We help x do y by doing z"; this is an effective way to express a value proposition.

There are multiple ways to express a value proposition. One useful approach proposed by Steven Blank is to express the value proposition as: "We help x do y by doing z," where

- x = the customer
- y = the value the customer receives
- z = how one helps create that value for the customer

Another approach advocated by Cooper and Vlaskovits is to express the value proposition in terms of the customer (C), the problem (P), and your solution (S). A third approach suggested by Geoff Moore involves stating the proposition in terms of:

- For (target customers)
- Who (statement of need or opportunity)
- Our (product/service name) is a (product category) . . .
- That provides (key problem-solving capability or benefits)
- Unlike (the product alternative or status quo). . .

Too often, aspiring entrepreneurs try to keep their idea secret; they are afraid that someone else will "steal" it. In doing so, they usually fail to get valuable feedback from potential customers or thought leaders that will help them refine their idea and make it better received by customers. Later on in this chapter, the desire to protect intellectual property through patents, trademarks, and nondisclosure agreements is discussed. Although certainly important, these protections should be appropriately balanced against the need to get an idea fleshed out and applied in reality.

> Keeping an idea a secret is usually a mistake. One needs feedback from others to refine, strengthen, and test the idea.

Another key factor to success is getting one's idea out there in the marketplace relatively quickly to gauge market interest and continually refine that idea based on actual customer feedback. Some start-up entities can fall into the trap of delaying product release until they feel the product is nearly perfect, only to find they are late into the market with a product that may work well but does not meet customer needs.

Two other critical aspects of turning a good idea into a successful company are building an effective team that creates the right culture for the organization and effectively executing the company's plans. Those aspects are described in more detail in upcoming sections.

THE TEAM

An effective team is a critical factor in the success of a start-up. The core of that team is the management team itself. It is a rare situation where a company's founder

> The chief executive officer (CEO) needs to be the chief evangelist to customers, a credible leader to investors, and a motivational leader to employees.

is able to develop a well-functioning organization without a strong and diverse management team. That team will operate most effectively if it brings together a mixture of skills, experience, and perspectives.

A typical start-up organization will have a CEO who will usually, but not always, be one of the cofounders. That person not only needs to be passionate about the idea but also able to effectively motivate his or her senior management team and staff. Being CEO involves balancing a variety of competing product development, operational, and financial priorities in an environment of uncertainty and risk. Ultimately, the CEO needs to be able to tell the company story:

- To customers, as the chief evangelist who excites and engages
- To investors, as a credible leader who delivers results
- To employees, as a motivational leader who sets the culture

This is not an easy task, which is why a strong leadership team is also important. Other key members of the senior management team are a head of product development, a chief financial officer (CFO), a leader of customer service, and a head of sales and marketing. Each of these people brings a different set of expertise to the team.

An effective leader of product development not only needs to understand how to create good software but also how to translate sometimes poorly defined customer needs into a workable product. An effective CFO needs to be able to work well with the board and investors and also lead the development of a realistic budget and keep a close eye on cash flow needs.

A strong customer service leader recognizes the prime importance of happy customers, who if treated well will overlook inevitable product glitches and become the leading evangelists for the company's products and services. If a start-up organization does not deliver excellent customer service from the beginning, it is quite difficult to recover from the negative market perceptions.

Perhaps the most underrated and difficult position to fill with the right person is the head of sales and marketing role in healthcare start-ups. Although in the earliest stages, the CEO is often the most effective salesperson for the company, the head of sales and marketing becomes critical to moving the healthcare system from early sales to a sustained sales effort. This person is most effective if he or she introduces a structured sales approach with sound pipeline forecasting and creates the right image for the hospital system and product in the marketplace.

The CEO should be supported by an engaged board of directors. Working with the board of directors can consume a significant amount of the CEO's and senior management's time. This time commitment increases the importance of having a board that works well together and is not pursuing an individual agenda to the company's detriment.

A well-structured board will typically include the CEO; two investor representatives (assuming the company has received financing); and two outside, independent directors. Boards that are much larger than five to seven people or include too many members of management can become unwieldy and discourage frank, open discussion.

The CEO should view the board as an important source of candid advice and contacts. Accordingly, it is important for the independent directors to bring relevant experience to the discussion, as opposed to simply being well-known people or friends of the CEO. Given the challenges facing the CEO, it can be helpful if one of the independent directors is a person the CEO feels totally comfortable using as a sounding board for any sensitive topic or personal frustration.

> An engaged board of directors that works well with the management team can be critical to the success of a start-up organization.

The most effective board members become actively engaged with the company and are willing to offer guidance to the CEO about what he or she is doing well and should consider doing differently. Outside directors are usually compensated with a very modest amount of stock in the company, whereas investor directors typically do not received additional stock or compensation.

Start-up entities often choose to create an advisory board to bring additional credibility to the company. These advisory boards typically meet semiannually or quarterly, and the members make themselves available as needed for conversations with the CEO and senior management. Although advisory boards can be very helpful, they do require time to manage and coordinate. Therefore, it is important to have members who are willing to contribute their expertise and not just recognizable names to show on the company's website.

Choosing the right outside experts to work with can also be critical to the organization's success. These outside experts include the company's law firm and lead attorney, accounting/auditing firm, and any consultants that may be hired for marketing studies or other activities. Although these experts bring important specialized knowledge, it is important to keep in mind that management is responsible for making business decisions and in deciding how much risk to take. Being overly cautious or relying too much on outside advice can have a negative impact on the progress of an entrepreneurial organization. It is also important to understand the motivations of the experts hired to make sure they are consistent with the goals of the organization.

Finally, outside business partners can be considered part of the team of the organization. Business partners can help the organization more quickly penetrate a new market, provide talent that it may not be able to currently afford, and add credibility. However, it is important to seek partners who are "real" partners that will help the organization, rather than partners in name only, where the main output of the relationship is a joint press release and wasted time.

THE BUSINESS MODEL

An effective business model helps the management team turn a good idea and a well-defined value proposition into a successful organization. The business model starts with the value proposition discussed earlier but then needs to address these questions:

- How do we generate revenue and price our product or service (revenue model)?
- How do we sell our product or service (distribution model)?
- How do we support our customers (support model)?
- How do we generate a sufficient profit margin (profit/cost model)?

The revenue model should clearly define how the company intends to generate revenue from the idea via the product or service delivered to customers. That involves defining the company's consumers (providers, payers, employers, patients, advertisers, others), their ability to pay (how much in relation to the value delivered), and type of payment to be received (per transaction, monthly, quarterly, yearly, one time). Investors tend to value continuing revenue streams significantly more highly than one-time payments. Table 16.1 identifies common pricing models and their relative advantages and disadvantages.

> A good business model should incorporate revenue, distribution, support, and profit/cost models.

Along with deciding on how the product or service will be priced, one needs to decide how it will be sold or distributed. Will the company hire its own sales/marketing force or rely on distribution partners? Will it do in-person visits or sell over the Internet? Will it take advantage of social media in the sales process (Table 16.2)?

Patient/client support can be critical to the success of a business model. Particularly for early-stage organizations, poor customer service can have an inordinate negative impact on the organization's growth and can be difficult to recover from.

Table 16.3 identifies several different models for customer support and discusses the relative advantages and disadvantages of each.

The final component of the business model is the profit-cost model, or how will the company make money? Deciding on the profit-cost model involves answering the following questions:

- Is this a high-margin or low-margin business?
- How complicated is the supply chain?
- How important is technology internally and in the product or service?
- How capital-intensive versus labor-intensive is the business?
- How much can or should the business outsource?
- How easy or difficult is it for the managers to differentiate based on perceived value?
- What are the profit expectations of current and future investors?
- What are the expectations of customers in terms of responsiveness and service?
- How quickly are the circumstances likely to change in the market and industry?

Through answering these questions, it is possible to decide on what type of infrastructure needs to be built; how many employees, in what areas, will likely be required to run the business; and what metrics should be used to determine progress. This information can then be translated into an operating budget for revenue and expenses, a capital budget for capital investments, and a cash flow budget to maintain a sufficient cash balance to grow the organization.

COMPETITION AND DIFFERENTIATION

To successfully implement the business model, one needs to develop an in-depth understanding of the competition and what differentiates "you from them." Aspiring entrepreneurs will sometimes say that they have no competition for what they are doing. That is usually not a good sign. If there is no competition, there may very well not be a market for your product or a compelling enough problem that needs to be solved.

TABLE 16.1   ADVANTAGES AND DISADVANTAGES OF COMMON PRICING MODELS

Pricing Model	Advantages	Disadvantages
Upfront fee plus annual maintenance	Large early payments and ongoing relationships	Lumpy revenue and need to sell 80% new each year
Subscription fee (monthly, annual)	Consistent revenues, go into next year with 90% booked assuming renewals	Subject to renewal rate, support expenses front loaded
Annual fee plus transaction fee	Revenue goes up as relationship expands in scope and volume	Subject to renewal rate and volume decrease, support expenses front loaded
Percent attributed savings	Big dollar amounts possible	Hard to clearly demonstrate savings, delayed payments
Freemium	Risk-free adoption can lead to rapid growth in users	Only small portion of users may upgrade
Advertising based	Risk-free adoption can lead to rapid growth in users	Need strong brand name for good rates
Consulting	Monthly revenues with significant markups	People go home at night and projects end

TABLE 16.2   ADVANTAGES AND DISADVANTAGES OF A
DISTRIBUTION MODEL

Distribution Model	Advantages	Disadvantages
Direct sales—traditional	Control of message, process and pricing, flexibility to change quickly	Expensive, sales management challenges, need higher product price
Distribution channels	Less expensive, broader reach, multiple partners	Limited control of message and process, less flexibility
Mixed direct/channel	Benefits of both direct and channels to maximize sales	Channel conflict, could have worst of both worlds
Direct sales—Internet	Same as traditional + lower cost	May not get enough traffic, lack of personal interaction
Social media	Broader reach, buzz creation	May be short lived, can go negative

TABLE 16.3   ADVANTAGES AND DISADVANTAGES FOR
PATIENT-CLIENT SUPPORT

Support Model	Advantages	Disadvantages
General help line	More efficient, handle higher volume, can refer more complicated calls to the right person	Impersonal, lack of past knowledge/relationship, lower level role, less commitment
Assigned account manager	Personalized service, knowledgeable about client, feels accountable, increases likelihood of renewal and add-on sales	More expensive, more training, sometimes unavailable, client dissatisfaction if changed or not good
Self-service	Least expensive, many customers find preferable and quicker	Difficult to do for more complicated problems, many will want someone to talk to, frustration if doesn't work
Hybrid	Best meets need of the customer for that specific situation	Requires good software and good communication

When evaluating competitors, it is important to be realistic about their strengths and weaknesses. A comparative chart where there is a check mark for your product or service for each feature being compared and none for your competitors is not likely to be credible or realistic.

> Objectively evaluating the competition and identifying what differentiates "you from them" is important in successfully implementing the business model.

If one's product or service simply mimics that of a competitor through a "me too" approach, it will be much more difficult to achieve success. That differentiation can be on one or multiple factors. Differentiation can be anything from sophisticated analytics to exceptional service to solution simplicity.

Table 16.4 illustrates a typical competitive matrix where one identifies the factors for comparison, ranks those factors in terms of customer importance (high to low), and indicates how the business performs in relation to key competitors.

INVESTMENT CAPITAL SOURCES

Almost all new entrepreneurs need to find sources of funds to start their company and to grow the company over time until it reaches a point of cash flow self-sufficiency, which may be years in the future. Historically, the most common funding sources have been "friends and family," angel financing, and venture capital. Crowd-funding (see subsequent discussion) is a relatively new source of funds for start-up organizations. Private equity is typically for much later stage, well-established organizations.

TABLE 16.4   TYPICAL COMPETITIVE MATRIX[a]

Factor	Importance to Customer	Our Company	Competitor A	Competitor B
Quality	High	4		
Customer service	High	5		
Product capabilities	High	4		
Expertise	High	5		
Reputation	Moderate	4		
Stability	Moderate	3		
Technology	Moderate	3		
Price	Low	3		

[a]NOTE: 5 is best; 1 is worst.

"Friends and family" is often the initial source of funding for a start-up. It can be a much quicker and less expensive way to raise initial funds because investment decisions are based on faith in the entrepreneur and legal documentation and restrictions are usually kept to a minimum. Funds raised from "friends and family" will range from $10,000 to $200,000 for a small portion of the company. The entrepreneur should be transparent about the riskiness of a start-up (likely to lose their investment) in discussions with friends and family members to be able to preserve those relationships should things not go well.

In a follow-on round or in lieu of a "friends and family" round, angel investment is another common source of early-stage financing. Angel investors are wealthy individuals or groups of individuals who provide seed or other early-stage capital. Angels are often previous entrepreneurs or semiretired or retired executives whose interest is often not just in financial returns. A typical angel investment round ranges from $50,000 to $1,000,000. More than a decade ago, angel investing began to replace venture capital investing for early-stage funding. An angel round requires substantially more paperwork than a "friends and family" round and will have more requirements placed on management.

> Common financing sources for a new venture are "friends and family," angel investors, and venture capitalists. Crowd-funding is a new source of financing.

Venture capital financing is an alternative for entities who need a larger initial investment and/or are beyond the initial investment stage and want a more structured investment partner. Venture capital firms are organized partnerships that have a dedicated investment staff and raise their funds from limited partners such as pension funds, universities, and insurance companies. The legal requirements for a venture capital round are significant as are the expectations for performance of the management team. A typical investment from a venture capital fund is more than $1,000,000. Because of the risk involved, venture capital firms expect high returns from their investment.

Crowd-funding, or collaborative funding via the Web, is a relatively new funding option for some start-up entities. In the donation-based crowd-funding model, individuals donate online to the start-up in return for future products, perks, or rewards. In other words, the crowd-funders receive no ownership interest. This donation model may be attractive to a company that needs some initial capital and can get individuals personally excited about its product or social mission.

The newer crowd-funding model is investment crowd-funding where individuals invest online in return for an ownership stake in the company. The legal requirements of this new model are evolving to protect the interests of typically unsophisticated investors. This model can be particularly attractive as an alternative to raising money from "friends and family" and can usually be done much more easily and less restrictively than an angel or private equity round. Some of the leading crowd-funding sites that facilitate fundraising are Kickstarter, Indiegogo, RocketHub, Crowdfunder, and Peerbackers. These sites will take a percentage of the funds raised as an administrative fee for their services.

INVESTMENT ROUNDS AND COMPANY VALUATION

The first official round of capital (typically post–"friends and family") is called the seed round. It provides capital for management team salaries, research and development, proof of concept, prototype development, and initial milestone achievement. It will typically fund the company for 6 to 9 months and will involve giving up 10% to 20% of ownership in the company and ranges from $200,000 to $1,500,000. The average seed round in 2012 was $342,000 for 13% ownership in the company.

The next round is referred to as the series A round. It provides capital for continued development, the hiring of key staff, initial business development efforts, and additional milestone achievement. Series A rounds typically range from $3 million to $10-plus million. Subsequent rounds are referred to as series B, C, rounds—and so on. They are geared toward market expansion, revenue growth, and building scale in the business. In these rounds, the technical risk related to the product is replaced by sales, operational, and general execution risks.

In many ways, the valuation of a company for early-stage financing is more of an art than a science. Initial valuation is often based on the investor appraisal of the company CEO and senior management in conjunction with the attractiveness of the value proposition and potential market. The investors will also consider the expected time to market, anticipated path to profitability over time, and the estimated capital needs and burn rate for the company. If it is a "hot" area with a proven CEO, the valuation will be much higher than if it is an unknown market with an inexperienced management team.

Valuation of later rounds (e.g., series A, B, C) can use much more specific data such as achievement of milestones, reaction of the market to the product, and revenue growth and other growth metrics (e.g., number of users, number of clients). Investors will also look at the clarity of the path to break even and profitability, how effective management has been in building the management team, and how good the management team has proven to be at execution.

> The valuation of an early-stage company is more of an art than a science. It can depend on intangibles such as the track record of the CEO and his or her team as well as the attractiveness of the company's market space.

It is useful to understand the language used in valuation discussions. Premoney and postmoney valuation are commonly used terms:

Premoney = Company value before new investment
Postmoney = Company value after new investment
Premoney plus new investment = Postmoney and postmoney =
    New investment/percentage of company

A capitalization table, or cap table, shows the amount of investment, shares, and ownership of each equity holder (management and investors).

Dilution is an important concept in valuation. The founders and any previous investors typically become diluted (own a smaller percentage of the company) in each new financing round. Founders are often given the opportunity to invest in future rounds to lessen dilution. However, even though the ownership percentage goes down, the monetary value of that ownership goes up if the valuation of the company increases from the prior round—an up round. If the company is not doing as well as expected, there can be a down round where the company valuation is lower after the new round of financing.

Most such entities also set up an option pool to reward nonfounder employees should the company do well. The option pool is designed to attract talent and to motivate performance throughout the organization. The options typically have no monetary value until there is some kind of an exit event (e.g., company acquired). A typical option pool contains 10% to 20% of the shares in the company and in effect dilutes the ownership interest of the investors and founders. Some companies give options only to senior management and other companies give options to everyone in the organization.

COMPANY VALUATION EXAMPLE

Let us review an example of a seed round and then a series A round valuation. The CEO and cofounder of a healthcare start-up company is seeking a $200,000 investment from an angel group of investors. Before the financing, she and her cofounder each own 50% of the company. She plans to use the $200,000 to build out an initial prototype of their product and to secure a beta site. After multiple presentations and discussions with the angel group, they jointly decide that the angel group will put up the entire $200,000 for 20% of the company.

In this example, the postmoney valuation is $1,000,000 ($200,000/20%) and the premoney valuation is therefore $800,000 ($1,000,000 postmoney – $200,000 investment). The CEO and her cofounder are diluted from a 50% ownership each to 40% each (80%/2, which is valued at $400,000 each ($800,000/2 premoney). The angel investors end up with 20% of the company, valued at the $200,000 they put in. Accordingly, after the seed round, the cofounders owe 80% of the company with a valuation of $800,000 and the investors own 20% of the company with a valuation of $200,000.

After 6 months, the company has done a good job of achieving its milestones, has developed the prototype, and has received preliminary approval from a beta site for implementation. The CEO is now seeking a series A round of financing from the same angel investors of $500,000 for another 20% of the company to fund further product development, beta implementation, and staff expansion.

TABLE 16.5   FINANCING ROUNDS

	Before Seed Round	After Seed Round	After Series A Round
Management:			
New Investment	$0	$0	$0
Total Valuation	$0	$800,000	$1,600,000
Ownership percentage	100%	80%	64%
Investors:			
New Investment	$0	$200,000	$500,000
Total Valuation	$0	$200,000	$900,000
Ownership percentage—new	0%	20%	20%
Ownership percentage—combined	0%	20%	36%
Premoney valuation—total		$800,000	$2,000,000
New investment		$200,000	$500,000
Postmoney valuation—total		$1,000,000	$2,500,000

This represents an up round of financing—the postmoney valuation has grown from $1 million after the seed round to $2.5 million ($500,000/20%) after the series A round. The premoney valuation is $2.0 million ($2.5 million postmoney – $500,000 new investment). After the series A round, the cofounders now own 64% of the company, down from 80%, but with a valuation of $1.6 million compared to the previous $800,000. The investors own the remaining 36% (a diluted 16% from the seed round plus 20% from the new round), with a combined valuation of $900,000 ($400,000 for the seed round investment and $500,000 for the new investment).

Table 16.5 summarizes the results of these two rounds of financing:

THE INVESTOR PITCH

The presentation or "pitch" made to investors to obtain financing is critical to both securing that financing and receiving a reasonable valuation. In the past, investors required detailed business plans before they would consider an investment. In recent years, that requirement has often been relaxed to a strong slide presentation complemented by more detailed supporting financial and market information. Most investors prefer a relatively short pitch from management that concisely describes the value proposition, business model, and management team and provides summary financial projections.

> An investor pitch should be short and concise and describe the value proposition, business model, management team, and financial projections.

The following structured approach is modeled on the pitch format suggested by former Apple evangelist and current venture capitalist Guy Kawasaki:

- Slide 1—Title page
  - Show your logo and contact information. Create the right first impression when people walk into the room.
- Slide 2—Overview or elevator pitch
  - Present your value proposition. What does the company really do? Any proof of market interest?
- Slide 3—Problem/opportunity
  Describe your customer's "pain" and the opportunity to reduce or eliminate that pain if they work with you.
- Slide 4—Unfair advantage
  Describe your competitive advantages. Indicate why those advantages are important.
- Slide 5—"Demo"
  Focus on "what" and "how," not "why," because that has already been covered. Take approximately 10 minutes. The "demo" is very important because it makes your idea real.
- Slide 6—Sales and marketing
  How will you roll out your product or service? What have you done thus far? What expertise do you have in sales and marketing?
- Slide 7—Competition
  Who is your competition? How do you compare with regard to things important to your customers?
- Slide 8—Business model
  Describe how you will make money. Describe your revenue, distribution, and customer support models. Keep it simple, understandable, and realistic.
- Slide 9—Forecast
  Show customers, employees, revenues, expenses, and profit-loss for 3 to 5 years. Be reasonable with realistic assumptions but exciting enough to interest investors.
- Slide 10—Team
  Who is on your senior team? What skills do they bring and why are they credible? What new talent do you need to build out the team?
- Slide 11—Status and milestones
  Where is the company now? What are the important events that will indicate real progress?

It is the rare start-up entity that secures financing after only one or two investor pitches. The entrepreneur should be prepared for multiple pitches to multiple potential investor organizations and not get discouraged that the process is taking longer than initially expected. With a strong and well-supported pitch, the entrepreneur should be able to find the right financing partner to move the company to the next stage in its development.

LEGAL STRUCTURE

Entrepreneurs need to make the decision of what legal structure to establish for their start-up venture. There are five primary alternatives—a C corporation, a limited liability company (LLC), an S corporation, a partnership or sole proprietorship, and a nonprofit corporation.

A C corporation, or C corp, is the most common type of corporation. It is a legal structure that shields personal assets of shareholders, directors, officers, and staff from judgments against the company. The structure includes various reporting requirements such as annual meetings and corporate minutes. The main downsides are the higher cost, double taxation of profits and dividends (corporate and individual) and greater reporting requirements than other organizational structures.

> A C corp and LLC are common legal structures for a start-up organization. Limitation on personal liability should be a key consideration.

An LLC is a popular legal structure for early-stage start-ups. It provides liability protection similar to a C corporation but allows profit and loss to flow through to the owners for tax purposes, avoiding double taxation. It also is less expensive to set up and maintain than a C corporation and offers greater operational flexibility. However, it cannot have shareholders and thus would need to be converted to a C corporation to receive venture capital financing.

An S corporation, or S corp, is similar to a C corporation in terms of providing limited liability. An S corporation is similar to an LLC in that an S corp provides profit-loss pass-through. It can have shareholders but with only one class of stock and with a maximum of 100 shareholders. It is more difficult to convert to a C corporation than it is for an LLC.

A partnership and sole proprietorship has an owner(s) who is(are) personally responsible for business debts, a huge disadvantage in many circumstances. The partial offset is minimal reporting requirements and pass-through of profit/loss to the owner(s).

Finally, a new venture may be able to be set up as a nonprofit corporation, the most common of which is a 501(c)(3) corporation. A nonprofit provides limited liability for officers and directors, is exempt from federal and state income and sales taxes, and can take tax-deductible donations from individuals and corporations.

Table 16.6 provides a comparison of some of the key attributes of the different organizational structures. It summarizes the advantages and disadvantages of each structure.

TABLE 16.6   ATTRIBUTES OF DIFFERENT ORGANIZATIONAL STRUCTURES

Organization Type/Key Attribute	C Corporation	S Corporation	Limited Liability Company (LLC)	Partnership or Sole Proprietorship	Nonprofit Corporation
Limitation on personal liability	Yes	Yes	Yes	No	Yes
Limitation on type of stockholder	No	Yes	No	No	NA
Limitation on number of stockholders	No	Yes	No	No	NA
Taxable entity	Yes	No	No	No	No
Pass-through entity	No	Yes	Yes	Yes	NA
Annual meetings, minutes required	Yes	Yes	No	No	Yes

INITIAL EQUITY DISTRIBUTION

An important question that start-up organizations face is how to divide the initial equity among the founders. A number of factors come into play, such as:

- Contribution to the development of the idea and value proposition (level and importance of past commitment)
- Previously developed intellectual property provided to the company
- Expected contribution to product development and launch, sales, operational execution, and strategic management (level and importance of future commitment)
- Previous track record and significance of management position (e.g., CEO more than the CFO)
- Unique value offered by that founder (e.g., how replaceable will he or she be if necessary)

Although there can be a tendency to divide the equity equally among the founders, that may not be the right choice from a long-term perspective given the factors above.

One should carefully consider how equity in the company is distributed. Several "do's and don'ts" should be kept in mind.

Some "do's and don'ts" for equity distribution are:

- Do
  - Objectively evaluate individual contributions—past and future
  - Structure the company to properly motivate people (be seen as fair)
  - Be as transparent as possible
  - Consider stock options for all employees, not only senior executives
  - Seek advice from attorneys and trusted outsider advisors
- Don't
  - Just spread the equity equally
  - Delay the decision as long as possible
  - Only reward people for past contributions
  - Make decisions without a lot of thought

There are three principal kinds of stock related instruments—common stock (restricted and unrestricted), stock options, and preferred stock.

Founders and early employees receive common stock—common stock that is restricted; it cannot be sold or traded until there is an acquisition or another liquidity event. This restricted stock typically vests over time and has various tax advantages compared with stock options. Investors such as angels may also receive common stock that is not restricted because they contributed capital in return for that stock.

Stock options represent an option to purchase common stock at a fair market price that is set when issued. Early in the company's existence, this price is close to zero. Options typically vest over time and are not usually exercised until there is a liquidity event such as an acquisition.

Preferred stock is what venture capital investors and sometimes angel investors receive when they invest in a company. Preferred stock has a liquidation preference, which means that the preferred stockholders get paid first out of any proceeds before the common shareholders. The preferred shareholders sometimes have dividend rights, which enhances their financial return, and they may also receive other special rights as well.

VESTING AND NONCOMPETE AGREEMENTS

The common stock and stock options received by the founders and other employees typically vest over time. Vesting is the process by which a founder or employee accrues nonforfeitable rights to the stock or stock options. This vesting is important to both the investors and senior management. Vesting recognizes that not every founder or employee will stay involved in the company over the longer term, discourages key employees from leaving prematurely, and takes into account that a founder may need to be replaced if he or she is not making a sufficient contribution to the company's success. Quarterly vesting over 3- to 5-years is typical.

Investors usually require noncompete, nonsolicitation of employees and confidentiality agreements from the founders and key employees. These agreements are
typically 1 year in length and may be difficult to enforce if longer. They should also
be reasonable in scope to be enforceable. The agreements may also include severance for the founders and key employees if they are let go without cause. Severance
pay may range from 6 months to 2 years of salary, depending on the person's position and industry mobility.

INTELLECTUAL PROPERTY

Patents, trademarks, and copyrights are types of intellectual property of most interest to entrepreneurs and investors. A patent is an exclusive right granted by a government to an inventor to manufacture, use, or sell an invention for a certain number of
years in exchange for a detailed disclosure of the invention. (See Chapter 6.)

The inventor usually assigns the patent rights to the company. Since 1995, US
patents have been issued by the US Patent and Trademark Office for 20 years from
the date of filing; it often takes 3 to 4 years from the time of filing to issuance.
Patents offer legal protection against infringement of an invention and may add
credibility with potential clients and investors. However, patents are often expensive in terms of legal and filing fees, can require a significant amount of time from
technical and other company staff, and can easily be turned down.

A trademarks or service mark is defined as a symbol or word or words legally
registered or established by use as representing a company or product. In the
United States, registered trademarks (indicated by the symbol ®) are issued by
the US Patent and Trademark Office and typically take approximately 1 year from
application to issuance if there are no conflicting marks. Trademarks (indicated
by the symbol ™) are established for use by the company but are not registered.

Copyrights are a form of intellectual property protection for original works of
authorship, such as written documents, graphics, or pictorial representations created by the company or its employees. The copyright notice consists of the symbol
© followed by the year of first publication and the owner's name.

EXECUTION

Entrepreneurs often underestimate the importance of execution to their venture's
success. Numerous companies with strong ideas have failed because of a lack of
execution. Effective execution necessitates a clear focus on the key drivers of your
organization's development and growth.

Developing realistic milestones related to the company's business plan helps
keep appropriate focus on execution. Those milestones should specify concrete
and quantifiable actions and outcomes in such areas as product development and

launch, pipeline development, customer engagement, financing, and management
team creation. They should include expected dates of completion, specify metrics
for measurement of completion, and
identify the people responsible for their | Many organizations fail not because
accomplishment. It helps to track prog- | their leaders do not have a good idea
ress against the milestones on a regu- | but because they do not execute well.
lar basis and take additional actions or | Consider some important "do's and
recalibrations if their attainment is in | don'ts" about execution.
jeopardy.

A lack of sufficient attention to managing ongoing cash flow can lead to a failure
of execution. Especially during the early stages of a company's history, sales revenues are difficult to predict. Too many companies incur expenses in expectation
of deals closing at a particular time and then experience a cash flow crunch when
those sales do not materialize. Closely managing expenses according to a realistic
budget will help an organization survive the unpredictable peaks and valleys in
demand for its products and services.

A strong emphasis on customer service is especially important during the initial stages of an entity's development. Early on, even if customers are not paying
or paying a discounted amount, they are taking a risk in working with you. Given
the inevitable glitches in any new product or service offering, companies need to
respond as quickly and transparently as possible to resolve those issues to customers' satisfaction, or at a minimum, make them aware of their plans to resolve the
issues. As mentioned earlier, it is quite difficult for a start-up to recover from a
perception of poor customer service.

The culture supported by senior management for the organization can have
a substantial impact on the company's ability to execute its plans. Although
there is no one model for an effective culture, there are clear signs that the
culture is hurting the company's progress. Lack of accountability, playing
politics, shifting blame, unclear direction, and morale issues are just several
indications of problems with the company's culture. How a company makes
decisions is a central part of its culture. Start-up entities often have to make
critical decisions quickly and with imperfect information. Who is involved
in those decisions, how timely they are made, and how they are communicated throughout the company can greatly influence the company's ability to
execute.

It may be helpful to consider some "do's and don'ts" regarding execution.

- Do
  - Take reasonable risks. Start-ups are inherently risky ventures.
    Taking reasonable, not irresponsible, risks is part of the process of
    execution.
  - Focus on your patients/clients' needs, but do not let them dictate
    strategy. The key is to understand customers' needs and then
    translate them into an approach that supports the business model.

- Hire trusted people you can work well with. Unproductive conflict or lack of trust among senior managers as well as staff can easily derail a start-up.
- Focus on creating the right culture from the start. Senior management's actions help instill a productive culture for the organization. Start-up organizations have the unique opportunity to create a culture from scratch. It is much harder to change a culture once it is established.
- Don't
  - Mislead investors/board members or withhold information from them. Once their trust is lost, it is very difficult to win it back. Plus, they can help deal with the inevitable problems and roadblocks the company will face.
  - Let the perfect be the enemy of the good. Then the company will likely run out of money before gaining traction in the marketplace. It is better to continually adapt based on initial failures and successes.
  - Overcustomize products or services. This approach will likely be cost-prohibitive. Instead, try to parameterize the approach so it seems to the customer that the company is flexibly meeting his or her specific needs.
  - Become easily discouraged or euphoric. Ups and downs are inevitable in a start-up company. The key is not to get too euphoric about the ups or too discouraged about the downs.

THE EXIT

The sad truth is that most start-up organizations fail and close down relatively shortly after they are started. The concepts discussed in this chapter will hopefully help avoid some of the pitfalls that lead organizations to fail.

If one is able to build a viable growth organization, the most common exit strategy is to be acquired by another company. Although some successful companies are able to "go public" through raising capital on a stock exchange, going public involves substantial additional expenditure, both during the process of going public and in running a public company. Accordingly, most investor-backed companies choose to go the acquisition route.

> Unfortunately, most start-up organizations fail. However, with a good idea and value proposition, a strong team, a solid business plan, and effective execution, one is much more likely to have a successful exit.

There are two main types of buyers—financial buyers and strategic buyers. Financial buyers are primarily interested in the profit generation potential of the organization in the future and will base what they are willing to pay on some multiple of revenues or earnings before interest, taxes, depreciation, and amortization (EBITDA).

Revenues are often used for earlier stage organizations that have not yet turned a profit and EBITDA for more established companies that have a multiyear track record of earnings. The multiples that investors use are often based on industry segment benchmarks, past acquisition multiples, attractiveness and riskiness of the company, strength of the management team, and an in-depth evaluation of the customer base and future projections. In the end, it is primarily numbers driven.

> Most successful growth companies go the acquisition route rather than go public. Acquirers are typically either financial buyers or strategic buyers and have somewhat different perspectives.

Although strategic buyers are also interested in the numbers, they are often more interested in how they can leverage the company's products, services, or expertise in their existing business. It may fill a current hole in their product line less expensively than building it themselves, may help them move in a new strategic direction more quickly, or may assist them in responding to a competitive threat. For these types of reasons, strategic buyers are often willing to pay a higher acquisition price than a financial buyer.

What is realistic timing for an exit event? Normally, 5 to 7 years is the expectation that investors have for an exit event. Although some companies are acquired earlier, especially in "hot" areas, 5 to 7 years are typically required for a company to prove its value proposition, develop a significant market for its product or service, and generate consistent profits. Some companies may not be acquired for 10 years or more, but usually not by choice. Investors, many of whom are invested in 10-year funds, need to show a return in a reasonable time and will strongly encourage or even force management into an acquisition event.

CASE STUDY

Like many other nonprofit institutions, Bolton Health Care allocated a small portion of its endowment to alternative investments such as private equity, venture capital, and hedge funds to try and maximize financial returns through diversification. HealthFocus Capital, a local venture capital fund, was one of those in which Bolton had a limited investment.

The managing director of HealthFocus had recently reached out to Dr. John Klingler, the CEO of Bolton Health Care, to get his advice on whether HealthFocus should provide seed financing to a new healthcare venture. That company offered text messaging software to improve communication between nurses and the family members of patients about the patient's status while in the hospital. Not only did the managing director want advice, but he was also wondering whether Bolton Hospital (part of Bolton Health Care) would be willing to serve as a beta site for the communication software, at a reduced fee, if HealthFocus did end up funding the start-up company.

On the top of the Dr. Klingler's mind was the recent proposal from his chief experience officer, Tracey Chandler, about the need to improve the patient experience of care in part by more effectively engaging the patient's family. Maybe being a beta site for the start-up company would be a win-win situation. As he contemplated this situation, he wrote down a list of questions he wanted some answers to before he gave his advice to the managing director of HealthFocus.

Questions

- How much experience does the start-up's management team have? Will they be able to deliver on their promises?
- What is the business model? How will they make money and price their services? How will they support us?
- How will HealthFocus and Bolton Health Care determine whether the beta site is successful? What things should Bolton be measuring and expecting? Would the nursing staff be supportive?
- How does this text messaging product compare to other competitors? What are the differentiating factors that are important to us? Could Bolton Health Care just offer this service itself?
- Why should Bolton Health Care devote its internal resources to such an endeavor? What are the potential risks and rewards?

After getting good answers to these questions, John Klingler feels confident that he could reach a decision. His first call was to Tracey Chandler.

At the same time, the CEO of the start-up company, Chris Sanders, is contemplating how she should be making the most effective pitch to both HealthFocus and Bolton Health Care.

Questions

- What should she include in her slide presentation?
- What commitments should she be willing to make?
- How would she determine whether the beta site was successful?

SUGGESTED READING

Johnson MW, Christensen CM, Kagermann H. Reinventing your business model. *Harv Bus Rev.* 2008 (Dec);86:50–59.

Kawasaki G. *The Art of the Start 2.0: The Time-Tested, Battle-Hardened Guide for Anyone Starting Anything.* New York, NY: Penguin Group; 2015.

Ries E. *The Lean Startup: How Today's Entrepreneurs Use Continuous Innovation to Create Radically Successful Businesses.* New York, NY: Crown Business; 2011.

17

Risk Management

JOSEPH S. SANFILIPPO AND STEVEN R. SMITH

KEY POINTS

- Risk management includes identification and analysis of potential losses as well as programs that minimize their occurrence.
- A first step is collection of information about areas of "at risk."
- Risk management approaches need to be consistently implemented.
- The goals of health organizations include reduction in causes of losses and adverse events as well as the protection of the organization.
- Negligence is often the basis for liability. It is primarily based on failure to adhere to a reasonable standard of care under the circumstances.
- Healthcare organizations should establish safeguards against system failure.
- Healthcare professionals should always be aware of the disgruntled patient or employee.
- Risk management includes avoiding litigation and administrative complaints.

RISK MANAGEMENT: WHAT IS IT AND WHY SHOULD WE CARE ABOUT IT?

Risk management is the process of identifying; assessing and analyzing potential losses; and seeking to eliminate, minimize, or manage them. Risk management is a standard part of modern businesses, including health organizations.

Any health organization, no matter the size or whether for-profit or nonprofit, must have a formal, written risk management program that is implemented effectively.

Developing a risk management program requires time, effort, and dedication; hence it is not cost free. But it is more expensive *not* to have one. Among other things, without one the organization is at risk for lawsuits, employment complaints, and fraud and abuse claims. Such problems, of course, also put the management of the organization at risk. When something goes wrong, the hindsight bias of boards and the public will make it appear that management was "asleep at the switch." The worst of all worlds is to have a risk management plan that is ineffective or not implemented. It gives a false sense of security and invites ridicule or worse when something goes wrong. On the positive side, a good risk management plan not only reduces the likelihood of the worst threats to the organization, it will likely improve the quality of service provided to patients.

Risk management may present tension between error reduction and individual responsibility. Some risk management approaches focus more on individual responsibility, in terms of identifying and holding people responsible for their mistakes. This approach is illustrated by the National Practitioner Data Bank (NPDB), which requires reporting about individual practitioner problems. The other approach looks more for systemic changes that reduce problems—less holding of individuals responsible and more encouraging self-reporting of errors in order to make systemic changes. An example is the Federal Aviation Administration's approach to reducing air accidents, which includes use of checklists, is oftentimes appropriate. Some commentators see a tension between error reduction/patient safety and risk management, with risk management emphasizing holding individuals responsible and patient safety advocates looking for systemic change. One solution to this apparent dichotomy is a preventive or "compliance" program. "Compliance" or a compliance office should be part of risk management, but it is only part of the response to potential risks of the organization.

BASIC PRINCIPLES OF RISK MANAGEMENT

There are many systems of risk management. Which system is the best one depends on many factors, including the size, culture, and nature of the business of the organization. In fact, more than the perfect fit, the best system for the organization is one that will be embraced as an ongoing part of the work of the organization and will be implemented faithfully. The following are some elements of a workable risk management system in healthcare.

All Risks

The risk management system should be designed to consider all of the risks the organization will face. Some health organizations have seen risk management as being related solely to professional malpractice. Of course, that is one area of significant risk, but it is far from the only one. It is a mistake to become too focused on that alone.

A large range of other risks need to be considered. Examples include violation of the fraud and abuse laws; employment discrimination; wage and hour, Employee Retirement Income Security Act (ERISA), and other fringe benefits rules; tax laws; fire and flood; theft and embezzlement; and death of key employees. The list could go on and on, but the point of a very broad concept of risk is clear. (See Chapter 6.)

Organizational Buy-In

The leadership of the organization must enthusiastically support risk reduction and make it part of the everyday lives of employees. In most healthcare organizations, this will mean devoting resources and personnel to the effort. In larger organizations and practices, an office charged with risk management is probably necessary. It is often desirable to have a consultant or other professional assistance in understanding the risks of the organization and developing the initial risk management plan. Again, the critical point is that there is not "a stable plan once and for always"—it has to be a living and changeable plan. The risks organizations face change, the business (practice) changes and the law changes. With all of this change, the plan must change, too.

Risk Assessment

The first step is usually to collect, in a systematic way, information about all of the areas in which the organization may be at any kind of risk. This, of course, must include all parts of the organization. Brainstorming about "what could go wrong" may be a good technique. Perhaps the idea that "a meteor could hit the building and cause a fire" is not a risk worth considering, but a rock sliding down the hill, or a truck running off the adjoining highway, crashing into the building, and starting a fire are events that should be considered.

The second part of the assessment is to consider the significance of the risks so that the greatest risks can be identified. There are two parts to this—considering first the probability of something happening and second, the severity of loss if it does happen. So, the probability of a tornado hitting the building may be low—but it would be devastating. On the other hand, the probability of someone spilling coffee in the cafeteria may be nearly 100%, but it seems to have very low severity. The coffee spill, however, illustrates the problem of the "hidden risk." That is, an event that can easily cascade from a small problem to a large one. The coffee spill may not be bad, but if it is not promptly attended to, it can become a big problem if someone slips on it before it is cleaned up.

The Current Plan

A next step is to review any current plans for managing the risks that have been identified. Even in the absence of an existing plan, there will be bits and pieces of risk management planning for specific problems. Gathering that plan or all of those pieces in one place will allow a consideration of the completeness and appropriateness of the existing plan and approaches. What areas are covered well by the current plan? Where are there weaknesses in the current plan? What risks remain unaddressed?

Assessing the current plan should also advance the process of determining where the biggest risks are to the organization—particularly those that are not currently addressed adequately. It is these, of course, that future planning should address most urgently.

The Risk Management Plan

The next steps involve creating risk management plans for areas that together will become an integrated risk management plan. This ordinarily involves the heads of department(s) considering the specific areas, under the general direction of a steering committee or officer. Any plan will go through several iterations to be both effective and efficient. Creativity should be encouraged, perhaps through roundtables and brainstorming.

The *efficiency* of the risk management program is important. An ounce of risk prevention may be worth a pound of cure, but there can be some inclination in the risk management program to overdo it. This is especially true in organizations (practices) where managers are disciplined for negative events in their departments. Purchasing insurance for events that are not likely to happen and, if they do happen, will not have serious consequences, may be foolish from the organization's long-term perspective; but it may seem worth it to a manager who fears being criticized for leaving the risk "uncovered" if that rare event does happen. One role of the supervising management in risk management is to emphasize efficiency in considering costs as well as benefits.

Part of efficiency is establishing priorities. Based on a realistic assessment of the importance of the risks and the cost of addressing them, the office manager or steering committee should establish the priorities. Funding and time are always scarce commodities, so they need to be deployed in a way that gets the best risk management "for the buck."

Another consideration is the unintended consequences of the plan. This involves thinking through every aspect of actions that the plan calls for. For example, having exhaustive "incident reports" that go to an administrator and attempt to detail every mistake that anyone made could have the unintended consequence of creating a record of negligence that might be used against the institution in the event of a lawsuit. Unintended consequences are, in the end, another "cost" of options that need to be calculated in developing a plan.

Implementation and Review

The plan, no matter how well drafted, creative, and efficient, no matter what the level of enthusiasm and buy-in, will not implement itself. Formal structures are essential if the plan is to be effective; there must be specific assignments for implementation with oversight and follow-up to make sure that it is done properly. It must be ongoing. In addition, periodic reviews for adjustments to the plan are important.

Some parts of the plan will not work as intended—they will need to be modified. The organization or practice will change and it will undertake new activities not considered when the plan was developed. The environment in which the organization operates will change, sometimes significantly, as new competitors emerge, new technology is developed, reimbursement is adjusted by third parties, and new laws create unanticipated risks. When circumstances change, the plan should always be open for modification. In addition, it periodically should be reviewed from top to bottom at intervals depending on the nature of the organization/practice.

Part of the implementation of the plan requires that the organization determine the structure of the ongoing risk management program: who will do what, what report lines will there be, and the like. The place of outside reviewers and consultants should also be considered. In addition, funding and staffing commitments must be considered and finalized.

The process of considering risks, assessing their seriousness, and creating a plan to manage them can have a salutary effect on the organization. It allows a sense of cooperation, with joint effort and cross-department discussions regarding the good of the organization and its service to its patients. At the same time, there are personnel risks as well. For example, to the extent that risk management becomes a "blame game" it is almost certainly going to become an institutional negative. Managers and human resource departments should consider potential problems in helping to design the process and the overall strategy for risk management. Box 17.1 gives advice about healthcare safety.

Box 17.1   ADVICE REGARDING HEALTHCARE SAFETY[a]

Ask questions if you have doubts or concerns.
Take a relative or friend to help you ask questions and understand answers.
Make sure you understand what will happen if you require surgery.
Tell your healthcare provider about all medications, including
    over-the-counter drugs, dietary supplements, and allergies.
Inform your healthcare provider regarding reactions to anesthetics.
When in doubt, get a second opinion.
Keep a copy of your own health history.

[a]This is advice from Medline Plus, a service of the US National Library of Medicine,
National Institutes of Health.

SOME SPECIFIC AREAS OF RISK MANAGEMENT IN HEALTHCARE ORGANIZATIONS

Each healthcare organization has its own sets of risks and values to be managed. This section briefly considers some of those areas. This list, of course, is not comprehensive. There are a number of very valuable sources of information about these risks; some are noted in the Suggested Reading at the end of the chapter.

Malpractice Risks

For many healthcare organizations, malpractice is not necessarily the greatest risk the organization/practice faces, but it is what many think of as "the big risk," so it receives special attention. Risk management related to malpractice has two general parts—avoiding professional negligence and dealing with claims once something bad has happened.

From a statistical perspective, most physicians will be involved in a medical malpractice suit at some point in their careers. This is the unfortunate reality; in a survey conducted by the American College of Obstetricians and Gynecologists, it was revealed that 89.2% of their members had been sued for malpractice during their career. Medical risk—that is, the risk of an adverse outcome versus the risk of being sued—must be distinguished. Adverse outcomes occur despite "best practices and best efforts." Fortunately, only 2% to 4% of adverse outcomes result in legal risk (i.e., a suit).

As it relates to reducing malpractice liability, it generally means negligence. The chapter on applied business law sets out the elements of negligence: duty, breach, causation, and injury. So avoiding malpractice means interrupting one of these elements, usually by eliminating the breach of duty. (See Chapter 6.)

Negligence is usually based on the failure to provide a reasonable standard of care under the circumstances. This "standard of care" is generally defined by what the profession itself sees as reasonably careful practice. Although not perfect, the measurement is usually what the actual practice is among similar professionals. Physicians, for example, would be held to a different standard of practice than nurses. In effect, it means that those who are specialists (or hold themselves out as) are likely to be held to a higher standard of care in that area of practice. The "assertions of expertise can be important—when professionals or professional organizations claim to have special skills, expertise, or training, the law will generally hold them to that level of skill, regardless of whether they actually have it or not. Claims of expertise in a clever advertising campaign must, for example, be undertaken with care.

Earlier in Chapter 6 (Applied Business Law), it is noted that there is ordinarily a duty to patients, not a general duty to everyone. It is, therefore, important to know when a professional relationship begins and the duty to a patient begins. It is equally important to know when a professional relationship ends. A healthcare professional cannot just "abandon" a patient. If the professional wishes to terminate the relationship, that must be clear, the patient must have a reasonable time to find other providers, and the professional must provide the next professional with the records necessary for treatment.

In Chapter 6, other topics of discussion included the "duty to protect" or the "duty to warn," which is a very limited duty that a provider may have when there is an identifiable victim who is in immediate danger from a patient. Risk management plans should take specific account of the risks associated with dangerous patients.

> The law recognizes that there may be different, legitimate approaches to medical care.

Some physicians may treat a cancer with chemotherapy, others with radiation, and still others with a combination of chemotherapy and radiation. Legitimate "schools of thought" that are based on reasonable medical or scientific support provide a standard of care. This neither justifies bizarre practice (treating a viral infection with a copper bracelet) nor does it continue to support outdated and discredited therapy (bleeding to cure pneumonia). But it does mean that there is not a single approach that all practitioners must use. The increasing use of evidence-based medicine and formal practice guidelines may, over time, affect the degree to which other schools of thought are acceptable for malpractice purposes. Deviations from formal guidelines are probably increasingly going to have to be justified when things go wrong.

Healthcare organizations should also have in place an effective mechanism to ensure that practitioners are permitted to practice only in areas in which they have received adequate training or certification. Beginning new procedures may be a "red flag" for an organization to review preparation for that area of practice.

Pressures from Medicare, managed care, limited reimbursement, financial pressures, or the like are not justifications for failing to provide good, professional care. For example, the fact that private insurance says it will not cover a hospital stay is not a legitimate legal basis for discharging a patient for whom continued hospitalized is clearly indicated. "The reimbursement made me do it," in short, is not a legitimate defense for poor or inadequate care.

The process of ensuring the highest possible level of practice and, even more, eliminating careless practice, is a central part of malpractice risk reduction. Patient safety and error reduction efforts, discussed in the next section, are very important to this end and exist in most healthcare organizations. Risk management suggests that if they do not exist, they need to be developed; if they do exist, they need to be taken seriously. Going through the motions, half-hearted efforts to make sure they work well, or (worst of all) using the process to protect or cover up weak practices is risk "enhancement," not risk reduction.

Safeguards Against System Failure

The following measures help protect against malpractice:

- Read, address, and sign off on culture and laboratory, pathology, and radiology reports.
- Use referrals or consults appropriately.
- Ensure that a fail-safe mechanism is in place if a patient cancels an important office visit.
- List medications and allergies.
- Add to record critical medical history not documented in prior records.

Malpractice risks are also affected by the hiring of professionals and granting practice privileges. The failure to exercise rigorous quality standards in these areas will create long-term problems for risk management. On one hand, engaging in, or keeping those engaged in, careless practice endangers patients and creates substantial risk for the organization. On the other hand, failing to note problems as they are developing and then taking precipitous action invites complaints and lawsuits based on employment or contractual rights.

When malpractice issues do arise, having excellent records and a process of handling complaints and errors is beneficial. Even when things have gone wrong, these processes can substantially reduce the possibility of a malpractice claim, and we will look at that later in this chapter.

Document the discussion. This *cannot* be overemphasized.

Caution: Disgruntled Patients or Employees

Not all patients and employees are equally likely to file complaints or take legal action. The studies of malpractice claims, for example, show that only a small proportion—perhaps 10% to 15% of those claiming injury by negligent treatment—will take legal action. In part, those who file are "disgruntled patients" and may be reacting to not being honestly dealt with, a perceived sense of indifference to their plight, or unfair billing/credit practices. These actions may also, of course, be related to patients' psychological makeup. It is a realistic element of risk management to consider the emotional reaction of complaining or disgruntled patients.

Listening to patients and having them involved in the decision-making process regarding their management must be emphasized. What is the patient perspective? In a study by Hickson, et al (see Suggested Reading) in which patients were interviewed in association with malpractice claims, specifically they felt:

- Rushed
- Ignored
- Received inadequate explanations or advice

In addition, physicians who had experienced a malpractice claim spent less time during routine visits than did physicians with no prior claims. Patient assessment was reflected as follows:

Physician would not listen	13%
Physician would not talk openly	32%
Physician attempted to mislead	48%
Needed (more) information	20%

Physicians with no malpractice claims were more likely to have oriented patients to the "process of their office." "We will talk the problem over and I will leave time for your questions" was succinctly conveyed. Terms more commonly heard from "no malpractice claim physicians" include "tell me more about . . .," "what do you think caused that to happen," and "what do you think about taking these pills" (Levinson, et al; see Suggested Reading).

"Whistleblowers," notably including those who may file False Claim Act complaints, are frequently disgruntled employees or former employees. Indeed, disgruntled employees are prime sources of information about false claims and other fraud and abuse charges. These are people who have access to internal information that may make a case for false claims, discriminatory practices, or other violations of the law. If they feel they have been mistreated, disciplined unfairly, or otherwise abused, they have the motivation to use this inside information for their own advantage, to even some scores, or just to cause trouble for the institution. Risk management, therefore, should take into account not just the problem of false claims but also how personnel policies may affect the likelihood of "whistle-blower" claims being made. (See Chapter 6.)

Patient Safety and Error Reduction

Patient safety has evolved into a specific discipline within medicine that focuses on reporting, analysis and prevention of medical errors. The latter oftentimes result in adverse events. It is estimated that in the United States annually, 44,000 to 98,000 "unnecessary deaths" and more than 1,000,000 instances of harm occur. All of this translates to one in ten patients experiencing a medical error. According to the Institute for Healthcare Improvement, the estimated cost of "medical errors" ranges from $17 to $29 billion annually. The Medicare and Medicaid programs are increasingly taking quality and error reduction into account in the reimbursement for services. Under the Affordable Care Act, healthcare systems with poor records will be penalized.

Significant efforts in addressing patient safety have occurred in the specialty of anesthesiology. Specifically, the Anesthesia Patient Safety Foundation was established by the American Society of Anesthesiologists, and it has become the leading medical specialty to address patient safety since 1984. See Box 17.2, which sets out some of the primary reasons that errors occur in the healthcare setting.

Efforts in the right direction to minimize medical care errors include use of electronic medical records (EMRs), alerts regarding interaction of drugs or dietary aspects, allergy checks, and dosage alerts. Advances in health informatics along with EMRs are designed to have a profound positive effect in minimizing medical errors.

Box 17.2   WHY DO HEALTHCARE ERRORS OCCUR?

Variation in training and experience, fatigue, depression, and burnout
Time pressure
Failure to acknowledge the prevalence and seriousness of medical errors
Technological advances and the requirement for prerequisite higher
    level of education
Communication failure
Decrease in nurse-to-patient ratios
Similarity in drug names
Reliance on automated systems to prevent errors
Information-sharing problems
Cost-saving measures by healthcare systems
Competency of select healthcare providers
Development of procedures with increased risk(s)

Reports of "near misses" are also important. Although the "miss" means that no injury, illness, or damage occurred, valuable lessons can still be learned from what almost went wrong—this is a concept learned from airline safety procedures. The Association of Operating Room Nurses has implemented a voluntary "near miss" reporting system, Safety Net, focused on medications, transfusion reactions, communication issues, wrong patient/procedure events, and technologically related errors.

Quality improvement initiatives is one other effort in this area. Community pharmacies are using automated drug dispensing devices, computerized drug utilization review tools, and electronic prescriptions to decrease errors. In the arena of obstetrics and gynecology, as another example, improvements in patient outcomes have occurred, with fetal mortality rates declining by 1.4% annually with fetal death rates at 6.22 per 1000 live births. Established measures or indicators of quality and safety have been instituted. These are:

- Developing a culture of patient safety
- Implementing safe mediation practices
- Reducing surgical errors
- Improving communication among healthcare providers
- Partnering with patients to improve safety
- Making safety a priority during clinical practice

A continued effort to incorporate evidence-based medicine in clinical practice is paramount to good patient care. Box 17.3 summarizes the elements of evidence-based medicine.

Pay-for-performance (commonly known as P4P) systems associate compensation with measure of quality. A number of pilot programs are underway to assess efficacy of such an approach. This has also been equated with avoidance of "high-risk" patients and thus cutting back on care. Incentive-based programs rewarding healthcare providers for quality care and excellence in cost-effective care remains a key goal.

Box 17.3   EVIDENCE-BASED MEDICINE IN CLINICAL PRACTICE

Summarizing evidence into checklists
Identifying and mitigating local barriers to comply with the checklist
Measuring and providing feedback
Ensuring all patients receive the items on the checklist by reorganizing
    work, improving culture and monitoring performances (Pronovost; see
    Suggested Reading)

Patient Bill of Rights and Risk Management

The patient bill of rights may be an important element of risk management. This sets out reasonable expectations of patients. Once adopted or accepted by an organization, all members of the organization must know, accept and implement these rights. The failure to adhere to the basics of these principles invites complaints and litigation.

The Affordable Care Act results in significant changes in the way medicine is practiced. In one sense, it puts consumers more in charge of their healthcare. On June 22, 2010, President Obama announced new interim final regulations, meaning the Patient's Bill of Rights. This includes a set of protections that are applicable to healthcare coverage with a start date of September 23, 2010. The Department of Health and Human Services collaborated on the Patient's Bill of Rights. See Box 17.4 for more information as well as Chapters 3, 6, and 7.

Overall, now patients are given specific rights regarding their healthcare coverage. There is a guarantee for patients for access to information, fair treatment, and autonomy with regard to the medical decision-making process.

The American Hospital Association has also developed a "Patient Bill of Rights" with the goal of more efficient and more effective patient care. Healthcare is a partnership between the patient, his or her physician, and the hospital system. Factors that must be taken into account are good communication; respect on both sides; standard of care; respect for the patient's rights and the care provided; patient input as appropriate into the decision-making process with awareness of communication limitations; and culture, race, language, religious, age, gender, and disabilities. Ask and be informed regarding business relationships among hospital educational institutions.

Box 17.4   THE PATIENT'S BILL OF RIGHTS

Obtain considerate and respectful care.

Obtain from physicians and other direct caregivers appropriate, current and understandable information related to diagnosis, treatment, and prognosis except in emergencies.

Make decisions about the plan of care before and during treatment.

Have an advanced directive (e.g., living will, healthcare proxy, or durable power of attorney for healthcare) as related to treatment or designation of a surrogate decision-maker.

Have privacy, including case discussion consultation, examination, and treatment.

INSTITUTION RESPONSIBILITIES
- Consent to or decline to participate in research studies.
- Expect reasonable continuity of care.
- Be informed of hospital policies and practices that relate to patient care treatment and responsibilities.
- Be informed of available resources for resolving disputes, grievances and conflicts.
- Be informed regarding hospital charges for services and available payment methods.

PATIENT RESPONSIBILITIES
- Provide information about past medical history.
- Participate in decision-making.
- Ensure that the healthcare institution has a copy of their written advance directive.
- Hospital has a duty to be reasonably efficient and fair in providing care.

Reporting Obligations

As part of risk management, every health organization must have specific plans to ensure that it makes, and records that it has made, required reports. As noted previously, the federal government and states have reporting obligations for many conditions, including child and adult abuse, gunshot wounds, and a variety of communicable diseases. Each obligation has its own designated reporting agency, the timeframe in which reports must be made, and the like. The failure to make required reports may be a serious matter, and these are among the most important risk management policies the institution has.

On November 14, 1986, President Ronald Reagan signed Public Law 99-660 which was the legislation that led to the NPDB. (See Box 17.5 and Box 17.6.)

Fraud and Abuse Risk Management

For the modern healthcare organization, the big risks may be associated with unintentionally violating reimbursement rules or wandering into fraud and abuse of Medicare/Medicaid and other governmental programs. The chapters on applied business law and ethics noted the extraordinarily complex rules that apply—and that they are constantly changing. And the violation of the rules can have costly consequences, potentially including loss of Medicare eligibility.

Therefore, risk management systems must pay particularly close attention to these significant risks. The risks are not limited to the process of reimbursement but may affect almost all parts of the organization. For example, accepting

---

Box 17.5   PRACTITIONERS ARE REPORTED TO NATIONAL PRACTITIONER DATA BANK

Physicians, including residents in training
Dentists
Nurses/allied health professionals
Chiropractors
Podiatrists
Pharmacists and pharmacist assistants
Psychologists
Physician assistants
Nurse practitioners
Physical therapists

---

computer hardware from an associated hospital for an EMR program may seem perfectly harmless to the information technology (IT) department—but it may be a violation of antikickback rules. A good primer on fraud and abuse issues is available from the Inspector General of Health and Human Services at https://oig.hhs.gov/compliance/physician-education/roadmap_web_version.pdf.

Employment Risks

Employees represent risks in that the organization is responsible for the actions of the employees. Employees also represent another class of risks—the organization has many legal obligations *to* as well as *for* employees.

Employees require a very substantial range of protections from injury, notably under the Occupational Safety and Health Administration and various safety rules. There are federal and state wage and hour laws that involve pay, overtime,

---

Box 17.6   MALPRACTICE REASONS REPORTED TO NATIONAL PRACTITIONER DATA BANK

Anesthesia-related issues
Diagnosis-related issues
Equipment malfunction
Medication-related sentinel errors
Blood product complications
Significant obstetrics-related problems
Sentinel surgical problems

and record-keeping. Taxation and benefits are subject not only to withholding, Social Security contributions, and so on, but ERISA has many obligations regarding fringe benefits, particularly retirement accounts. Employment discrimination and harassment rules deserve particular attention from a risk management standpoint. Claims based on age, gender, ethnicity or race, sexual orientation, or disabilities are not uncommon in health organizations. The failure to have employment policies that address complaints may expose the organization to significant penalties.

Some healthcare organizations have employees represented by labor unions, or whose workers seek to be represented. Federal labor laws provide considerable detail about fair labor practices. The contracts with the union will provide contractual rights for the covered workers. Any risk management or other compliance program should take into account these obligations to avoid expensive errors in dealing with unionized workers.

Financial Risk Management

Issues related to audits, debt collection, and financial controls are discussed elsewhere in this book. We pause only to point out that there are substantial risks to health organizations that fail to adhere to good financial practices. Nonprofit organizations must also be sensitive to the obligations imposed by the Internal Revenue Service Form 990, described in the chapter on applied business law. Of course, publicly traded organizations have securities law risks to consider.

Business Recovery and Continuity

A full consideration of risks includes the possibility of a massive interference with the normal operation of the business—including natural disasters (earthquakes, tornadoes, floods), large fires, and bomb threats; the list could go on and on. For healthcare institutions, the need to consider such risks is especially acute because the demands for its services are likely to increase in the event of a disaster. "The business of medicine cannot just shut down." The community will expect it to be ready. That means more than keeping the lights on in the emergency department. The odds are that most of the institution could not operate without IT, phone service, personnel emergency contacts, and so on.

Beyond keeping services going, "Business 101" continuity has to consider payroll, organization of leadership in the absence of some critical managers, and access to cash and supplies. This business continuity process is sufficiently complex that it can be spun off into a separate process, but it really needs to be comprehensive.

Compliance and Risk Management

Compliance officers or departments are an important part of ongoing risk management. These officers oversee day-to-day compliance with various regulatory requirements of the organization. But it is not appropriate just to turn over all of risk management to this office. Risk management has to be an integral part of the institution, not one department.

Record-keeping

Documentation remains a hallmark in successfully defending any complaint against the institution, including a malpractice case. Inclusion of healthcare provider "thought process" is appropriate and clinically useful information.

Never, ever alter a chart or record, because this may make it or the case indefensible. Healthcare providers must avoid blaming each other. Criticism mentioned in passing by a clinician can be the impetus for a patient to seek legal counsel with a resulting suit. If an opinion regarding another providers care is rendered, it should reflect a thorough review of details of the case and honest, fair and objective assessment. (See Chapter 6.)

Legal Audits and Annual Checkups

A good technique of risk management is to have periodic reviews of the legal questions and the forms and procedures that may affect legal exposure. These preventive processes will save time, money, and legal exposure in the long run. Ideally, they are conducted annually.

AVOIDING LITIGATION

Risk management is aimed not just at winning lawsuits or administrative complaints. It is even better to avoid complaints. Although it is practically impossible to avoid *all* litigation, there are many steps that can be taken to reduce substantially such claims being filed. (See Chapter 6.)

Malpractice

In medical malpractice, there is good evidence that usually something more than negligence and injury is "at work" when a lawsuit is filed. It was noted earlier that a claim is filed only in a small proportion of instances in which there is negligence. In fact, most people are disinclined to file malpractice suits. They generally begin with respect for the healing professions. They know that filing a suit will be a protracted, difficult, and time-consuming process that will reveal private information and require that they relive painful experiences.

Some people injured by medical errors have a strong economic need for resources for future medical care or family support. It appears, however, that the incentive actually to file a malpractice claim or a complaint with a licensing board is (1) related to the hope "that nobody else will be treated as I was," (2) a "search for answers" regarding what happened, or (3) a sense of anger or even retribution for mistreatment. Those feelings often arise from being disrespected, kept "in the dark," or being misled. Ironically, when things go wrong, there is often a reluctance to talk with the patient and the patient's family, and that exacerbates the problem. Poor communication is an invitation to distrust for disgruntled patients. Poor debt collection practices may also create hostility that leads to claims being filed.

The failure to communicate with the patient can lead to dissatisfaction and problems. The informed consent process is a good opportunity to engage in effective communication, including a chance to address patient misunderstandings and concerns. For example, unrealistic expectations about the risks of outcomes of treatment can wrongly lead to the conclusion that the treatment was mishandled. The informed consent process is an ideal time to align expectations with reality.

Other Areas

Malpractice claims are only one area in which an organization should consider mechanisms to avoid claims. A good example of another area is employment-related errors. Indeed, a good risk management plan will consider how potential claims and complaints in any area will be handled, keeping in mind that disgruntled patients and employees are opportunities to reduce risk exposure.

Apologies

Lawyers have traditionally told health clients not to admit to mistakes or to apologize for them. Under common rules of evidence, such "confessions" may be "declarations against interest" that can be admitted at trial as admission of liability: hence the old advice, "just keep quiet." We have long felt that this advice denies an element of the humanity of healthcare workers and might be counterproductive, and our feelings have been borne out in a number of studies. Many states have now adopted "apology statutes" that prevent apologies from being considered admissions.

The process of communicating with those who may have been harmed through negligence (or otherwise) is an element to be considered in risk management. This may include an apology, if it is genuine, and even the offer of adjustments to the bill or other financial settlement. Such plans, however, must be coordinated with insurance carriers to ensure that the insurance contract is not violated.

Insurance

Insurance coverage is a natural part of avoiding the cost of litigation and of paying claims. Indeed, insurance coverage has traditionally been a centerpiece of risk management. Various types of insurance cover liability claims of many kinds as well as property destruction and business continuity. Among the types of insurance that should be considered are general liability and umbrella, fire and flood, directors and officers, errors and omissions, workers compensation, professional liability, property, and business disaster/recovery. The kinds of insurance and amount of coverage depend on the nature and size of the organization, and this analysis generally requires the assistance of an insurance consultant.

FORMING, JOINING, OR LEAVING A PRACTICE

Most healthcare practitioners will join and leave a number of practice settings over a career. Many will participate in the formation of a practice group. These are moments of considerable risk. They involve complex legal, financial, taxation, ethical, professional, and liability issues. Even a simple exposition of those issues would take many pages.

Despite the enthusiasm of the moment that is ripe with anticipation and excitement, it is essential to have solid legal review and advice before undertaking any of these changes. Some medical societies offer advice on forming practices. The California Medical Association, for example, has such a publication (for purchase) at http://www.cmanet.org/resource-library/detail/?item=medical-group-how-to-form. As good as some of these resources are, it is risky to try to finalize these arrangements alone.

PRACTICAL ADVICE

In closing, we outline several suggestions for avoiding losses and the disruption of claims against health organizations. Good risk management plans include consideration of most of these areas.

- Have a current, comprehensive plan of risk management for all areas of the organization or practice. Implement the plan faithfully and review it periodically.
- Understand and carefully abide by all ethical obligations. Seek ethical consultation when in doubt. Formal consultations are available from some organizations, and informal consultation with colleagues may be helpful (with caution regarding confidential information).
- Engage in good, professional practice at all times and have processes in place to identify when that standard is not being met. The essence of malpractice is failing to engage in practice that is acceptable to good professionals.
- Do not allow pressures from Medicare, managed care, limited reimbursement, or the like be an excuse for the failure to provide good, professional care.
- Avoid conflicts of interest (or dual relationships). In some specialties, notably mental health areas, this is a particularly sensitive area, but all professionals must keep in mind the inherent risks of dual relationships.
- Maintain patient confidentiality. Understand legal limitations and constraints on confidentiality and on communicating medical information.
- Be compliant with the Health Insurance Portability and Accountability Act (HIPAA). The Security and Privacy Rules of HIPAA now apply to almost all health organizations. Changes in the law during the past few years have resulted in increased penalties for violations of privacy laws. Many states now have privacy rules that go beyond the federal requirements.
- Carefully maintain *all* records—including patient care, employment, financial, and corporate records. Be sure that records stay up-to-date and are subject to "records retention" policies tailored to the type of record. Avoid any changes in documents that are intended to alter them. If records are relevant to a dispute, claim, or lawsuit, be sure that the records are retained and are secure.
- Have reporting systems in place to ensure compliance with all legal obligations to report child or elder abuse, as well as other laws that require a variety of reports to governmental agencies. Document that the required reports have been made.
- Practice only within areas of current competence and stay up-to-date with literature, new practice techniques, and so on. Risk management systems in organizations should have mechanisms for limiting practice to those areas in which practitioners are adequately trained and certified.
- Comply with the Americans with Disabilities Act and all disability laws.

- Undertake debt collection with great caution. There are laws limiting debt collection practices, but debt collection can also lead to antagonism that invites legal complaints.
- Avoid inappropriate relationships with pharmaceutical companies. There are increasing legal and ethical limitations on these relationships in clinical practice and research.
- Supervise assistants, employees, residents and others carefully. Both principles of negligence and vicarious liability suggest that the "hiring" organization will be responsible for their errors.
- Understand the particular challenges of treating minors and adolescents. Parents ordinarily have the right to consent to treatment and to receive information regarding the treatment of their children. There are several exceptions for older minors and for certain kinds of treatment. These vary among the states.
- Maintain liability insurance consistent with the practice and organization. Depending on the organization, a variety of other insurance will be important to have. Annually review the adequacy of insurance coverage.
- Maintain good relationships with patients and be open to their concerns and problems. Be especially cautious with troublesome patients. It is a serious mistake to stop communicating with difficult patients in the face of an error, criticism, or unpleasantness.
- Avoid abandoning patients. If they should see another professional, be sure that there is an appropriate referral and follow up. Also avoid even appearing to "dump" patients. Institutions should know and fulfill their Emergency Medical Treatment and Active Labor Act (EMTALA) obligations.
- If you receive a demand letter, subpoena, lawsuit, threat, or the like, consult with an attorney and provide the necessary notification to the insurance carrier. Each of these legal processes carries special obligations and rights. Do not guess at what it means.
- Maintain an ongoing relationship with a qualified attorney who can provide routine legal advice and conduct "annual examinations" as a preventive measure. This will not only reduce the risk of violating the law or incurring liability, it will help bring peace of mind.
- Work with the general counsel or legal division within your institution (medical center) to provide oversight when dealing with controversial areas (e.g., aspects of assisted reproductive technology/in vitro fertilization).

Good risk management is a complex but essential process. Managers will do a great service to their institutions to take it seriously and make it a routine part of the organization.

In summary, risk management is an essential part of modern healthcare organizations. There are many effective approaches to risk management; one is described in this chapter. Whatever approach is taken, however, it is essential that it be implemented consistently and strongly supported by management. In healthcare organizations, the most common goals of risk management are to reduce the causes of losses and adverse events, ensure that the organization is protected when such losses occur, and reduce claims against the organization. There are several special issues for health organizations, including malpractice, the disgruntled patient, fraud, and abuse claims.

CASE STUDY

Dr. X is a full-time hospital employee who completed residency training 3 years prior to accepting a staff position in a specialty that includes both medical and surgical aspects of care. Two years into his contract, it is noted that his infection rate is indeed two standard deviations above the mean. The rate of return to the operating room on average occurs at one patient every 1 to 2 months. Transfusions are significantly more frequent than other practitioners in the same hospital. Indeed, this physician is on the "radar screen" of risk management!

Questions

- How would you proceed?
- What information should be obtained by the internal peer review committee in this small-town hospital?
- Should external peer review be obtained?
- Should the physician's privileges be suspended immediately or pending evaluation?
- What risks does the hospital/employer have?
- What safeguards need to be in place to prevent this?
- Should provisional status be granted for the first year of this type contract?
- Does this have an impact on the patient's bill of rights?
- Should this physician's patients be informed of this problem?

SUGGESTED READING

Gaba D. Anesthesiology as a model for patient safety in health care. *Med Care*. 2000;320:785–786.

Glitter G, Goldstein EJ. The elements of medical malpractice. *Clin Infect Dis*. 1996;23(5):1152–1155.

Hickson G, Clayton E, Githens P, et al. Factors that prompted families to file medical malpractice claims following prenatal injuries *JAMA*. 1992;267:1359–1363.

Hickson G, Pichert J, Federspiel C, Clayton EW. Development of an early identification and response model of malpractice prevention. *Law Contemp Prob*. 1997 (Winter);60(1):7.

Levinson W, Roter D, Mullcoly J, et al. Physician-patient communication. the relationship with malpractice claims among primary care physicians and surgeons. *JAMA*. 1997;277(7):553–559.

Nepps M. The basics of medical malpractice, a primer on navigating the system. *Chest*. 2008;134(5):1051–1055.

Pronovost P, Holzmuller C, Ennen C, Fox H. Overview of progress in patient safety. *Am J Obstet Gynecol*. 2011; wwww.AJOG.org.

Sanfilippo JS, Robinson CL, ed. *The risk management handbook for healthcare professionals*. New York, NY: Parthenon Publishers; 2002.

Theodos TF. The patients' bill of rights: women's rights under managed care and ERISA preemption. *Am J Law Med*. 2000;26:89–108.

Williams D. Practice patterns to decrease the risk of malpractice suit. *Clin Obstet Gynecol*. 2008;51(4):680–687.

US Department of Health and Human Services: Quick Guide to Health Literacy. 2011 National Healthcare Quality and Disparities Reports.

World Health Organization. World Alliance for Patient Safety. www.who.int/patient safety. Pages 9–27. Retrieved 2008.

Youngberg BJ, ed. *Principles of Risk Management and Patient Safety*. Sudbury, MA: Jones & Bartlett Learning; 2011.

Extended Case Studies

CASE STUDY 1: THE CASE OF SYNERGISTIC HOSPITAL CORPORATION OF AMERICA

Synergistic Hospital Corporation of America is composed of three hospitals consisting of 700 beds, a 65-bed nursing home, and three home healthcare agencies, with a total of 310 employees. The total operating budget is $40.3 million. The corporate headquarters are located in Columbus, Ohio, but the system is located throughout the state of Ohio.

Dr. Roy Jameson has been the president of Synergistic Hospital Corporation for the past 3 years. He was unanimously appointed by the Board of Trustees of the corporation because they wanted to inject "new blood" into the system. He was seen as "youthful," in his early forties, energetic, intelligent, very articulate, effective, and well-liked. The Board saw him as someone who could easily attract other energetic, accomplished employees at all levels.

The previous president, Dr. Martha Aimsley, had been in office for 15 years with a less than stellar record. During her tenure, Dr. Aimsley had allowed a large debt to accrue and old equipment to be retained, and there was a turnover of key physicians and other employees who were disgruntled about a variety of unresolved issues. Medicare and other insurance reimbursements were not on par with competing hospitals in the region. There were no Centers of Excellence in any of the system's component parts, and electronic medical records did not exist at all in two hospitals, despite federal payments and incentives to implement them. These and other inadequacies were largely hidden from view of the Board, who relied on Dr. Aimsley's input and counsel to guide them for years. It was not until the Board decided to hire an outside consultant to review the current state of the system that the Board was apprised of Dr. Aimsley's failings, which surprised them. The corporation terminated Dr. Aimsley with what had been seen as a "golden parachute" and asked her to vacate her office within 3 weeks. Mr. Mark Byler, the current chief operating officer (COO), became the interim president and chief executive officer (CEO).

Shortly thereafter, the Board conducted a nationwide search for Dr. Aimsley's replacement. Ultimately, it decided to hire Dr. Jameson, a renowned surgeon from the Cleveland hospital to replace her. A search into his background revealed the following information: he was Chief Medical Officer (CMO) in Cleveland for 7 years prior to being that hospital's president and CEO for 5 years. While CMO, he continued with a small clinical practice as a general surgeon. He also had published four significant, peer-reviewed articles in prestigious national and international medical journals.

Dr. Jameson had successfully dealt with many challenging physician-related problems and had simultaneously quelled serious nursing union organizing efforts in two hospitals. As an effective role model and also as a leader, he improved the quality of patient care by decreasing medical errors, thereby decreasing potentially costly malpractice suits. He effectively kept insurance reimbursements at an equitable level with surrounding similar hospitals in the Cleveland area for 3 of his 5 years in office.

Not all of the physicians at the Synergistic Corporation felt totally positive about Dr. Jameson. Many believed that he lacked the experience, expertise, and forward-looking ability to create a well–thought out vision for the hospital. Nonetheless, the turnover rate was minimal while he was in office.

After his hiring by the Synergistic Corporation, Dr. Jameson's reputation narrowly "survived" a very difficult, contentious, and prolonged malpractice suit due to a surgical oversight error. His patient died shortly after intestinal surgery due to infection and internal bleeding. The family finally agreed to an out-of-court settlement simply to stop the lengthy, intense, agonizing acrimony between them and the hospital lawyers, especially because the hospital was their "community hospital." The family feared that extreme levels of negativity would harm their ability to seek future care in that hospital.

Currently, Dr. Jameson faces many challenges to his leadership knowledge, skills, and abilities. In the nursing home in Akron, Ohio, the CEO, Andrea Martinez, is having trouble with the physical plant and also with many staff. The heating, ventilation, and air conditioning (HVAC) does not always work appropriately. Staff at all levels complain that it is too hot in the summer and too cold in the winter. Ms. Martinez does not have the funds to rebuild the entire system, so she has been replacing parts in a piecemeal fashion each fiscal year. Despite huge expenditures, the HVAC still does not function acceptably. This is particularly problematic for the elderly patient population.

In terms of the employees, although they seem dedicated and willing to work hard, the poor environment is demotivating them. They no longer want to "go the extra mile" to work extremely hard; many just come and go, and in fact cannot wait to leave after their shift. The quality of their work suffers as well. Although their reactions may be understandable on some level, their decreased work ethic and level of productivity are unacceptable. No one really knows how the geriatric population there is dealing with these environmental issues.

Furthermore, because of the heavy expenditures to the physical plant, monies have not been available to increase employee salaries at all levels to a competitive rate with other hospitals. The current set of employees have been working hard, in general, and the medical and nursing staffs in particular, have been working extremely diligently, with long hours, usually "extra hours," and few complaints. Still, salaries are a huge issue.

The annual holiday party and summer picnics have been canceled because of fiscal constraints. In the past, these events have served as a "shot in the arm" for employee morale. The opportunities for all employees to get together in an informal, fun atmosphere has always had a positive effect. This is no longer the case.

Ms. Martinez has gone to Dr. Jameson several times over the past few years to plead her case and ask for increased budgetary funds to address her challenges, because revenues, even with a mixed-payer base, do not cover expenses or plans for the future. Although he is kind, a good listener, and wants to help, he has not been forthcoming with specifics or cash to relieve her difficulties. She is not sure how much longer she is willing to lead her hospital without some key changes now or in the very near future.

Mr. John Brink is the CEO of the Columbus Hospital (a Synergistic hospital), a position he has held onto for approximately 6 years. A former chief financial officer (CFO) for 10 years at the Buffalo Medical Center, Brink has shown himself to be a strong-willed executive. He takes a situation that he deems to be unacceptable (i.e., failing or underperforming), and after seriously contemplating and evaluating possible scenarios for intervention, he calls in the key players and pressures them to devise solutions to their own problems. Sometimes this takes a long time, because Brink is rarely quick to act, not wanting to make an error. Although this has been effective in many situations and helpful from a leadership perspective, other situations have not been resolved properly. When the individuals involved have difficulty coming up with plans to correct the situation, Mr. Brink seems to sit back and wait for them to work even more diligently at improving the situation and ensuring that it does not recur. He does not even suggest possibilities. However, often, the state of affairs and the players are stalemated. At times like this, it seems that he himself is stalemated.

In the past, Mr. Brink usually went to Dr. Aimsley for assistance and direction. She would often provide answers. Some would be effective, others not, but at least she would offer assistance and guidance. And that is what Mr. Brink needs: direction and guidance. Without it, he is unable to move ahead.

Well, that was then, and now is now. When Mr. Brink goes to Dr. Jameson for advice, he usually gets the same treatment he himself gives other people: "what do *you* think you should do?" Mr. Brink needs answers—specific answers—because he is very perplexed and frankly does not know what to do, although he fears telling Dr. Jameson exactly how upset and perplexed he really is. Mr. Brink rarely exposes his true emotions to anyone, certainly not his direct boss. The result is considerable thinking and soul-searching but little in the way of positive answers, direction, or clues. Without specific, direct ideas or suggestions from someone, in this case from Dr. Jameson, Mr. Brink cannot function; he is unable to take action to deal with a challenging situation.

Dr. Jameson, CEO of the entire corporation, knows the value of setting high goals and expectations for his team. In these situations, he prefers to ask them to set their own goals, believing that they will be far more willing to move ahead on goals they have created, rather than the ones he, in "corporate," has created for them. As a result, at times he obtains dynamic goals and creative results from some people who report to him directly. But this is not true of everyone. Nonetheless, being the optimistic thinker and leader that the Board expects, he does not pressure everyone to perform to the same high standards that some of his team does.

Dr. Jameson has problem-solving issues with Ms. Maria Antonio, CEO of the third hospital, this one in Cincinnati, Ohio. The Board hired Ms. Antonio for much the same reasons as they hired Dr. Jameson. She is smart, personable, and young. She relies on Dr. Jameson, however, for direction and forming a vision, not only for the overall corporation, but for her hospital. She has many new and exciting ideas about where the hospital needs to grow. She wants to start a women's service line with renowned experts in breast and ovarian cancer, reproductive issues, pre- and postnatal care, and wellness, especially for single mothers. These are dynamic and forward-looking goals, the kind that please Dr. Jameson, and Ms. Antonio seriously wants to please her boss. She is acutely aware of the political importance of being kept in the good graces of one's boss. However, she has learned that the hard way. She can easily recall a prior boss's displeasure with her lack of productivity, lack of energy, and lack of involving others in her plans and actions. She had been seriously criticized for these problems in the past. But to her credit, she has overcome those shortcomings, or at least that is how she presented herself the past few years.

Now that Ms. Antonio is more comfortable having been appointed CEO of this 250-bed hospital, she seems to have fallen back on her previous problems, ignoring the skills she used to "get to the top." A real "go-getter," she is more accustomed to going at it alone. She comes up with an idea and uses many resources to put her plan into action. Unfortunately, she does not consult with her senior team to get their views on what projects to select and how to put them into action. She firmly believes that she is smarter than most people, and dislikes being fettered by them in her efforts to "move ahead" and put her ideas into action. Actually, she probably is smarter than most of her employees.

The result is that sometimes Ms. Antonio falls flat on her face. For example, in her energetic surge in wanting to hire a well-published oncologist with a national reputation to begin to build the cancer service line, she failed to seriously investigate past accomplishments of Dr. Looker, the physician she hired. Ms. Antonio claimed to the Board, the press, and the hospital employees that Dr. Looker was women's answer to cancer, much the way Jonas Salk was welcomed as the savior to the polio epidemic. Investigative journalists, spurred on possibly by jealous cancer researchers, uncovered faulty scientific and statistical techniques that Dr. Looker used in reaching certain conclusions. As a result, she was forced to retract two of her peer-reviewed and published articles. At one point, Dr. Looker's medical license was in doubt due to allegations against her for sexual discrimination. Although she survived those challenges, her reputation was damaged. When the true picture of this physician was exposed, a very embarrassed Ms. Antonio was forced to terminate her.

During this time, Dr. Jameson became acutely aware of Ms. Antonio's lack of abilities to be the successful CEO that he hoped would bolster his team and support his own vision for the future. Secretly, he hoped she would fill in the voids in his own character and skill base. That was not to be.

Ms. Henrietta Stone, CEO of the larger of the two home healthcare agencies owned by Synergistic, has been in that position for only 2 years. During that time, however, she has taken the "bull by the horns" and has brought real changes to a fledgling organization. First, she created a six-person team composed of three nurses, one physical therapist, one social worker, and one respiratory therapist. She empowered them to look at every policy and procedure that guided how the home health agency functioned. She wanted a written report within 7 weeks, along with specific and measurable suggestions for change; those changes needed to be accompanied by type and numbers of resources used in the process of change, the number of and level of employees who would champion the change, and the time frame involved without any leeway for lack of action. In fact, this latter factor, "action," is the one word that described Ms. Stone.

Ms. Stone has been an effective counterpart for the CEO of the "sister" home healthcare agency. She believes in change—but not change for the sake of change. She "manages by walking around," learning at least the first name of each employee, and serving as a resource to the staff whom she met with during her walks. She goes out of her way, sometimes to a large extent, to find the resources to help team leaders lead and resolve problems. At agency-wide meetings, Ms. Stone always finds some employee to praise. She then turns to that person's team leader to ask him or her to explain to the rest of the employees exactly what that person did that was outstanding. Then she encourages discussion about the situation involved.

This key recognition factor has motivated not only the employee being discussed but others who also want to be singled out for praise as a result of their efforts. In fact, this idea of identifying outstanding employees has motivated the entire team to strive for higher levels of productivity, quality care, and patient satisfaction.

In addition, Ms. Stone has identified problems as well. She spoke with numerous team leaders to find an example of something someone did that was unacceptable, incorrect, or problematic. Then she spoke with that person and asked his or her permission to discuss that situation at the meeting. The goal was *not* to embarrass the employee but rather to use the situation as a teaching tool. When the situation was described, often by the very person involved, or other times by the team leader (if preferred), the goal was to present the issue, identify the dilemma the employee faced, and determine what went wrong. Then, enforcing the educational value and component of the meeting, Ms. Stone facilitated a conversation among the employees as to what suggestions or actions that person could have taken to have avoided a negative outcome. In this way, everyone learned that they, too, could easily have been in that same situation, and everyone learned how to avoid the same negative result. This was a positive learning experience for everyone, including the individual who made the original error.

Mr. Stone's counterpart, Paul Jenkins, a former physical therapist (PT), is now CEO of the third home health agency. His style differs from Ms. Stone's. Nevertheless, even when Dr. Jameson or someone has pointed out to him Ms. Stone's superior style, Mr. Jenkins is reluctant to change, if at all. He had been an excellent PT, and that is probably why he was promoted to the top job. That process is common in many organizations; the highest biller, the most productive researcher, the best known physician is promoted up the ladder, often to their highest level of incompetency. Known as the "Peter Principle" (think Peter Pan), these less than competent individuals, often uneducated in management concepts, become less than stellar leaders; in fact, they are often incompetent!

Although Mr. Jenkins was somewhat outgoing with his patients, now as the leader, he is reluctant to walk around asking questions of his staff, offering to assist with problems or obstacles or serving as a key resource. Like Dr. Jameson, Mr. Jenkins has a vision for his organization but is reluctant to share it with others. It is almost as if he created it alone but is uncertain if it was helpful or effective, so that he does not let others in on his views. In fact, he basically creates the vision by himself, thinking that because he is in charge, he is the best person for the job, the best person to take charge of creating such an important document as the vision for the next 5 years. The result is that because no one really knew what it is, no one could aspire to improving themselves, looking forward to the future or to change, or to working in a newer environment. Employee morale seems to decrease as time went on. So does motivation.

Another factor that makes Mr. Jenkins stand out is his belief, spurred on by his view that he is the best person for the job, that he really does not need to involve other people in his decision-making or problem-solving. Not only does he express some degree of selfishness in these areas, he tends to put down other people who voice opinions different from his own. This is especially true if Mr. Jenkins feels challenged by an employee. Rather than discuss differences of opinion or entertain other viewpoints, even when positive, Mr. Jenkins would mock or reprimand people for their opinions and suggestions. Employees quickly learn not to question him, especially in meetings. If they do, not only are they ridiculed or embarrassed, they risk losing their job.

Dr. Jameson has wanted employees throughout the system to recognize him and be willing to express issues and concerns to him. He is intent on walking around all facilities to get to know the strengths, limitations, and challenges employees faced. In the first year or so, he was able to "make the rounds" to each facility at least 1 to 2 days per month. He soon grew to understand more completely what the system wanted from him, and to his credit, he tried hard to respond to its needs. Employees particularly liked it when he told them he was "person-centered" and wanted to help them anyway he could. They knew him to remove certain obstacles in their way of success that even their own direct bosses could not. They were very pleased with him. Part of their satisfaction came from the reality that as CEO of the entire corporation, he had the power to spend money more freely, create or facilitate the creation of teams to investigate problems, and address their concerns. Everyone seemed pleased with his results, including the executives at the organizations he visited.

CEO Jameson served as a role model for some of his executives to "get out of the office" and engage employees at all levels on a more personal basis. After all, if the executives did not know or understand the issues, how could they possibly address or correct them?

During one particularly "difficult" year, many employees began to bypass their own bosses and seek out opportunities to meet with Dr. Jameson, usually to complain about intolerable situations in their work setting. Actually, Dr. Jameson created this situation. Recall that in previous years, he would frequently visit each site and invite comments, questions, and problems. Now that he no longer called on the various sites, many employees felt empowered enough or dissatisfied enough in their situations to go to corporate headquarters in Columbus to complain and seek answers to their issues. It seemed that these complainers came from everywhere except from Ms. Stone's agency. Their issues were so compelling and so problematic that, on the advice from the former interim CEO, Mr. Byler, who is the current COO, Dr. Jameson decided to form a task force to investigate what was happening. He could not afford a mutiny, a strike, or even high levels of turnover, for the latter is one of the factors that alerted the Board to investigate Dr. Aimsley's stewardship.

Therefore, Dr. Jameson asked each CEO to nominate three individuals who would form a system-wide task force to determine what problems, if any, the organization was confronting. He did not specify a timetable for producing a report or recommendations for change, fearing that such a deadline would hamper the members' progress by pressuring them to reach a conclusion.

The team met six or seven times over the next 9 months. No one was really in charge because Jameson believed in a democratic decision-making process. But no one complained either. Each member was free to investigate their own choice of sites. Each decided on a series of questions to ask employees at every level. The team's intent was clearly not to intimidate anyone; all they wanted was to obtain honest information about their views of the strengths and limitations of each site.

After about 6 months, Mr. Byler asked Dr. Jameson if he had any results from the team. Mr. Byler had not received any feedback or even temporary views of any situation. He encouraged Dr. Jameson to call a meeting of the investigative team to determine its progress. At that meeting, he discovered that three of the members had been on a 2-week vacation, and when they returned to their site, they were encumbered by problems that had arisen during their time away. Four other members were frankly too busy with healthcare issues to devote much time to their projects. Two others had interviewed approximately 50% of the employees they had intended to work with. Three other members had in fact made considerable progress with their interviews and were in the process of pulling together summaries of their findings.

In brief, the team really had not made much progress. For the first time, Dr. Jameson was visibly upset and in a raised voice, explained why he was disappointed in their lack of progress. He had given the team a great deal of freedom and leeway to fulfill their tasks. He did not want to pressure them. As a result of his being a "nice guy," not wanting to be demanding, the team did "not come through" for him. He let them know how disillusioned and dissatisfied he was. Contrary to his usual style, he set a deadline of one month for the team to pull together a final report.

The members individually and as a team were equally as shocked with Dr. Jameson's behavior. They thought that they were taking on this first-ever evaluation process and were volunteered by their bosses to participate in this project. Some really did not want to be on the team at all but felt powerless to refuse their bosses' request. Team members believed that they were too busy to do this extra work, which involved taking time to travel to the various sites; create their own set of questions; and deal with schedules, schedule changes, people not showing up for the meetings, and other headaches. All the while, this was taking time away from their pressing jobs.

During the month that was supposed to be devoted to continuing the interview process, only 50% of the members completed their task. A final meeting took place in which they were supposed to share their results with each other and compile a final report. Because all of the data were not "in," any report of significance or merit could not possible have been written. Finally, three of the team members sat for almost 2 hours and put together a poorly written report that was devoid of hard facts—merely a summary of a representative number of system employees and some meaningful suggestions for change. But at least they were able to offer Jameson some proof that they had at least tried to complete the task.

When Dr. Jameson read their findings, clearly he was upset, even more so than during the meeting 1 month ago. The results were almost meaningless. Sure, there was a list of some positives and some negatives, and even some suggestions for change, but overall, it was not a document that could serve as a basis for beginning a process of "correcting" or improving the system's problems. Actually, there was not enough information of significance to even understand what key issues, if any existed.

Within 1 week, news of this failed survey attempt had reached several members of the Board. At a full Board meeting, the chair as well as most attendees were furious at the waste of time and money spent on producing a document of almost no value. The Board wanted to take action, but they did not know how or what they should do. After much debate and handwringing, they decided to contact the consultant they had engaged years ago to review Dr. Aimsley's effectiveness.

Dr. Jameson was shocked at the Board's decision and action. He did not think this was at all necessary. When he looked back at his accomplishments in the first few years, he was pleased. He had started a process to create a realistic vision that would catapult the system into the next several decades as far-sighted and effective—the centers for quality care, patient safety, and patient satisfaction. But then something happened; the honeymoon that had lasted so very long with indications that it would continue into the future, did not. His trajectory slowed down and was even misguided at times. He was known to be very transparent in his actions and plans in the beginning of his tenure, but later on, for some unknown and unspecified reasons, he began to withdraw from that position. He ceased his "management by walking around" behavior; he held fewer "town hall meetings" at the various sites, and his e-mail communications were fewer in number and frequency.

Some of the members of the Board have become aware of this change in attitude and behavior. At first, they gave Dr. Jameson "much leeway" to "do his own thing," even when his "thing" represented a change in their outward view of him. After all, they had faith in him and truly wanted him to succeed. They believed that he had all of the skills to be a very effective system leader. Then later, many simply hoped the problem would go away and Dr. Jameson would turn out to be the ideal CEO whom they had envisioned and wanted. Above all, they did not want to undergo the pain they experienced with Dr. Aimsley, her termination, the long national search for a successor, and the "getting up to speed" time that Dr. Jameson took.

The reality of the matter is, in fact, that an outsider's objective view of Dr. Jameson's successes and failures had to be obtained, despite the potential suffering that the Board and the organization would have to endure.

Imagine that *you* are the consultant hired to identify the strengths and limitations of Dr. Jameson's style and those of the organization as a whole. Make a long list of your findings.

Questions

- What suggestions for change, large and small, would you recommend?
- Why did you arrive at those conclusions?

CASE STUDY 2: RISK MANAGEMENT

A female patient has undergone a minimally invasive surgical procedure, which entailed hysteroscopic resection of a uterine fibroid. The surgeon's operative notes reflect that the surgical procedure was uneventful. There was no evidence for perforation of the uterus—the system utilized was a fluid management system that would identify a rapid loss of fluid volume if perforation were to occur. Furthermore, the operative report does not reflect any problems with distention of the uterus intraoperatively. The surgeon has some familiarity with the fluid management equipment because prior to this event, the operative hysteroscopic and fluid management sales representative had been in the operating room, facilitating acquiring education related to the procedure at both physician and nursing levels. The sales representative was unavailable the day of this procedure.

Postoperatively, the patient is noted to have excessive abdominal pain refractory to analgesics. The attending physician deems it wise to admit the patient for observation. The patient experiences difficulty urinating, and a Foley catheter is reinserted into the bladder. Twenty-four hours postoperatively, the patient is noted to have an acute abdomen, and she is still hospitalized. Computed tomographic scanning is obtained and suspicious for a bowel injury. The patient is taken back to the operating room and noted to have a bowel and bladder injury. The latter reflects undiagnosed uterine perforation. All repairs (bowel and bladder) are accomplished via minimally invasive surgery and the patient has minimal scarring on the abdomen.

The surgeon notifies the risk management office of the event and is told the patient had to be notified of details of the findings, equipment-related problems, and so on. The surgeon strongly opposed this discussion, fearing setting the stage for a lawsuit. The risk management office told the surgeon that state law requires that such discussion occur.

This case raises a number of legal issues and illustrates some of the complexity of liability issues in medicine.

The Liability for the Injury

Perhaps the most obvious legal issue is whether there is civil liability for the injury the patient received in the first surgery. Let us look at each of the participants regarding possible liability. For most of the participants, the question will be one of negligence liability. Was there a duty to the patient, and did a breach of that duty cause injury?

THE SURGEON
The perforation of the bladder and bowel. It is not clear from the facts whether the surgeon has been careless (negligent) in the way the surgery was performed. Not every bad outcome suggests negligence, of course. So the fact the injury occurred does not prove negligence. If the patient were to sue for the injuries, she would have the burden of proving negligence (through the records, the testimony of those who saw the surgery, and expert witnesses) in

the way the surgery was performed. The plaintiff would also have to have to demonstrate that the negligence caused the perforation. Finally, the plaintiff would have to prove damages. Here it is fairly clear that an injury occurred and that the injury had consequences—subsequent surgery with the attendant cost, loss of wages, and pain and suffering. At the same time, the outcome is ultimately successful and although circumstances are not trivial, they are not catastrophic. Thus, the cost of the injuries, and the potential liability, would not be massive.

Failure to detect the perforation. The most apparent basis for liability is the failure to detect the perforation. The surgeon and operating room team fail to notice that something is amiss—that there is a deficit mismatch (i.e., between intake and output, failure to note cavity collapse).

There is also a question of the failure of the fluid management system, which should have noted a rapid loss of intra-abdominal fluid that was not recovered in the outflow system. The case suggests that the surgeon and the nursing staff were not yet completely trained in using the system but went ahead and used it, probably without adequate supervision. Assuming that a sales representative is an acceptable way of obtaining such expertise with this equipment, it is notable that not even a sales representative (nor any other medical personnel with the necessary expertise) was present. It is ordinarily negligent for physicians to use new techniques or equipment without adequate training. ("See one, do one, teach one" should not be taken too literally.)

The next question is "Did the negligence cause injury?" If proper use of the equipment or more appropriate observation would have resulted in the immediate discovery of the perforation with the ability to repair the bowel and the bladder injury, then there may have been negligence. Indeed, knowing that they were not completely trained on the fluid management system, a reasonable medical team would probably have been extra vigilant to ensure that any suspected perforations were noted and such information conveyed to the surgeon.

If there was negligence in the failure to detect the perforation, there was an injury associated with having to undergo a second surgery and any other injury that resulted from a delay in the detection of the perforation. Note that the injury is not the need to repair the perforation, only the consequences in determining that it occurred. That is so because the (possible) negligent use of the equipment could not have prevented the perforation but would have resulted in the immediate discovery of it.

Informed consent. The case does not describe the informed consent that was used prior to surgery. Assuming that the consent included a discussion of the procedure proposed, the risks and benefits, alternatives, and the consequences of doing nothing, the failure of consent would unlikely be the basis for liability in most states. Depending on the nature the status of the fluid management system, in some instances, some mention of that equipment would have been appropriate. The most obvious example is if the equipment were considered investigational or novel.

The Surgical Team

If other members of the surgical team have been careless in the performance of their duties (and the case does not suggest that), their negligence, in all likelihood, would be attributed to the hospital or (less likely) the surgeon.

The Hospital

The hospital could be liable based on vicarious liability for any negligence of the nursing staff or other employees. In addition, if the hospital has given inappropriately practice privileges to the surgeon or has allowed the surgeon to perform procedures without adequate training and certification, it may be liable for that negligence.

Surgeons who are not employees of the hospital are commonly considered independent contractors, and the hospital is not vicariously liable for those surgeons. Of course, if the surgeon is an employee of the hospital, there would be vicarious liability. In addition, if the hospital has led the patient to believe that the surgeons are employees or other agents of the hospital, there may be vicarious liability based on "apparent" or "ostensible" agency.

The hospital undoubtedly provided the fluid management equipment. If that equipment has not been properly maintained or inspected, and that caused the malfunction of the equipment, the hospital could be subject to liability for that failure.

At some point the surgeon and hospital would be required to inform their malpractice insurance carriers of the possible claim and liability. The policies describe when that time is, but it probably is not yet necessary.

The Device Provider

The manufacturer of devices may be legally responsible for defects in the equipment. If the fluid management system is defective in design or manufacture, for example, the manufacturer could be liable for the injuries caused by that defect. In this case, there is no suggestion of such a defect, but it would be important to check the equipment for such defects.

Dealing with the Patient

The goal, of course, is not to win malpractice lawsuits. Rather, it is to avoid the suits altogether. The discussion between the physician and the hospital risk management office (described in the last paragraph of the case) is an opportunity to reduce the likelihood of a lawsuit. There are two questions:

1. Should the physician or hospital discuss the error with the patient?
2. If so, what should the physician or hospital say?

Patients who believe they have been misled, ignored or kept "in the dark" are more likely to be dissatisfied and more likely to file complaints or lawsuits. Genuine concern and apologies, on the other hand, are likely to reduce the suspicion and search for "what happened" and thereby reduce the risk of legal complaints. In the ordinary course of things, the surgeon in the case probably has it wrong—discussion with the patient is more likely to reduce the risk of a lawsuit than set the stage for it.

Quite apart from the state law to which risk management personnel refer, the practical considerations would argue in favor of a conversation with the patient in this situation. It is almost certain that the patient understands or suspects that something went wrong in the first surgery—after all, it required a second surgery. Trying to hide the reasons for the second surgery are more likely to cause trouble than an honest explanation.

What should be disclosed and the nature of the conversation is critically important. That should be understood and agreed upon among risk management personnel, the physician, and hospital staff. A few guidelines should be followed. First, honesty and a fair sense of openness are critical. The genuine regret about the difficulty the patient experienced should be communicated, including, if appropriate, an honest apology. Defensiveness and misleading statements are poison. The level of detail about what went wrong should be agreed upon by the risk management office and the physician. It is important to give the significant known facts without overwhelming detail.

There must be a single, consistent message and explanation. Not to put too fine a point on it: if the disagreement between risk management personnel and the physician is reflected in the communications with the patient, it will be a disaster. There needs to be an agreement on who is going to say what to the patient and possibly the patient's family. Given the circumstances, the parties may need to practice or "role play" the conversation. It would also be appropriate to discuss whether the institution is prepared to make any accommodations on the bill (e.g., ensuring that the patient will not be charged extra for the additional expense of the perforation to a settlement for the additional pain and suffering).

Many states now have "apology statutes" that prevent apologies to patients and related discussions from being used against the physician and hospital if a lawsuit is filed. The discussion with the patient should be structured to fall under this state's apology statute.

It is true that many states are requiring greater disclosure to patients. The disagreement between the physician and the risk management office focuses in part on the specifics of this state's law. Given the disagreement, it is important that the requirements of the law be clarified.

The physician's disagreement with risk management personnel illustrates a circumstance in which it would be desirable for the physician to be able to contact her or his own attorney (not the hospital's attorney) for advice and counsel. Among other things, the physician's attorney could tell the physician what the state law is about disclosure. In addition, it would be prudent for the physician to discuss the benefits and risks of engaging in a discussion with an attorney. If the physician has an ongoing professional relationship with an attorney, such consultation could be done quickly and efficiently (inexpensively).

Regulatory Issues and Error Reduction

Risk management personnel would presumably ensure that all of the regulatory requirements of disclosing and investigating the problem that caused the perforation. Federal and state governments, as well as Medicare and Medicaid and other federal reimbursement programs, now provide a number of record-keeping and reporting requirements, and the failure to keep the records or make the required reports may result in penalties. Some federal programs and private insurance contracts are excluding reimbursement for certain kinds of medical errors, which must be identified. These reports are commonly filed by the hospital. Some of the reporting requirements may play a role in the decision to offer a settlement to the patient, or the structure of a settlement. For example, the National Practitioner Data Bank requires reporting "of some" physician malpractice payments.

The hospital's regulations undoubtedly require internal reporting of adverse outcomes. The involvement of the risk management office suggests that those reports have been undertaken already. Beyond the value of this for legal or regulatory risk management, it is an important element in the effort to reduce future adverse events. Error reduction generally would not focus on individual physician error, but what went wrong—how the bad outcomes could have been prevented and what the changes in the "system" of delivering care could reduce the possibility of future problems.

The importance of a risk management office and the risk management process also makes the apparent antagonism between the physician and that office unfortunate. It is essential that they work together, and the physician may wish to consider what steps should be taken to ensure that there is not an ongoing tension. With the proper relationship, the office (or hospital) can be of considerable assistance to the physician and to the cause of better care.

Preventive Law Notes and Lessons

There are several lessons that can be learned from the case. Here are the 10 most important ones.

1. The use of new techniques or equipment requires proper training and should not be undertaken without adequate supervision before the training is complete.

2. Not every bad outcome is a result of negligence. Still, it seems likely that there were errors that resulted in the perforation and the failure to recognize the problem during the first surgery. The positive aspect of the case was the level of care in recognizing that something was wrong, responding quickly to that problem, and correcting it without major harm to the patient.

3. The legal interests of the surgeon and hospital appear to be consistent in this case, but they may not stay that way. For example, if there is a complaint, the hospital may be inclined to blame the surgeon for not using the fluid management system correctly, and the surgeon may want to blame the hospital for not maintaining the equipment properly.

4. When possible errors occur, they should be faced. Here the question arose of how to inform the patient about the problem, and that is an important discussion to have. The goal is not to win lawsuits but to avoid claims of malpractice or misconduct.

5. The physician's inclination not to explain to the patient what happened is likely mistaken. Honest explanations and honest apologies, where appropriate, are more likely to reduce, not cause, formal complaints.

6. Antagonism between risk management personnel and the physician is, well, risky. Such problems must be resolved quickly and before more problems are communicated to the patient.

7. Time is of the essence in responding to the patient. The longer the delay in informing the patient what happened, the greater the risks of suspicion, distrust, and antagonism. There is not a lot of time to come to a conclusion about what should be provided (information and support) to the patient.

8. The informed consent, although not discussed in the facts of the case, is an important, if hidden, element of this case. On one level, the possibility of perforation should have been disclosed as a possible risk of the procedure. On another level, if taken seriously, the consent process is an opportunity to engage in serious communication with the patient before the surgery. It also was important that the "informing" part of the consent process not create expectations of perfect care or that nothing can go wrong.

9. When things go wrong, there is a natural tendency to avoid disclosure, not report negative events, alter the records, and the like. It is, however, just the time when accurate, honest record-keeping and reporting is essential.

10. For the surgeon, an established, ongoing relationship with an attorney would have allowed quick, easy consultation, and good advice about responding to the problem. Establishing such a relationship is a good preventive measure.

Questions

- Does this case represent malfeasance or malpractice?
- Were risk management personnel justified in their approach to management of the problem?
- What are the three most valuable lessons learned from the case?
- What would you have done differently?

CASE STUDY 3: CASEY DENTAL ASSOCIATES

Dr. William Casey has just come out of a long meeting with his business manager, Linda Baker, and he is quite concerned. She has shared with him that his practice has been losing $10,000 a month on monthly revenues of approximately $90,000. Just 6 months ago, he had opened a new office and expected his profit to be growing rather than shrinking. Did he make the wrong decision? He wondered what he should be doing to at least get back to a break-even level for his practice as a whole.

Casey Dental Associates is located in Massachusetts and operates two offices—one in Wellesley, an upscale suburb 17 miles outside Boston, with plenty of parking space, and a second recently opened one in Downtown Crossing, a shopping and business district in the heart of Boston, located right on the subway line.

Dr. Casey is the owner and CEO of Casey Dental Associates. He is semiretired and does not see patients anymore, but he enjoys managing his practice and being a resource and mentor for his staff. He spends about half of his time working at the practice and the rest enjoying his retirement.

Currently, Dr. Casey has two dentists who are employed by him as associates. Each dentist is employed at one of the offices and is responsible for the day-to-day clinical operations of the local office. Dr. Jen Marks graduated from Wellesley College and Harvard School of Dental Medicine and is in charge of the Wellesley office. Dr. Dave Rogers graduated from Hofstra University and New York University College of Dentistry and is in charge of the Boston office. Dr. Casey's vision is to make the dentist who shows the most leadership promise a full partner within the next year.

The organization chart for the practice is shown in Figure A.1.

Each of the offices has two dental hygienists, one dental assistant, and one front-office staff person. Dr. Casey oversees the business manager, who splits her time between both offices and directly oversees the front-office staff to ensure appropriate money handling at the desk, recording of financial and insurance information, and so on.

Because there is some seasonality to running a dental practice, Dr. Casey and his dentist associates look at a typical month in building their annual budget and evaluating ongoing results.

Dr. Marks earns a salary of $8,500 per month, Dr. Rogers, $7,500. All the non-dentist personnel earn the same salary for their position regardless of whether they

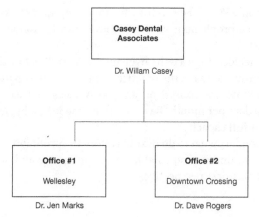

Figure A.1
Organization chart for Casey Dental Associates.

Monthly Expenses—Typical Month:	
Salary for Dr. Casey	$8,000
Dentists' salary	$16,000
Business manager salary	$5,000
Hygienists' salary	$20,000
Dental assistants' salary	$6,000
Front-office staff salary	$5,000
Fringe benefits (at 20%)	$12,000
Office rent	$8,600
Laboratory fees	$6,000
Clinic supplies	$2,000
Malpractice insurance	$1,000
Dental materials	$2,000
Other overhead	$8,400
Total monthly expenses	$100,000

work in the Wellesley or Downtown Crossing office. The rent for the Wellesley office is $2,000 per month higher than Downtown Crossing because of its premier location and extra space. The laboratory fees are the expenditures to pay IDOC and North Shore, the two laboratories being used for all prosthetic work. Other overhead consists of electricity, gas, cleaning service, snow removal, and other similar expenses.

In a typical month, Casey Dental Associates provides dental care for 400 patients, 240 at the Wellesley office and 160 at the Boston office. All those patients see a hygienist, and 25% of them return for follow-up dental work. The average charge for a hygiene/prophylaxis visit is $90 and $540 for follow-up dental work (net of collections).

Dr. Casey has decided to price the hygienist visits well below the normal $120 rate in the community to make the practice attractive to new patients. Currently, hygiene appointments are booked on an hourly basis and each office is open approximately 20 days per month. Based on that schedule, a hygienist will see six patients per day at full capacity.

As Dr. Casey ponders what to do next to restore the profitability of his practice, he thinks he need to understand what his best options are and how best to compare those from a business perspective.

Questions

- Classify Casey Dental Associates costs into direct and indirect categories and also into variable and fixed categories.
- What is the full cost of an average patient at Casey Dental Associates?
- What is the break-even patient volume for Casey Dental Associates as a whole?
- Evaluate the following alternatives from a differential analysis perspective:
  a. Closing the Downtown Crossing office
  b. Raising the prophylaxis price to the market rate
  c. Making one hygienist part time at the Downtown Crossing office
  d. Shifting from 1-hour hygiene appointments to 45-minute appointments
- What would you recommend that Dr. Casey do?

CASE STUDY 4: THE COMPLEX HEALTHCARE SYSTEM CHALLENGE

You have just finished your Master of Science in Healthcare Administration at a well-known university. During the past 2 years, you have been working at the manager level for a large department within a complex healthcare system. Your new employer, excited about your additional expertise, has decided to promote you to a vice president of quality for its flagship hospital. This is a significant promotion and you are excited about the opportunity to really make a difference—you accept.

When you meet with your new boss, the president of the hospital, she asks what experience you have had in dealing with difficult situations in your past role and specifically with staff who are having difficulties with interpersonal interactions. You discuss that in your prior manager role you had some over-sight over these issues but that they were largely handled by the lead administra-tor of the service line; occasionally you were brought in to these conversations but rarely did you lead the process, and it was never with physicians or pro-viders. The president, looking somewhat concerned, states that she has become aware of an individual surgeon who is becoming increasingly disruptive in the operating room. She has even heard from a board member, who has a niece who works in the operating room, that the situation is becoming quite uncomfort-able. You are tasked with investigating the situation and dealing with the issues. As a first effort in your new role and the high visibility to your leader, you are quite interested in making sure the process is fair and that the outcome is good.

Meeting with the leader for the operating rooms, you learn that the individual in question is a very busy, highly connected surgeon for a major service line. As it turns out, the surgeon's father was also a beloved leader in the organization who happened to be chief of staff for a number of years before retiring recently. His son had gone to medical school nearby and completed a residency at the hospital. He is also highly politically connected throughout the organization and in the community.

You are informed that over the past few months the surgeon in question has become increasingly agitated in the operating room at times, even throwing instruments and refusing to performing "time outs" prior to the procedure. Nurses have been brought to tears, and several of the best team members have recently quit and gone to a competitor hospital.

On further investigation, you learn that the surgeon's operating time has increased for similar cases and that there are some questions about outcomes. You also note that his patient satisfaction scores, which previously had been above the 60th percentile, have slipped to the 23rd percentile over the past year. There are only four surgeons in this particular service line, and the surgeon in question performs the majority of cases and has productivity over the 90th percentile. You have also come to learn from the service line leader that these are very difficult physicians to recruit.

Questions

- How would you begin to further investigate what you have learned at a high level from the operating room and service line leaders? Who would you be most interested in speaking with?
- How would you engage the physician in dialogue? Are there others that you would have present for the interaction with the physician?
- You are finding that the operating room nurses are reluctant to speak openly with you, given the fear of retaliation. What would you do to create a sense of security? How would you work with the operating room leadership to ensure that these and other nurses are free to report any incident that they are concerned about? Do you have concerns that

a "culture of silence" might be more pervasive than just this operating room team?

- How would you go about evaluating the concern about quality issues for this physician? What metrics would you consider? Given the small size of the service line, would you engage an independent third party at this point?
- How would you structure a performance improvement plan for this physician? Would you invoke changes in compensation or incentive and why?
- If the situation improves after intervention, how and for how long would you monitor for sustained improvement?
- How would you protect the service line and ensure patient access, given the difficulty in recruiting other physicians?

Having successfully managed the issues in the prior situation, the staff are beginning to become increasingly comfortable with bringing issues forward and appreciate the opportunity to participate in the "culture of safety" that you are building. Because of the comfort, an emergency department nurse comes to meet with you about a patient who had presented some time ago with a myocardial infarction. Curious about the situation, you pull a more recent chart of another patient with a similar diagnosis and are quite surprised with the difference.

CASE STUDY 5: A TALE OF TWO PATIENTS

Patient 1

A 48-year-old man experiences acute chest and arm pain while working at home. His wife recognizes that he is probably having cardiac symptoms and calls 911. The ambulance arrives within 13 minutes and the paramedics, after a brief examination, agree that this is likely cardiac in origin and put him in the ambulance. Travel time is 12 minutes.

Upon arrival at the hospital, he is immediately taken to the emergency department (ED), where an electrocardiogram (EKG) is run. The ED physician and the nurse believe that the EKG shows ST-segment changes consistent with a myocardial infarction (MI). Because only a cardiologist can officially diagnosis a ST-segment MI, he is called. He arrives several minutes later, agrees with the diagnosis, and notifies the cardiac catheterization laboratory. Thirty minutes later, the patient is taken to the laboratory, but unfortunately he dies en route. The total elapsed time from the 911 call to cardiac arrest has been more than 90 minutes.

Patient 2

A 54-year-old man is at home and experiences chest pain and shortness of breath. His wife calls 911, and the ambulance arrives within 2 minutes. The man is immediately placed in the ambulance and a 12-lead EKG is run and transmitted to the hospital ED physician. The ED physician concurs that it is a probable MI and notifies the cardiac catheterization laboratory team. Upon arrival at the hospital ED, the patient is immediately transported to the laboratory, with the already waiting team. The total elapsed time from the 911 call to his procedure was 37 minutes.

The difference? The first patient had his heart attack before Core Measures began and before the "time is muscle" initiative that stressed that a percutaneous coronary intervention be done within 90 minutes.

Questions

- What are Core Measures and why do they matter?
- What are the current and future divisions for value-based purchasing and how does this affect hospital reimbursement?
- "Time is Muscle" is a broad-based performance improvement initiative to decrease the time from first call to intervention. As the hospital leader responsible for quality, how would you run a performance improvement effort to improve the results?
- How and what transparent processes/metrics would you use to drive change working with the administrator of cardiology?
- How would you begin a process in your new organization of building a quality and patient safety culture? Who would you engage and what process would you use to create alignment, accountability, and sustainable change?

References to tables, figures, and boxes are denoted by an italicized, *t*, *f*, and *b*